e
d
e
l-
)-
d
a
s
)r

al
ll
ll

Social structure and rural development in the
Third World

Social structure and rural development in the Third World

Guy Berger

CAMBRIDGE
UNIVERSITY PRESS

CAMBRIDGE UNIVERSITY PRESS
Cambridge, New York, Melbourne, Madrid, Cape Town, Singapore, São Paulo

Cambridge University Press
The Edinburgh Building, Cambridge CB2 8RU, UK

Published in the United States of America by Cambridge University Press, New York

www.cambridge.org
Information on this title: www.cambridge.org/9780521392587

First published 1992
This digitally printed version 2008

A catalogue record for this publication is available from the British Library

Library of Congress Cataloguing in Publication data
Berger, Guy.
    Social structure and rural development in the Third World/Guy Berger.
        p.   cm.
    Includes bibliographical references and index.
    ISBN 0–521–39258–6
    1. Rural development – Developing countries. 2. Social structure –
Developing countries. I. Title.
HN981.C6B47 1992   91–31982
307.1′412′091724 – dc20   CIP

ISBN 978-0-521-39258-7 hardback
ISBN 978-0-521-06633-4 paperback

To my wife Jeanne Berger and my parents
Lucy Gough Berger and Nathan Noté Berger

Contents

Introduction

This monograph investigates the significance of social structure and economic development, with specific reference to rural development. It makes use of a concept of development analysed as productive capacity and a concept of economic structure analysed in terms of three 'Moments' of production. Beginning with theoretical issues, the study moves on to a general definition of development, and from there to basic social and economic concepts. These are then used to theorise the capitalist mode of production and its role in development and underdevelopment in the Third World. Finally, the role of agriculture in development is discussed, and different experiences of planned rural development are analysed.

The approaches dealt with during the argument include the modernisation school; the dependency and underdevelopment theorists; the 'articulation of modes of production' framework; the 'laws of motion' protagonists; and those who adopt a 'class struggle' emphasis. Numerous debates have raged between and within these different approaches, involving a confusing range of phrases – 'growth without development', 'underdevelopment', and the 'development of underdevelopment' to list but a few. Among other difficulties in many of these approaches, one can note four major problems.

(a) There has been a lack of clear philosophical principles. In particular, the status of theory in relation to material reality has been largely ignored. On the one hand, this is evident in theories that have been too general to be useful for historically specific empirical investigation (for example, Wallerstein, 1974, 1977), and have instead imposed reified relationships and processes on to empirical analyses (see, for example, Banaji, 1976a). On the other hand, a large number of studies dispense with theory entirely, and are the poorer for this.

(b) Where theory has been used, the relationship between macrodevelopment, microdevelopment and intermediate levels of development has been neglected. The units of analysis put forward have often not been adequate for understanding the specificity of each of the parts and of the whole, nor the relationship between them. This has had its negative

1

effects, such as in cases where rural development is studied in isolation from industry, and rural development projects are examined independently of their broader linkages and wider significance (see examples in Richards, 1979: 272 and Amin, 1974: 32).

(c) In much of the writing, 'development' as the locus of the debates has not been properly theorised. Writers have become caught up in 'metropole-satellite' versus 'dual economy'; 'laws of motion' versus 'articulation of relations', etc.

(d) A fourth problem is that each approach has tended towards exclusivity. Colin Leys, for example, urges writers to rid themselves of 'the ideological handicap of dependency theory' (1980: 109; see, similarly, Kitching, 1985: 148). This hostility between protagonists has inhibited them from acknowledging insights elsewhere in the spectrum. Where a synthesis has been attempted, it has been on an eclectic basis and with little regard to theoretical rigour and consistency (for example, Roxborough, 1976).

The significance of these four problems is that development theory itself needs to be developed. For this monograph, this has meant starting with basic definitions, re-working existing concepts, innovating different ones and integrating the contributions of various approaches into a new body of theory.

This study draws substantially from Marxism, although for Marx the vantage point was political and the major concern was with state power and the relations of production, and not with development as such. Neither he nor Engels took on the task of explaining properly quite how, why and when capitalist social relations could – as they observed (*The Communist Manifesto*, 1986: 37) – revolutionise production. Similarly, much Marxist writing on development has ended up discussing the development of social structures, rather than the social structure of development. The success with which Marxism can help explain economic development is therefore a kind of sub-hypothesis of this monograph. At the same time, this work departs from Marx's use of concepts such as 'base and superstructure' and 'the state', relying instead on the insights of neo-Marxists like Cutler et al. (1977) and Jessop (1982). It also develops new arguments around Marxist concepts such as relations and forces of production, exploitation, class, subsumption, the (alleged) primacy of productive forces, capitalism and the Agrarian Question. In addition, this work makes use of a number of original theoretical constructs – such as the model of three Moments of production and the phenomenon of 'system dynamics' – and these are central to its arguments.

The scope of this study is almost exclusively with social structure and development in relation to capitalism, and even here it concentrates primarily on class issues. Whether issues of gender or geopolitics could be incorporated into the framework is an important question that is not, however, confronted here. It should also be noted that most of the research was done in 1980–2, and many new contributions to the debates have since been published. I would hope, however, that the manner in which problems are tackled and the theoretical solutions that are proposed are of some long-term value.

1   Development: defining the terrain

Theory – its role and scope

A beautiful scene catches the eye – lushly covered units with mealies
standing 2,4 metres high, ready to be picked. Cows grazed in the
thick pasture.

('The New World of Keiskamma', *Daily Dispatch*, 1 April 1977)

This is a journalist's idyllic view of a rural development project in South
Africa's Ciskei bantustan. In contrast, serious analysis needs to go
beyond what Poulantzas (1976a: 68) calls 'the noisy illusion of the evident'. Thus, numerous writers have argued for the necessity of theory,
and against empiricism, on the basis that there is no 'innocent' investigation of reality. Whether he knows it or not, every social researcher uses
generalisations and abstractions in identifying, selecting and ordering
'the facts'. Empirical information does not exist as 'raw data' independently of more abstract assumptions.[1]

However, the use of theory is no guarantee that the resulting knowledge corresponds accurately to reality. Firstly, while criteria may be
proposed to validate the knowledge produced by a given theory, there is
always the problem of validating these criteria in turn (Althusser, 1976:
137; 1970a: 56–7). Secondly, every theory bears the traces of social values
that lend significance and ordering to phenomena in its field.[2] The sociology of knowledge applies no less to development theory than to other
theories, as shown, for example, in the discussion by Goodman et al.
(1984) concerning the changing history of development theories in Brazil,
and the study by Kitching (1985: 145–6) on the political context that
underpins the debate around Kenyan development.

It would appear then, that the epistemological character of theory, and
indeed of knowledge in general, is precarious. Yet this does not mean
that all theories are of equal value. Within a given historical period,
certain theories are socially recognised as being more or less accurate
than others, particularly in the face of the test of practical application.
Marxist theory serves as a broad theoretical framework for the investi-

gation in this monograph. While not ignoring points made by its critics (some of which I tackle in my arguments), this choice is based on the fact that Marxism has some social recognition as a credible theory, and indeed much development literature is based on its perspectives. However, I also borrow (with modifications) from other theories and attempt to synthesise the various insights.

Using theory often involves the danger that empirical relationships are treated as manifestations of the theoretical. A negative example in this regard is the way that, within Marxism, Lenin's theory of capitalist differentiation in the Russian countryside has been incorrectly read into what have been quite different historical experiences (Williams, 1984: 2; see Kitching, 1982: 163 for a similar situation concerning Marx's *Capital* and studies of the genesis of capitalism). While theories play a key role in identifying and ordering empirical facts, it is not the case that they determine the facts. The concept of 'simple commodity producing household' does not, for instance, provide us with the fact of a particular family farm. On the contrary, there is a specific material reality to the family and a number of shared real characteristics among it and its fellows. It is this reality which underlies the unit's categorisation as a simple commodity producing household (and not as a capitalist enterprise, for instance). As an interface between theory and reality, empirical research cannot be redundant and ancillary to theory (Mouzelis, 1980: 368).[3]

In deploying theory, there is, of course, the danger of selecting only that empirical data which confirms the initial hypotheses (see Popper, 1973: 260). For example, dependency theory has been said to block the analysis of phenomena that do not conform to its assumptions (Leys, 1980: 109; Phillips, 1977: 13). In countering this problem, I have tried to be open to the diverse empirical facts encountered, and to alter my assumptions where need be. At the same time, I have tried to construct my particular theory of development in such a way that it can be evaluated in relation to a wide variety of empirical cases. My aim has been to specify general relationships which may be recognisable in a number of situations, which would then make for the validity of applying the theory there.[4]

As will become apparent in the body of this work, there is no attempt at a grand and universal *theory* of development that would cover all modes of production. Certainly, my theorisation of capitalist development – like any other – does require a general *definition* of development. As soon as any definitions are considered less abstractly, it is clear that they are composed of numerous layers of determinations which depend on the specifics of each situation (see Marx's *Grundrisse* discussion on production, 1973: 85–100). This does not negate their value, of course: on the contrary, definitions are a wholly necessary and legitimate dimension of theoretical work. Hence, early in my argument, I devote considerable space to clarifying definitions, not least 'development'.

Theoretical investigation takes place not only in terms of the issues discussed above, but also with regard to philosophical principles. Some Marxist principles, as adapted from Cornforth (1968: 78), draw attention to:

i.   The structure of interconnections and relationships in society.
ii. This structure as a complex of processes rather than 'ready-made' things.
iii. The dynamics of these processes as linked to dialectical contradictions in the structure.
iv. Quantity and quality as two distinct dimensions of developing structures.
v.   The historical character of social processes, especially the origin and likely development of social structures.

The relevance of these points – especially that of contradiction – will be evident in the main body of the argument. Some remarks can be made here, however, about interconnections – the existence of which requires a theory to have a range of concepts that enable the researcher to perceive the wood as well as each of the trees. Theory has to provide a comprehensive specification of the relevant units of analysis and the relations between them (Larrain, 1979: 65). For example, one needs to be able to analyse a specific rural development scheme without losing sight of the significance of the international context. The principle of interconnections is bound up with the Marxist point of view of the totality and the primacy of the whole over its parts.[5] The whole is constituted by the active relation between the parts, but is also 'greater' than these parts. It acquires a particular kind of character from its parts, and *vice versa*.[6] This monograph investigates whether Marxist concepts are able to specify the effective wholes and parts in each unit of analysis, and the interrelations between them, with regard to social structure and development.

With this methodological review, I proceed to my own theory of development, beginning with a general definition of the topic.

Defining development

In my view, 'development' should be understood in an economic sense, and not in terms of political, ethical, ideological or other criteria. This is not to say that the *issue* of development is an exclusively economic consideration. Rather, it is to argue that the *concept* should designate solely economic characteristics of social life, considered in abstraction from their extra-economic dimensions. What constitutes 'development' therefore is an economic rather than (for example) a political, ecological, spiritual or other phenomenon. While development has extra-economic significance, such considerations are not part of its definition here.

This perspective shares some common ground with modernisation theory which has come under attack for the priority it accords the economic at the expense of political and ethical issues involved (see Berger, 1976: 53; Phillips, 1977). The critique is that modernisation theory perceives development simply as economic growth and, further, that it assumes this to be the end in itself. Consequently, it is argued, extra-economic considerations are side-lined, and seen only in terms of whether they help or hinder economic growth. Many of the critics of modernisation theory are what one could refer to as 'humanists', who argue that the economistic approach of modernisation theory needs to be overturned so that economic growth is seen as a means to extra-economic goals. They put these goals at the centre of their analysis, with the result that development is defined ultimately in relation to a variety of social or moral values. For example, some 'humanists' would argue that development should be measured in terms of improving the quality of life, rather than in technical indices of economic growth. The two yardsticks, in their view, are not necessarily synonymous.

The 'humanist' critique has in some cases opened the way for a radical position to emerge in which development ultimately need have nothing at all to do with economic factors. Here, development is so bound up with extra-economic ends that economic factors are in no way a precondition for them. As the 1971 TANU Guidelines argue:

for people who have been slaves and have been oppressed, exploited and disregarded by colonialism or capitalism, 'development' means 'liberation'. Any action that gives them more say in determining their affairs and running their lives is one of development, even if it does not offer them better health or more bread. (Tanzania, 1971, cited by Seidman, 1978: 320)

The danger of this position is that once the link to economic factors is lost, 'development' comes to have an entirely relative meaning. What counts as development for some people does not for others. In contrast, I believe that development should have a consistent general meaning across all situations, and that crucial to this is the link between development and economics. Development with simply a moral or other extra-economic meaning risks making us overlook what Marx (in a different context) observed: 'the middle ages could not live on Catholicism, nor the ancient world on politics' (1972: 86, footnote 2). It is not surprising that most 'humanists' see economic factors as necessary (albeit not sufficient) elements of their definition. I take it therefore that the concept of development should have an intrinsic economic dimension.

More than this, however, my position is that development is linked not only to economic factors, but specifically to economic *growth*. Yet, for those who see development as including reference to extra-economic criteria, this is not necessarily so. For example, if development is defined as raising living standards for poor countries, this does not require growth *per se* – it could be realised by redistribution (rather than expansion) of the world's economic resources. In terms of such an approach, development is even compatible, up to a point, with a fall in a country's production. In this scenario, one may logically have 'development without growth', and even development with economic stagnation or recession. Such phrases sound paradoxical – yet they are a logical possibility of putting extra-economic criteria at the centre of the definition of development.

Most writers do in fact accept that economic *growth* must be part of conceptualising development – even where non-economic criteria form part of the definition. There is thus a widely held (and correct, in my view) assumption that development – at least in the long term – requires a minimum of economic expansion. If, then, economic growth is necessary to defining development, we can now turn to the question of whether it is sufficient – or whether extra-economic criteria are also needed.

The 'humanist' insistence that extra-economic considerations should be put up-front involves a critique of modernisation theory's failure to distinguish between growth and development. For example, development presupposes economic growth for both Le Brun (1973: 286) and Berg (1964, cited in Markovitz, 1976: 184, footnote 3). However, for humanist Le Brun, economic growth is necessary, but insufficient, to achieve certain socio-economic ends. For modernisation theorist Berg, it is both necessary and sufficient, because growth, in itself, constitutes development (in Le Brun's sense) eventually. His case rests on the 'trickle-down' theory: that everyone benefits eventually from growth. Berg's position has evoked much response for its historical flaws. Writers like Le Brun argue that growth is insufficient to count as development; on the contrary, they argue, it is quite possible to have *growth without development*.[7] It is in the light of such arguments that Brett (1973: 18) takes development to mean (*inter alia*) growth *plus* equity. These issues lead Berger (1976: 64–5) to criticise the 'ideology of developmentalism' by asking 'whose growth, who benefits, who decides?' Such questions imply a calculus of the human costs of growth, raising (in an ethical way) the political context of development (1976: 95, 254). It is in terms of these concerns that the humanists are concerned to build their moral and political values into the definition of development. Development thus becomes 'good' growth and 'desirable' modernisation (Todaro, 1983: 69–72; Berger, 1976: 52). What makes growth count as 'development' depends on its extra-economic concomitants, and one's moral assessment of these. For several reasons, I will argue below that this approach needs to be rejected.

One symptomatic effect of the problems in the humanist approach is that the term 'development' is used inconsistently. Development is used on the one hand to mean, *inter alia*, 'growth plus equity'; on the other hand, western capitalist countries are labelled as 'devcloped' – despite their lack of equity (Legassick, 1976: 437). Also, inequality and politics (in Berger's sense above) are not considered in terms of effectivity and determination in relation to economic growth but, rather, in terms of values alone. The emphasis is on the 'ought' rather than the 'is' (see Weber, 1948: 51; Phillips, 1977: 19). By calling on us to apply moral values and make (related) extra-economic considerations integral to our definition of development, the 'humanists' open a Pandora's box full of values to choose from. As Weber has argued, it is impossible to refute value judgements (1948: 4); consequently, a definition of development on the humanist basis is of limited value to analysts holding different values. The humanist definition thus directs us to the terrain of moral and political debate about economic growth, rather than toward concepts that might help us to explain this growth. It tells us more about analysts' values than about what is happening on the ground.

The humanist stress on values is largely a reaction to the claims of modernisation theory to value-free analysis and prescription. The humanists have correctly exposed that theory's implicit Eurocentric and consumerist assumptions, in terms of which development is conceived as high industrialisation, mass consumerism, urbanisation, etc., and is seen as an end in itself (see Frank, 1969b; Bernstein, 1971; Tipps, n.d.; Phillips, 1977: 11). Certainly, there are value assumptions in any attempt to define development (see next section). My critique of the humanists is thus not to defend the modernisation view that a value-free definition of development is possible. Values will, of course, influence the identification and the selection of criteria for what constitutes development. But where one is conscious of values, they should not lead to including extra-economic phenomena in the definition.

Although the humanist critique of economistic views of development does draw attention to the extra-economic significance of economic issues, it is one thing to be aware of the broader significance of economic growth, and another to make one's definition depend on it. According to

Weber, 'a phenomenon is economic *only* insofar as and only as long as our interest is exclusively focused on its constitutive significance in the material struggle for existence' (1948: 65, my emphasis). Indeed, by defining development solely in economic terms we are making an abstraction in order to highlight one aspect within the mixed-up character of reality. It is precisely this which makes it possible to see how development relates to extra-economic phenomena.

Development and underdevelopment as correlatives

I turn now to the semantics of 'development', arguing that both development and underdevelopment should be defined by reference to productive capacity. In its broadest senses, development suggests *attributes* that describe a certain state (for example, 'advanced') and the notion of *process* (as distinct from a lack of movement). At first sight these senses appear straightforward and uncomplicated, but they conceal highly complex issues.[8]

'Development' as a concept describing attributes

Taking firstly the attributes sense of development, the literature uses various grammatical forms to characterise a particular economic unit of analysis (be the unit a region, social formation or economic system). For example:

Economic Unit X	*Economic Unit Y*
developed/underdeveloped	developing/less developed/under-developed
(advanced/modern)	(backward/traditional)

Three assumptions are usually involved in these characterisations:

i.   The significance of X and Y is ultimately dependent on their relation to each other.
ii. Underlying this is the assumption that the two situations are comparable along a common yardstick.
iii. Comparability often involves the assumption that X and Y are separate and disconnected conditions.

Correlative meaning

The characterisation of one unit (as, for example, 'developed/advanced') gains its meaning largely in relation to the other ('underdeveloped/backward'). As correlatives, the attributes of X and Y are therefore mutually dependent (Myrdal, 1957).[9] In itself this is not problematic – indeed, it is fundamental to semantics (see Leech, 1974). However, in many cases in the literature, these correlatives are not defined around a concept of productive capacity, but solely in relation to each other. In particular, the attributes of one economic unit, e.g. country X, become the yardstick of comparison, and the orientation point in the relation.[10] The problem with this is that the relational character of meaning between X and Y is not equal and symmetrical. Unit Y (and everything 'beyond' Y – i.e. unit Z, unit AA, etc.) gets defined negatively – i.e. by default – in relation to unit X. 'Undeveloped', etc., thus becomes a catch-all label for any and every region (or other unit of analysis) which – when juxtaposed to the 'norm' – shows up as falling short (Mouzelis, 1980: 356–7). Clearly, this obscures differences within these 'undeveloped' countries, regions, etc.[11] The same problem emerges when 'developed' is used to group together all units that are not characterised by the attributes of 'undeveloped'. It therefore does not help to reverse the method, taking unit Y's attributes as given, and defining development negatively in relation to them.[12] In my view, what is needed in the first instance is a definition of development that transcends the specific attributes of units X and Y. And, contrary to much writing on development, it is in terms of productive capacity that a broader concept of development and its correlatives have to be defined for there to be more even-handed evaluation and comparison of given economic units.

Comparability

Regarding point ii. above, X and Y are assumed to be comparable in terms of their attributes and are assigned a rating in relation to each other on this basis. For this to be valid, X and Y cannot be 'apples and oranges'. Instead, they must be susceptible to being treated as equivalent units. This requires that all differences have to be ignored except for those which are comparable, and/or that a reductionism has to be applied in order for them to be ranked in terms of a single yardstick. In itself, there is nothing wrong with this. However, in much of the literature the procedure involves a reductionism that leads to atomised comparison and quantitative ranking. These steps are common in modernisation theory where X and Y are compared in terms of certain limited features, such as the Gross National Product (GNP), and where the differences between them are reduced to quantitative ones (for instance, X has a higher GNP than Y). The Adelman and Taft-Morris (1967) 'Ideal Typical Index' and Rostow's patterns of growth (1965) are classic examples.

In criticism of this approach, Amin (1974: 18) has pointed out that by defining development by an index such as per capita incomes, Venezuela appears more developed than Japan; Kuwait rates above America (see also Frank, 1969a). Mouzelis (1980: 354) takes the critique further by attacking not only the content of such indices, but also the use of indices *per se*. He advocates going beyond disparate indicators altogether and looking at the totality of economic, political and cultural structures of a country.

The point that emerges from this critique is that X and Y, exhibiting the attributes of development and its opposite condition, need to be contrasted qualitatively and as totalities, and not merely quantitatively or according to isolated components. It also means that productive capacity, the yardstick in terms of which they should be compared, needs to be defined in both qualitative and quantitative dimensions.[13]

Concerning the qualitative issue, productive capacity may be defined as the productive power of a given unit. Just as labour-power (i.e. capacity) is materialised in labour-time (see Marx, 1972: Part II), so productive capacity (power) is manifested in output. Described by Marx as the 'powers of social production', productive capacity results from 'science, inventions, division and combination of labour, improved means of communication, creation of the world market, machinery etc.' (1973: 307–8). These factors, in my view, may all be seen as part of the means and forces of production. 'Development' (i.e. of productive capacity) may consequently be conceived as the expansion and/or improvement (see next section).

Considered quantitatively, the question is how productive capacity can be measured and rated. If economic units produced identical items and used identical means of production, it would be legitimate to use *volume* of output as an index. But in the more realistic and complex case of diverse output between economic units, volume ceases to be a common measure. It is problematic to turn to monetary value of output to compare productive capacity because this measure is limited to certain societies only, and even there it serves only as a (often rather dubious) commercial value of output (as in GNP figures) rather than as an index of productive capacity. In fact, it is questionable whether there is a common measure for productive capacity between different economic units. It is, however, legitimate to measure the rate of expansion of productive capacity *internal to each unit* over a period of time. Such expansion would be manifested in increased output of existing products, enhancement of existing products, and the production of wholly new items. These indicators can be compared with the previous productive situation in that unit, and a quantitative assessment can be made. Comparing two units in these terms means comparing them relative to their own performance, rather than by any external standards of productive capacity. To sum up the argument above, comparing economic units for productive capacity requires acknowledging their qualitative distinction, and ranking them is legitimate only in terms of their respective rates of expansion of output.

Separate economic units
The meaning of any comparison or contrast is drastically affected by the extent to which X and Y are independent entities. Much modernisation theory assumes that X and Y are in some way separate from each other – each having its own independent attributes and determination. This assumption legitimises isolating and juxtaposing X and Y for the purpose of rating them against each other. This procedure is philosophically valid where X and Y are abstract mathematical units. But the whole meaning changes – for both qualitative comparison and quantitative ranking – where X and Y are not in fact wholly separate units of analysis. Where economic unit X and economic unit Y are part of a broader single system, it is misleading to separate and juxtapose them as if they had no connection. Instead, as parts of a unity, they would need to be analysed in intrinsic relation to each other and as integral parts of a wider whole.

Conclusion
To summarise this section, in using 'development' to refer to attributes, it is necessary firstly that the concept should be defined in relation to productive capacity, and not derive its significance from its relation to the more specific attributes associated with its correlatives. Secondly, atomised analysis and one-sided quantitative comparison of development should be avoided and, thirdly, separate units of analysis with independent attributes should not be assumed when this is not always the case.

'Development' used to describe a process
The sense of development as a process of expansion of productive capacity is crucial to understanding and defining development. To analyse development in terms of attributes (even as qualified above) is legitimate only inasmuch as one is aware that it involves arresting the dynamic in order to consider it as a given instant. Though artificially fixed and held, the attributes remain moments of the process. As a process concerning productive capacity, development gains several distinct meanings, depending on what its correlative is taken to be. I will discuss three possibilities here:

i.   Development as the correlative of a non-process (i.e. of non-development or stasis).
ii. Development as the correlative of a *hypothetical* non-process.

iii. Development as the correlative of a qualitatively distinct process (an underdevelopment process).

'Development' as the correlative of 'non-development'

'Non-development' – i.e. a lack of movement, a static ontological condition – can serve as a correlative in terms of which 'development' takes a particular meaning. 'Development' here is thus the opposite of 'stagnation' or 'stasis' and is synonymous with 'movement' or 'change'. Thus we have:

Process	Condition
development/movement/change	stasis/stagnation

Conceiving development in this way alters the attributes allocated to X and Y in the typology outlined at the start of this discussion. Instead of X being 'developed', and Y being 'developing', we now have:

unit X	*unit Y*
developing	stagnating
dynamic	static

One implication of this is that Y, a Third World country for example, cannot be labelled 'developing'. And even the term 'less developed' might imply that Y is still in motion. Instead, it is unit X which is 'developing'. Unit Y is a condition of stagnation and non-development and it is in this sense that the labels 'undeveloped' and 'underdeveloped' are sometimes used. 'Development', in this view, is simultaneously the movement out of Y, as well as the condition-of-being of X. It is both movement into the motion of economic expansion and the motion of this expansion itself. 'Development' for unit Y means that it emulates unit X in the sense of becoming dynamic. The positive side of this perspective is that X is not seen as having reached the end of a process – as being 'developed', full stop. But, on the negative side, any region, etc. in condition Y, i.e. unchanging economically, would be a highly unlikely and artificial situation. Marxism predisposes us to assume – correctly, I believe – that social reality is contradiction-ridden and thereby involved in history. Non-development is therefore really only a hypothetical condition. This is not to deny that productive capacity in a particular economic unit may stay static or even decline over a particular period. But to imply that there is a lack of movement would be misleading. It provides only a description of attributes of non-development, and no explanation of the process which must underlie these.

Development as the correlative of a hypothetical *non-process*

A different approach in the literature has (in effect) taken development as a correlative to non-development in the sense of the latter being a *hypothetical* condition. It therefore sees *all* economic units as developing in one way or another. But the question of distinguishing them and trying to capture the sense of development as a process is often then reduced to quantitative distinctions. Differences within economic motion have thus been analysed in terms of degrees of progress within a universal development process. Thus we have:

Process of development: developing/modernising
                                          $\xrightarrow{\hspace{2cm}}$ Y $\xrightarrow{\hspace{2cm}}$ X
Attributes at any given instant: less developed   more advanced

Here, *both* units X and Y are 'developing'. The difference lies in the pace and degree of expansion of productive capacity. The process of development is viewed as a continuum along which movement flows in the direction of Y to X. There is a veritable escalator carrying various (separate) social formations, regions, etc., into development. 'Development' is thus seen as an inexorable teleological movement through several stages towards (and beyond) the features that characterise the level that unit X has reached. The natural implication here is that the 'developing' countries, etc., stand a chance of one day catching up. The motor of this whole process is often not spelled out, but is assumed to be the working out of something already implicit – i.e. the unfolding of inherent tendencies. This conception has been criticised on several levels:

Firstly, the view that all societies can become 'developed' was shaken by the Club of Rome in 1974 and, more recently, by environmental research on how industrialisation may lead to global warming and damage to the ozone layer. The argument here is that the world's finite resources and eco-system will not allow every country to reach the present production and consumption levels of the First World. While this is controversial, it has at least some pertinence in that many of the world's 'developing' countries are too small or lacking in local resources to develop national productive capacity – unless they become an integrated part of a wider economic unit (Amin, 1974: 32, 376; Rodney, 1977: 112; Clegg, 1977: 365).

Secondly, to the extent that this perspective sees unit X as continuing to develop, it ahistorically assumes inevitable progress in the development of productive capacity. This is difficult to square with the history of economic crises and regressions, including contemporary decline such as de-industrialisation across parts of Britain.

Thirdly, this conception ignores the effects of the changed context on the situation in which the historical economic experience of the 'developed' countries has now been largely transcended (Dos Santos, 1969: 59; Geertz, 1963: 51). The Third World has a net disadvantage when compared to the West before it industrialised. There is now the stunting effect of foreign competition, and repeating western experiences such as using foreign trade, slavery and colonialism is not a realistic option (see chapter three).

Fourthly, this conception of 'development' has been criticised on a more fundamental level for failing to conceptualise qualitative differences in trajectory. It assumes that while X and Y are separate, they are not inherently different, and therefore that what applies to X is applicable to Y. Hence, to the extent that human intervention is given a role in speeding up the transition from Y to X, it is held that Y should consciously imitate (perhaps on a more intensive basis) the history of X. Against this, one can argue that the economic models based on X, and advocating a repetition of X's experience, derive from a unique history – a 'special case'. Consequently, these models are largely inappropriate to contexts foreign to that experience, such as the qualitatively specific internal economic processes of Y. It is in this light that Berger (1976: 249) and Mafeje (1977: 417) hold that development models have only limited exportability. It can further be noted that X and Y are often not separate and independent of each other. Instead, they are frequently inextricable (though qualitatively different) parts of a single complex process and the outcome is by no means an automatic expansion of productive capacity in each.

The significance of all this is that economic history cannot be interpreted as a unilinear process, and the distinctions in economic movement cannot be reduced to quantitative differences in development (Dos Santos, 1969: 62; Mouzelis, 1980: 373, footnote 5). Instead, X and Y involve qualitatively different economic movement – and not necessarily in the direction of expansion of productive capacity. Thus we may have:

In the light of these arguments, it is now pertinent to turn to the third sense of development mentioned above, where the term's correlative is the process of underdevelopment. This sense makes it possible to grasp the differences between qualitatively different economic movements. It also helps to distinguish when they are separate and unrelated, and when they are only distinctions within a single process.

Development as correlative of a qualitatively distinct process (i.e. of an underdevelopment process)

The term 'development' may be interpreted as referring to a particular type of movement – the correlative of which is a qualitatively different form of movement, i.e. *underdevelopment*. Development here means forward or progressive movement and gets its meaning from its relation to underdevelopment as reverse or regressive movement. In economic terms, development describes an increase of productive capacity, underdevelopment communicates a reduction.

Thus we have:

Increasing productive capacity

Development: X ———————————————→

Underdevelopment: ←——————————————— Y

Declining productive capacity[14]

The characterisation of unit X remains that it is 'developing' and at any given time is dynamic. But at any given moment, Y is also dynamic: it is underdeveloping. This provides a preliminary qualitative distinction between forms of economic movement. This conceptualisation also applies when units X and Y are not separate, i.e. where development and underdevelopment are part of a wider process which *simultaneously* leads to an increase of productive capacity at X and a decrease at Y.[15]

Summary

I have argued that if development is seen as a process, it is unrealistic to view underdevelopment as static non-development, despite the logical possibility of this. Instead, one should look at differences *within* economic processes, while also avoiding treating these differences as simply quantitative distinctions within a singular process of development. Using qualitative distinctions, development may be defined as an increase in the total productive capacity of a particular structure, and underdevelopment as a regression of capacity in a qualitatively different structure.

Conclusion: development as attributes and process

Following all the arguments above, 'development' in this monograph is used in a way that combines the senses of attributes and process. While its attributes concern productive capacity, viewed both quantitatively and qualitatively, the processual sense designates a movement that is qualitatively distinct to underdevelopment. This definition establishes a basic minimum of general meaning in terms of which I now consider the social basis of development and underdevelopment.

Social structure and development

Development involves an interaction of humans, means of production (including raw materials – the objects of labour), and the context of labour (geographical and ecological) (Nolan and White, 1979: 14). In interpreting the interplay of these elements, many writers have argued against a 'technicist' approach which ignores or underplays social issues.[16] While development is an economic concern, its explanation needs to be more broadly social. It is to the credit of some modernisation theorists (e.g. Hoselitz, 1964) that they have drawn attention to the institutional and cultural concomitants of economic growth (Nafziger, 1979; Berger, 1976: 51). How successfully they have related these, however, is another matter. In my view, focusing on social structure helps to make sense of the myriad social dynamics affecting development and underdevelopment. A social structure is dialectically constituted by social *relations*, which in turn are the general patterns present in concrete (and, to a greater or lesser extent, purposeful) social *relationships*.[17] It is in terms of these shared relationships and practices that individuals form, and are formed by, a social grouping in relation to other groups. This perspective contrasts with a pluralistic viewpoint which more-or-less randomly identifies a hodge-podge assortment of disparate groups and activities. By focusing on *relations*, the concept of social structure helps to explain the existence of social groups, their activities and their interaction.

There is a danger when theorising about social relations abstracted from a series of concrete relationships of developing a reified and formalistic concept of 'social structure'. In my view, this can be avoided provided that the concept is not confused with the real relations to which it refers, and still less with the concrete relationships and practices both sustaining and expressing these relations. Another danger is to treat social structure as rigid and unchanging (Williams, 1976a: 255). The concept of social structure should be dynamic because it involves the concept of contradiction – i.e. structural tensions between opposites which are related to each other within its unity (Mao, 1977: *passim*; Bottomore et al., 1985: 93–4; Colletti, 1975; Althusser, 1969b). The concepts of contradictory social relations, social groups and group practices are central to theorising the history of social structure as an historical object.[18]

The social structure is based on relations between the parts (various constituent groups and their practices) which make up the whole. However, the whole is also greater than the parts in that many constituent groups would not exist as such outside of their relations constituting the whole, and certainly would not be the same in a context involving different relations. At the same time, one cannot focus on the whole as if it had unidirectional determinancy over the character of the parts, as is evident in some accounts of global development (cf. Wallerstein (1974) and Frank (1969a, 1969c)) (see next chapter). Analysis needs to take both levels into account, looking at the dialectical relationship between them. However, that the whole is greater than the parts is significant because it enables us to conceptualise not only overarching relations between the parts, but also the dynamics that a given social structure gives rise to. An example here is competition – something that is not evident in the immediate relations between groups (and group practices), but is instead a dynamic generated by capitalist relations and which acts upon the whole and the parts as a function of the whole structure (see next chapter). To encompass this type of phenomenon, I use the term 'social *system*' to describe both the social structure and the dynamics it gives rise to. In the same vein, I refer later to the concept of 'economic system' and what I term the 'system dynamics' of competition, commercialisation and capital accumulation.

Turning now to an analysis of social structure, classical Marxism highlighted *inter alia* a 'base' economic structure and a political–legal 'superstructure'. According to Marx:

It is always the direct relationship of the owners of the conditions of production to the direct producers . . . which reveals the innermost secret, the hidden basis of the entire *social structure*, and with it the political form of the relation of sovereignty and dependence, in short the corresponding specific form of state. (1974: 791, my emphasis)

This quotation puts forward a key element of Marxist methodology, namely, that analysis needs to begin with the relations around production if it is to explicate the whole social structure (and, for the purpose of this work, how this entity relates to economic development). Marx further argued that:

The totality of relations of production constitutes the *economic structure* of society, the real foundation, on which arises a legal and political superstructure and to which correspond definite forms of social consciousness. The mode of production of material life conditions the general process of social, political and intellectual life. (1977a: 20, my emphasis)

This statement deals with both *structures* (economic, legal and political) and *consciousness*. When carefully analysed, it can be seen as specifying two distinct relations among these elements. On the one hand, there is the relation between structures (economic as the foundation for the legal and political structures). On the other hand, there is the relation between this entire *totality* of structures and consciousness. A pitfall in interpreting the model is to conflate these into a single relation, so that consciousness is seen as being determined by economic structures alone. A second pitfall is to see both relations in a transitively causal or expressive sense. In my view, consciousness (including ideology) is complexly determined by *all* the structures, not only the economic base structure. In addition, both consciousness and the superstructure are *determined* rather than caused.

Understanding the relations in the base and superstructure in a transitive, causal sense leads to the false – and unproductive – 'Marx–Weber' debate about the respective causal importance of the different components (see, for example, Popper, 1973: 107). In the development context, Berger (1976: 54) refers to the modernisation theorists' 'chicken–egg' question of which 'comes first' – economic growth or its social, cultural and psychological correlates. We could add here, political correlates too, given that theorists like Apter (1965) and Almond and Coleman (1966) have assumed that economic growth automatically causes certain political effects (see also O'Dowd, 1977). Because these assumptions are based on ahistorical, over-abstract and formalistic premises, the debate – phrased in chicken–egg terms – can only go round in circles.

A more sophisticated view (and one distinct from many Marxist interpretations) is to see the base structure as integrally *limiting*, rather than *causing*, the superstructure, and both these structures together having a similar type of relation to consciousness (Hindess and Hirst, 1975: 16). Such anti-reductionism has been theorised in the concept of 'conditions of existence' (see Cutler et al., 1977). A particular superstructure and consciousness are understood as the necessary conditions that a particular base structure would require in concrete existence *and vice versa*. But the economic base structure does not cause or call into being these conditions. Indeed, up to a point there are likely to be contradictions between them all.

The advantage of this more sophisticated view is that it stresses – without overexaggerating – the connections between i. the base, ii. the superstructure and iii. consciousness. This holism is valuable in that it shows, for example, that it is inadequate to analyse social structure only in terms of iii. without reference to i. and ii. Thus, the pattern-variable approach to economic development (Parsons, 1966), by defining its 'modern–traditional' dichotomy in terms of values (universalism–particularism; achievement ascription; specificity–diffuseness), must be judged as inadequate (see also Magubane, 1971). A value such as individualism, associated with modernity, needs to be seen against the real structural atomisation of people in an economy which isolates them as individuals in commodity exchanges with each other (see also Moore, 1969: 486–7). At the same time, neither i. nor ii. can be fully explained without iii. Thus, even if, for example, Weber gives too much weight to Protestant ideology in the development of capitalism, religious consciousness does have an efficacy in the practices and groups within the political and economic structures (Muratorio, 1980: 38; Zeitlin, 1968: 131–63).

Weber held that Marxist concepts are ideal types with only a heuristic use (1948: 103), and therefore that it was 'pernicious' to think of these concepts as empirically valid or real tendencies. Against this, one may argue that Marxist concepts are intended to assist in producing a 'reproduction of the concrete by way of thought' (Marx, 1973: 101), and for this purpose they are intended to *represent* dimensions of real phenomena. However, Weber's criticism is still valuable in pointing us away from treating the base and superstructure as reality itself. Some writers do assume that base and superstructure are meant to be distinct real entities (e.g. Kahn and Llobera, 1980: 94; Laclau, 1979). While Weber errs by seeing the model purely as an ideal type, these others go wrong by viewing it crudely as direct reality. Instead, the model needs to be recognised as an analytical concept in which the concepts of economic base, the superstructure and consciousness have been *abstracted* separately out of complex reality. In this reality, base and superstructure are certainly comprised of real relations, but mixed up and integrated with other aspects of the real. The model is a tool to analyse reality, and is not itself direct replica of that reality.

The economic structure: three Moments of production

The concept of economic structure, so central for social structure and development, can be fruitfully broken down into forces and relations of production and viewed in terms of three 'Moments' of production. In the ensuing theorisation of forces of production, productive labour, necessary and surplus labour, the concepts differ from many Marxist writings, including those of Marx himself. Marx argued that:

In the social production of their existence, men enter into definite relations that are indispensable and independent of their will, relations of production appropriate to a given stage in the development of their material forces of production. The totality of these relations of production constitutes the *economic structure* of society. (1977b: 20, my emphasis)

There are two distinct – though not in reality separate – structures in this totality of relations that Marx describes as comprising the economic structure. One of these is the structure of technical social relations around the means of production. This is designated in this monograph as the 'forces of production'. Used in this way, the term is not reducible to 'means of production' (see Hellman, 1979: 145–6). The second structure within the economic structure is that of the social relations around the performance of labour by producers for other people. I use the term 'relations of production' more narrowly than Marx (above) to refer to this structure as distinct from the forces of production. Both types of social relations, it will be argued, are pertinent to productive capacity, but in quite different ways. These two social relations structures are effective at what I have distinguished as three 'Moments' of production:

Moment A – relations of possession of and separation from the means of production,

Moment B – relations *in* production (i.e. *within* production),[19]

Moment C – relations in the distribution and utilisation of the product.

Looking at the forces of production in terms of the three Moments, it may be noted that the relations designated by the concept encompass Moment B, i.e. the specifics of co-operation within each labour process and the co-ordination of several labour processes within a single unit of production (Hindess and Hirst, 1975: 244).[20] 'Forces of production' also covers relations outside of the production process at Moment C, i.e. relations of distribution and utilisation of the products of each labour process/unit of production in terms of a societal division of labour. The 'forces of production' also encompasses Moment A – the technical relations of 'possession/separation' from the means of production. Finally, the concept of forces of production also includes the relations between *sectors* of production, such as those constituted in terms of *similar activities* in the economic circuit ('industrial', 'commercial', 'financial'), *size* ('small-scale', 'large-scale') or *product* ('services', 'manufacturing', 'mining', 'agriculture'). It is partly in the relation between sectors constituted by product that the 'Agrarian Question' of economic development is located (see chapter four).[21] The balance between sectors affects productive capacity in that, for example, a preponderance of commercial or financial over industrial activity may have adverse developmental significance. The 'forces of production' are directly linked to 'productive capacity' (or 'productive force'), but the two are distinct concepts. Productive capacity is (in part) but a consequence of the structure of technical social relations around the means of production, and a *function* of other factors including the relations of production. From the viewpoint of development, what is significant is *actual productive capacity in use*, i.e. as realised in material output.[22] The most efficient ratio in the division and allocation of labour to various activities is a key factor in the rate of expansion of productive capacity, and the character of the forces of production have special significance in this regard.

At the same time as material output is the actualisation of productive capacity, not all of it *raises* this capacity as such. Taking development to be a continuous process of expanding productive capacity, the most significant labour is that enabling increased, improved or entirely new output, and this is labour that culminates in new, advanced, material *means of production*. Development is thus bound up with the ability of a given economic unit to co-ordinate the forces of production in such a way as to maximise productivity in *this* area of work (not forgetting, of course, that this area cannot exist in isolation of others).

Like the forces of production, the concept of 'relations of production' also spans all three Moments of production. But it refers to the structure of social relations centred around the distinction (at Moment B) between labour that is necessary and labour that is surplus to the direct labourers themselves. In my schema, necessary and surplus labour are characteristic of *all* types of relations of production structures, and not in the sense that Marx's *Capital* uses them only in terms of capitalist structures (see Marx, 1972: chapter ten). A necessary condition of society's continued existence is that the class of direct producers perform a surplus labour beyond that needed to create the material goods for their immediate social reproduction. This surplus labour provides for the reproduction of dependants (the young and, to some extent, the sick and the aged). It also provides for those who perform activities which are indirectly necessary for the reproduction of the direct producers – such as organisational, co-ordinating, service, health, educational and other functions. The simple reproduction of a society therefore means that the labour of the direct producers may be conceptually divided into 'necessary labour' and 'surplus labour' (Hindess and Hirst, 1975: 26–7). This division, its proportions, and the allocation thereof, are pertinent to the development of productive capacity. For example, in some societies reproduction may be on an expanded scale where some surplus labour goes into development of the means of production (Friedmann, 1979: 162). In this particular respect, the concept of surplus labour overlaps with Baran's (1962) concept of 'surplus' (see next chapter).

That the direct producers perform surplus labour for others does not mean that relations of production are therefore relations of exploitation. Contra Meillassoux (1960) and Godelier (1969), exploitation is not reducible to the appropriation of surplus without counterpart (see Dupré and Rey, 1973: 151; Hindess and Hirst, 1975: 68). The appropriation of surplus labour becomes exploitative when the producers are 'separated' from the means of production, and only have access through accepting controls and conditions that alienate a proportion of their surplus labour to a 'possessing' class (in the form of work or as products) (Meillassoux, 1970: 103; Hindess and Hirst, 1975: 266, 232; Galeski, 1972: 189). This exploitation, and struggle against it, determines what constitutes necessary and surplus labour for the producers. The capacity to set the terms of exploitation is linked to the concepts of 'separation/possession' which refer to the effective ownership of the means of production. For example, within the context of feudal tenancy, a feudal hoe-cultivator can only initiate and control production once he has access to land (Hindess and Hirst, 1975: 238). An assembly-line worker under capitalism must generally be politically and economically acceptable to the owners of the means of production (or their agents) in order to participate in the labour process – although even then he is still excluded from control of it. While separation/possession are thus primarily bound up with the relations of production, they also have a technical dimension falling within the forces of production. The assembly-line worker and the hoe-cultivator differ in their respective capacities for individual control of the means of production and initiation of the labour process.

Class relations of possession/separation (i.e. Moment A) usually imply class power over Moments B and C. This involves control over the proportions of necessary and surplus labour (although not without an ongoing struggle) and therefore the extent of surplus labour, as well as the allocation and use of this surplus labour and its products. Exploitation usually involves the extortion of additional surplus labour than would otherwise be necessary to reproduce a society – for example, the 'extra' surplus labour to support unproductive members of the exploiting class, the above-average consumption of even the productive members of the exploiting class, and the political and ideological apparatus necessary for enforcing the possession/separation and exploitation (adapted from Morris, 1976: 298; Hindess and Hirst, 1975: 50; Wright, 1980: 179–80).

The difference between forces of production and relations of production can be illustrated in the example of small-scale cultivation where hired workers (who have no independent possession of the means of production) work alongside family labourers. The family possesses the means of production, controls the cultivation and has ultimate say over what is to count as necessary and surplus labour for the employees. Thus, although all labourers may, strictly speaking, perform the same work, they still differ in their relations to surplus labour. In other words, the forces of production are the same for everyone, but the relations of production differ (Cooper, 1978: 158–9; Friedmann, 1978: *passim*; 1979: 181, footnote 12).

Building on the discussion this far, it is possible to distinguish various 'stages' of surplus labour corresponding to the Moments of production:

Moments of production	*Stages of surplus labour*
A. Relations of possession/separation from the means of production	1. These relations constitute a foundation for the type and extent of surplus labour
B. Relations in production i.e. the labour process	2. Performance ⎫ of 3. Extraction ⎬ surplus 4. Appropriation ⎭ labour
C. Relations of distribution and utilisation of the social product ('post-production' relations)	5. Distribution of surplus product 6. Utilisation of surplus product

Exploitative surplus labour relations (in stages 2, 3 and 4) depend on class relations of possession/separation (in stage 1). Relations of distribution may also involve class relations of possession/separation – not of the means of *production*, but the means of *distribution*. Class control of distribution can be the basis for class appropriation (stage 5) of surplus product. But this is appropriation of surplus which has already been performed and appropriated in the labour process. There is thus an important – but in developmentalist writing often neglected – distinction to be drawn between exploitation in Moment B and Moment C (see Booth, 1975: 78–9; O'Brien, 1975: 27, footnote 1).

My concept of 'relations of production' refers to the social relations within and between *each* stage of surplus labour. This perspective differs from those writers who use the term to refer to only some of these stages. While most writers seem to take a position against reducing the relations *of* production solely to relations *in* production, they tend either to stress the interconnections between Moment A and B, *or* those between Moment B and C. Few approaches focus on all the interconnections, and one that does do so ends up denying meaningful significance to Moments A or B in characterising the relations of production.

For example, writers emphasising Moments B and C suggest that the 'relations of production' include relations of distribution, exchange and consumption (see Foster-Carter, 1978: 233; Nolan and White, 1979: 4).

Another writer (Bernstein, 1979b: 442) uses the concept in the same way, but adds the relations of utilisation of surplus labour. The inadequacy of stressing only Moments B and C has a mirror opposite in those who argue that 'relations of production' encompasses A and B. Thus, it is argued that the relations within production are never given at the level of the labour process alone, but depend on the distribution of the means of production (see Sklair, 1979: 330; Ennew et al., 1977: 308).

A third approach found in the literature uses the term 'relations of production' to refer to the whole structure of relations around surplus labour, but by ultimate reference to the very last stage: the utilisation of the products of surplus labour. The concept tends here to be used in the singular (*relation* of production). In this approach, utilisation is itself a function of the 'purpose of production' (which in my schema is bound up with the system dynamics of the whole). Thus, for Banaji (1980: 516–17), a range of relations of exploitation can be grouped under one relation of production insofar as they serve the same end.[23] Also, all forms of surplus labour are part of a capitalist relation of production if their products are ultimately used as capital (see also Roseberry, 1978: 79). In this view, therefore, a relation of production is not to be conflated or identified with a set of relations of exploitation. In my terminology, Moment B and Moment A are seen as secondary to Moment C, in particular to the relations of utilisation as affected by a system dynamic. While this approach has the merit of linking the stages of surplus labour into an overall structural whole, it is at the cost of blurring differences in exploitation relations between and within different labour processes. Both relations of utilisation and system dynamics may assist in *characterising* (rather than defining) a relation of production. But, even here they should not override Moments A and B. The problem that this raises is how to define the overall structure which unites the stages of surplus labour within it, and at the same time keep account of the heterogeneity within it. As will be discussed in the next chapter (on the concept of mode of production), the concepts of heterogeneous and homogeneous relations of production structures, and the articulation between them in an 'economic system', can help to clarify the issue.

Because economic structures involve a division between necessary and surplus labour, production is never a wholly technical process with only technically determined social relations (Hindess and Hirst, 1975: 26). Not only can there never be forces of production without relations of production, but Marxism assumes that at the very least all three Moments of production have an ideological component. It also holds that when the relations of production involve exploitation, then they involve a political–legal aspect. Examples here are the ideology of community redistribution under primitive communism and the juridical relationship of ownership under capitalism (Nolan and White, 1979: 4). Such political and ideological aspects of production relationships have two kinds of efficacy. Firstly, there are 'external' structural interventions by institutions outside production (judiciary, police, etc.). Secondly, there is efficacy in the form of a dimension or quality of the relations around surplus labour. Thus, superstructural relations can be said to have, in the concrete, a presence in the relations of production.

There are also other social relations which are pertinent to the relations of production. Long and Richardson (1978: 112) point to interpersonal and group relations outside production but essential to its maintenance. For example, kinship or associational membership may indirectly determine relations in all three Moments of production (1978: 188, 206, footnote 3). Such relations can link groups controlling resources with groups that do the actual production, i.e. bring together Moments A and B. Concrete relationships of production can only exist and be reproduced or transformed in conjunction with a host of other relations (Locke, 1976: 14). However, at the level of theoretical abstraction, it is important to bear in mind that development is an economic category, despite being crucially bound up with political and ideological factors.

The class structure

Central to the economic structure and to development are classes, constituted by groups of people sharing common locations in the relations of production, and specifically in regard to the control and extortion of surplus labour. Because class relations concern exploitation, the class structure is clearly not identical to the occupational structure as designated by the forces of production relations. A given technical function can perform a range of roles in the social relations of control and exploitation (Wright, 1980: 186). Forces of production have some influence on the class structure, such as where a particular occupation in the labour process can be an aid to enforcing class control. But it is the relations of production that define classes as such (see Hindess and Hirst, 1975: 134–5; Carchedi, 1975: 19–36). Seen in this way, the class structure thus refers to groups engaged in practices that are directly – and contradictorily – related to each other through exploitation.[24]

A thorough identification of classes requires account to be taken of relations at Moments A, B and C, as well as of how they reproduce themselves across these Moments, and whether they exhibit any system dynamics deriving from the whole. While class relations at Moment A, i.e. the relations of possession/separation, do not in themselves ensure exploitation, they do characteristically provide the foundation for this to occur in Moment B – the labour process (Meillassoux, 1970: 103). However, the relations at Moment A are not always totally congruent with the relations of exploitation in the actual labour process. There may be overlaps in production itself (i.e. in Moment B) between the conceptually exclusive class functions implicit in class possession/separation (at Moment A). Classes located in these places of overlap perform contradictory practices: for example, the 'new middle class' executes exploitative control in the labour process but is still an exploited class (Carchedi, 1975: 51; Wright, 1980: 183). As will be discussed in later chapters, overlaps also exist with rich peasants and also often among rural development scheme settlers.

Class relations structured in Moments A and B have a specific presence and effectivity in Moment C with respect to the relations of distribution and utilisation. With regard to *distribution*, there are differences such as between cases of surplus product given by a wage-labourer to his family, and a capitalist contributing to agents operating repressive and ideological control apparatuses. These distributive relations are distinct from class relations of exploitation within distribution, which depend on relations of possession/separation from means of distribution.

With regard to *utilisation* of surplus labour/product, there are again differences between classes pre-constituted in Moments A and B, particularly in the extent to which surplus product is used for productive or unproductive purposes. For example, capitalists' possession of means of production enables them to utilise much of the surplus labour they appropriate to consolidate and expand their possession. For wage-labourers, utilisation is generally limited to reproducing their families without transforming their separation into possession. Comparing class utilisation in different class structures brings out, for example, the different significance for economic development of a (consuming) feudal exploiter and a (reinvesting) capitalist exploiter. Consideration of distribution and utilisation also leads directly to an assessment of *reproduction* of the whole class structure. Indeed, a focus on class differentiation in terms of reproduction is common in the literature (see chapter four). This is valuable insofar as it shows how distribution and utilisation relations reflect and reinforce the other Moments of production. However, reproduction is just one dimension of these relations. Furthermore, while the notion of reproduction links Moment C back to A, such unity cannot automatically be assumed.

Class exploitation can exist within Moment C in the distribution and utilisation of surplus labour in the form of surplus product. An important distinction to bear in mind here is the difference between classes defined by their relations in Moments A and B as they relate to distribution and utilisation (as discussed above), and a class structure which is constituted in Moment C. The relations of exploitation in Moment C will articulate with the relations of exploitation in B, but they are distinct in that they involve 'fresh' exploitation. Exploitation in this situation occurs where one class (e.g. merchants) has exclusive possession of the means of distribution and on this basis compels other classes to yield a portion of their surplus product in the distribution process. These other classes are those based on Moments of A and B of production and, whether they be exploiter or exploited, may both be exploited by this class controlling the means of distribution (see Palloix, 1973: 83).[25]

Insofar as an exploiting class, constituted by exclusive control over means of utilisation (e.g. financial capitalists), exploits classes that use surplus product for *means of subsistence*, the exploitation is of a fixed amount of surplus already produced and appropriated. Insofar as the exploiting class exploits by controlling *the acquisition of means of production*, it can influence the actual performance and initial appropriation of surplus labour, as may happen to producers in rural development programmes where debt relations can serve to raise the rate of exploitation (see chapter four).[26]

Certain classes have consistent relations with each other and a presence in each Moment of production, as in the case, for example, for capitalist and proletariat classes. However, there are also groups that are not part of such a homogeneous relations of production structure at A, B and C. These are classes in what I term *heterogeneous relations of production* – i.e. classes which articulate to other classes only in one or two of the Moments of production. (The concept of a homogeneous and heterogeneous relation of production is further elaborated in the next chapter.) There are two different categories here:

Firstly, there is the question of relations between classes that are based in different Moments of production. The existence of an exploiting class based in Moment A and B does not preclude the existence of a different class in different exploitative relations in Moment C, for example, merchants and finance capitalists. At the same time, the existence of class exploitation in Moment C does not depend on class relations in Moments A and B. For example, simple commodity producers or co-operatives embodying no exploitation in their labour processes may be exploited in Moment C by merchants or usurers. Exploiting classes based in Moment C articulate within themselves and with the external classes which are already specific to a definite structure. This articulation constitutes a heterogeneous structure because while it involves real relations of exploitation, and therefore class relationships, these do not involve the same classes relating to each other at each Moment of production.

Secondly, there is the question of the relations between the classes which are part of different relations of production structures. Between the two situations, there may well still be articulation between one or other of the Moments of production. In order to identify comprehensively classes in these situations, it is necessary to examine the way that a heterogeneous relation of production may be created via intersections at Moment C (e.g. commodity exchange), Moment B (labour), or Moment A (overlapping relations of possession/separation) (see Poulantzas, 1973: 33; Meillassoux, 1970: 103). This is taken up in chapter three.

Just as the relations of production are only 'purely economic' as an abstraction, so with class relations and practices. Because class relations involve domination, subordination and exploitation – i.e. power relations – they have a political and ideological as well as economic character (Steeves, 1978: 124; Mamdani, 1977: 11; Crouch, 1977: 4; Wright, 1980: 212). The relations between classes also *inherently* involve relationships of control, exploitation, domination and subordination – and therefore conflict (Byres, 1981: 406). It is acknowledged that class behaviour is a far more complex, opaque and ambiguous phenomenon than many Marxists would concede. Class practices vary organisationally, ideologically and institutionally. Among the reasons for this, it can be noted that class practices and interests emerge in concrete class formation and creation, class consolidation, class reproduction, class development and class demise. Some classes and practices will exhibit features difficult to understand because they are transitional and uncrystallised (Mamdani, 1977: 10; Raikes, 1978: 286; Byres, 1981: 406–7). Multi-class membership by individuals is likely to affect their practices, as will seasonal changes in class membership, geographical mobility and interclass mobility (see Cliffe, 1978: 327; Charlesworth, 1980: 265; Alavi, 1973: 295; Clammer, 1978b: 15). This complexity is important for productive capacity and sometimes confounds rural development planning which assumes certain class trajectories for the people it aims at.

Class places, relations and practices are also affected by the whole gamut of relations that individuals are involved in and much variation in class practices is due to the influence of ideologies on class consciousness – i.e. the consciousness of a class as a class for itself. For example, class formation is less socially effective where no distinctive cultural characteristics have evolved to identify classes as groups with distinct lifestyles (Feldman, 1975: 165). This has special relevance to the political significance of many rural development strategies (see chapter five).[27] Notwithstanding the complex significance of these structural, institutional and ideological influences, the fact remains that a class structure and class practices involve people sharing similar actions and therefore classes are still of relevance as social forces – be their members 'conscious' or not.

2 Mode of production, surplus and capitalist development

The concept of mode of production

The concept of 'mode of production' is central to analysing the economic relations and associated patterns of development. For Marx:

The direct relationship of the owners of the conditions of production to the direct producers ... always naturally [corresponds] ... to a definite stage in the development of the methods of labour and thereby its social productivity. (1974: 291)

In my terminology, we may discern here a proposition that there is a correspondence between relations of production and forces of production. To this intermeshing also corresponds a level of productive capacity. In Marx's view, there is thus a limited functional compatibility between these elements (see also Godelier, 1972: 349; Marx, 1976b: 1024–5, 1035). In my view, it is when the correspondence between relations and forces of production structures spans Moments A, B and C – and is reproduced as such in conjunction with system dynamics deriving from the whole – that a 'mode of production' is constituted. This is what makes it possible to identify, for example, a *capitalist* mode of production with *capitalist* relations of production as opposed to a structure which might involve some seemingly capitalist features but does not constitute a mode of production. An articulated combination of a homogeneous relations of production structure with a homogeneous forces of production structure is the basic structure of the general concept of mode of production. It is, therefore, also the basic structure of modes of production in general, designating the essential relations common to the (less abstract) concepts of each particular mode of production. The correspondence of a mode of production to a level of 'social productivity' (i.e. 'productive capacity' in my terms) makes it a central concept for development studies.

The concept of mode of production is complex in two respects: firstly, its place in levels of abstraction and, secondly, its scope of reference. The first issue concerns the extent to which the concept of 'mode of production' and the concept of each particular mode of production may be elaborated upon without sliding into limited empiricist generalisations. The second issue concerns the relation of 'mode of production' to different units of analysis within the context of a myriad of economic articulations and interconnections.

As regards the first issue, the concept of the mode of production designates not a *juxtaposition* of relations and forces of production structures, but an articulated *combination* in a unified structural whole.[1] As such, modes of production are mutually exclusive and, although they are distinguished by relations of production, the differences between them cannot be reduced to this factor alone. A mode's *differentia specifica* has to be considered in the light of the concept covering more than the sum of its parts – such as the system dynamics generated as a function of the whole. For example, the capitalist mode of production (CMP) is different from other modes not only in its relations (and forces) of production structure, but also in the effects of these structures – such as competition. The obverse of this point is that an element like wage-labour is not on its own evidence of the CMP. Similarly, rent has a very different nature and function in the totality of the feudal mode of production as compared to the capitalist (Hindess and Hirst, 1975: 293, 296–7). It follows from the above that there are limits to theorising the general concept of mode of production, and that the effective constituent units of each specific mode will – to a certain extent – be mode specific (Duggett, 1975: 165; Hobsbawm, 1973: 219). It also means that investigating whether, for example, an articulation between capital and 'peasant' producers constitutes a capitalist unit of production in the CMP (see chapter five) requires a conception of the total specificity of the CMP.

This brings us to the second complexity noted above, namely, the scope of analysis. Marx uses 'mode of production' to refer to both the *entire base structure* in the base–superstructure model and to the (narrower) *labour process at the point of production* (Banaji, 1976a: 301). To see what distinguishes and what relates the 'mode of production' to the two units of analysis, one can profitably locate them all within the varying scope of the various Moments of production (see below). However, many writers have opted to approach the mode of production either in terms of the smallest units (labour processes) or the largest (the world economic system). Thus, a number of writers (for example Meillassoux, 1972; Terray, 1974; Sahlins, 1974; Chayanov (1925) 1966: 166) have used the labour process as a basis for deriving or generalising a broader mode of production. One common error here is to look only at the technical division of labour in the labour process, thereby ignoring the question of surplus labour. A second, more fundamental, error ignores the role of relations beyond the individual labour process – i.e. Moments A and C of production. This second error invalidates the basic method of this approach, even when it is not hampered by the technicist error (Cooper, 1978: *passim*; Hindess and Hirst, 1975: 61). One effect of this method is a mistaken proliferation of modes of production. For example, a feudal corvée labour system would be analysed as an articulation of two modes of production: one where the producer works for his family, and another where he performs surplus labour for the lord. Against this, the concept of mode of production is based on the premiss that the structure as a *whole* is crucial (Sole, 1977: 39). Thus, the two feudal labour processes just described are not independent adjacent processes but rather integrated and interdependent components within a feudal mode of production.

The problem with generalising the mode of production (or the 'economy' in a synonymous sense) from the labour process is that it assumes that the structure of the whole is no more than the aggregation of similar units (Friedmann, 1979: 159). In opposition to this, however, it is the ensemble of social relations (both forces and relations of production) which sets the conditions of existence of labour processes and their effectivity as individual units, and this cannot be neglected in theorising a mode of production (Ennew et al., 1977: 306). I would argue that labour processes should be located and characterised in terms of their wider conditions of existence, i.e. within a heterogeneous or homogeneous articulation with Moments A and C of production.

If the mode of production cannot be identified at, or derived from, the minimum unit on the scale, what about the other extreme? Here, dependency theorists have approached the question through their analysis of how economic units link up to form a total system (O'Brien, 1975: 112). For example, Wallerstein (1977: 5) argues:

A mode of production is a characteristic of an economy and an economy is defined by an effective ongoing division of productive labour. *Ergo*, to discover the mode of production that prevails we must know the real bounds of the division of labour of which we are speaking. Neither individual units of production, nor political or cultural entities may be described as having a mode of production, only economies. (Quoted by Foster-Carter, 1978: 239)

There is something to be said for stressing interconnections and effective totality. The problem is that remaining at such a level explains the economic structure in general at the expense of the particular. One can see the wood, but not the trees. It is not surprising, therefore, that the dependency approach has been criticised for detracting from the complexity of the whole (O'Brien, 1975: 12, 23; Foster-Carter, 1978: 239; Brenner, 1977: *passim*).

Laclau (1971) has tackled this problem by retaining the dependency stress on totality, but distinguishes this from the mode of production structure. He describes the totality by the useful concept of 'economic system', which designates a unified, structure and differentiated whole constituted by the articulation of a number of modes of production (and, I would add, heterogeneous relations of production structures). Such a concept of the economic totality can be characterised in terms of the dominant mode of production in the articulation – for example, one could speak of a 'capitalist economic system'. This is very different to identifying a capitalist mode of production with a capitalist economic system – which is what many dependency theorists do (Booth, 1975: 75). A capitalist economic system is fundamentally, but not homogeneously, capitalist (Obregon, 1974: 394–7; Mamdani, 1977: 138). And, as a *system*, this unit involves not a simple juxtaposition of elements, but a structure of relations which in addition is likely to be characterised by *system dynamics* deriving from the whole. In this view, the mode of production lies between the labour process and the economic system. With these distinctions made, I now turn to an analysis of the specific relationship between these different levels.

Mode of production and the articulation of labour processes

How, within an economic system, does a mode of production relate to its own endogamous labour processes, as well as to those that are linked to it but remain exogenous? Seen from the other side, the question is what makes a labour process part of a homogeneous, rather than a heterogeneous, relations and forces structure? Metaphorically, we need criteria to identify which trees are within the wood, and – by implication – which are merely on the fringes. One approach to the problem of distinguishing internal and external articulation has been simply to gloss over the difference altogether. Friedmann (1979: 160) proposes the term 'form of production' to cover both types of articulation, but it is precisely the differences between them that need to be theorised. And, contrary to what some writers have implied (e.g. Taylor, 1981: 389; Spiegel, 1979: 23), the need for conceptual criteria also does not vanish by seeing the articulation in historical and empirical terms.

The issue of internal articulation could be grasped easily if a characteristic labour process could be theorised for each mode of production. But the issue is complex because there can be (up to a point) some variation in the labour processes within a single mode of production, such as the different labour processes involved in a feudal mode which correspond to different forms of rent payment (labour, cash, kind). Another example is the different labour process involved in capitalist piece-work as compared to capitalist factory production. A related complexity concerns the question of whether all the labour processes within a mode of production should be characterised by the name of the mode – for example, as capitalist labour processes in a capitalist mode. This is more than a taxonomic quibble – it has implications for seeing the tendencies in the labour process (see Galeski, 1972: 22). Although some writers leave the issue hanging (e.g. Kay, 1975: 102), it is significant for the study of economic development.[2] Many writers take for granted the typicality of particular labour processes (and related units of production) for particular modes of production. Those who broach the subject have used various criteria to characterise 'internal' labour processes, including those of 'laws of motion', 'reproduction' and 'integration', but none of these is adequate on its own.

Banaji (1976a: 302) focuses on the 'laws of motion' of the mode as the key element in the relationship between a mode and its internal labour processes. For him, the typicality of labour processes for particular modes of production depends on whether they function according to the 'laws of motion' of the particular mode of production. Ultimately, his position distinguishes degrees of correspondence of motion of each labour process 'part' to the mode of production 'whole'. Thus he speaks about labour processes as varying in the extent to which they are an 'adequate' or 'crystallised' form of the mode of production. Banaji's view, however, is basically circular: the mode and the labour process correspond if they manifest the same laws. What these 'laws' are, how the labour process and mode of production might interact to produce them, and what the explanation is for different 'crystallisations' in different labour processes are all unexplained. This is not to say that the criterion of correspondence of the part (the labour process) to the 'laws of motion' of the whole is *per se* invalid (although I would prefer to interpret such 'laws' as system dynamics). However, it is inadequate as the sole determining criterion. This can be seen in the case of merchant capitalists exploiting a class of producers who maintain possession of the means of production – e.g. artisans. Despite often exhibiting characteristics of a capitalist system process (e.g. competitiveness and commercialisation), the producers here are not integrated within a capitalist relations of production structure. Instead, they relate to it as an external class relationship mediated through Moment C. As a structure of three Moments of production, this is a heterogeneous relation of production and not part of the CMP.

For some writers, a labour process is an internal part of a mode of production if it is physically reproduced within it (see Taylor, 1981: 389; Ennew et al., 1977: 310). One potential problem here is that the criterion of reproduction is broad enough to incorporate fundamentally different labour processes within a single mode of production.[3] For example, one finds that simple commodity producers, domestic labour, co-operatives and state enterprises can all be integrated into reproduction based on exchange of products with capitalist labour processes and sharing the superstructural context of capitalist property relations. To call all these 'capitalist' because of this only obscures important differences in their relations at Moments A and B and in their relations to the system dynamics of the CMP.

Some writers draw the line by specifying strict integration of a labour process into a homogeneous relation of production structure. This focus differs from the reproduction approach described above in that it rests not only on a physical articulation between a labour process and a mode of production, but on integration at the level of social relations. For example, Hindess and Hirt (1975: 104, 270, 305) argue that a unit which appears to be capitalist is only strictly so if its reproduction is dependent on capitalist exchange relations where means of production and labour-power are also exchanged.[4] One limitation of this view is that it ignores the issue of system processes as they relate to the labour process. But it also risks a labour process based on wage-labour exploitation being designated as *non-capitalist* if it has some integration with non-capitalist relations at Moments A and C such as plunder, unequal exchange or utilisation of labour-power that originate in other modes of production. Hindess and Hirst do not go as far as claiming such instances to be *non*-capitalist; they describe them as 'capitalist' in quotation marks to distinguish them from true capitalist labour processes. But the problem still remains that what constitutes a 'true' capitalist labour process – namely, in this view, absolute integration into Moments A and C – makes it difficult to grasp the possibility of more than one relation of production traversing a labour process – as with, for example, a labour process squarely within the CMP, but which also articulates (via heterogeneous relations) with non-capitalist relations of production in some respects (see chapter five). It would be wrong to assume that the labour process internal to a mode of production involves only one set of relations of exploitation in a concrete situation. An example is the combination of family and wage-labour in a middle peasant enterprise. In this case, we could speak of the articulation of differing relations of exploitation in a labour process only one set of which would be internal to a mode.

From the argument above, it may be concluded that defining a labour process as internal to a mode runs into difficulties if it is limited to any single criterion. The criterion of 'laws of motion' (or, better, system dynamics) leaves things too broadly defined. The criterion of 'reproduction' does likewise. And the criterion of 'integration' into Moments A and C is too narrow by itself and precludes consideration of multi-faceted articulation by a labour process. In my view, all of these criteria should play a part, so that a labour process can be established to be internal to a mode of production when i. it is integrally articulated into the structure of a homogeneous set of relations of production and corresponding forces of production; ii. its operation contributes to and is affected by the system processes ('laws') produced by this structure; and iii. its reproduction is within this structure and on the basis of products originating within it.

Having now established criteria for defining when a labour process is part of a mode of production, it is possible to investigate the range of variations within this.[5] In my view, variance needs to be located in the context of certain basic invariant relations in Moment B with particular regard to the three criteria noted above. The substance of this variance has been explained by Marx's concept of subsumption, interpreted in various ways. While subsumption is a concept originally linked to the theorisation of the capitalist mode, one can argue that, if conceived in its most abstract meaning, it has some general relevance. Some writers use subsumption to theorise the articulation between Moments A and B, while others focus on B and C. Depending on the emphasis, a different picture emerges as to the range of labour processes reproduced within a mode of production.[6]

Those writers who focus on subsumption of B to C tend to concentrate on the degree to which the actual labour process is subsumed under the system dynamics of the mode. For Banaji (1980: 516–18), a mode of production is defined by its motion, such as accumulation under capitalism. For him, this motion may exist in non-wage-labour labour processes, which means that they are therefore subsumed under – *and indeed are part of* – a capitalist relation (singular) of production structure. For similar reasoning regarding artisan producers subsumed to merchant capital, see Taylor (1979, in Mouzelis, 1980: 363) and Joffe (1980: 18b). These views contrast with Marx (1976b: 1019–20, 1037) for whom subsumption to the system dynamic of commercialisation did not render a labour process automatically part of the CMP, and indeed for whom this dynamic only became fully realised and indispensable when the labour process was within the CMP. I would support Marx's view here and point out that the Banaji approach conflates what are actually several different sets of class structures, and then concludes that the diverse labour processes do not actually differ from each other. As this does not even distinguish internal from external labour processes, it is, at best, only a partial method for distinguishing different degrees of subsumption within a mode of production.

Another approach taken by some writers is to analyse subsumption through the articulation of Moments A and B. Here, the concept of subsumption has been used to link the relations of possession/separation with the relations of production, in particular regarding the forces of production at each Moment (Hindess and Hirst, 1975: 226; Marx, 1976b: 1025–6; Asad and Wolpe, 1976: 484). In Marx's theory of the CMP, the producer is *formally* subordinated to capital by being separated from the means of production (i.e. conditions at Moment A). This is a negatively determined subsumption, though it is no less effective for this in enabling a capitalist to control the labour process. '*Real* subsumption' for Marx takes this control a stage further. It corresponds to the production of relative surplus value, which Marx saw as being based on large-scale production involving co-operation and a division of labour in the labour process (1976b: 1035; 1976a: 464–5, 486). What makes this different to formal subsumption is that the new *forces of production* at Moment B are such that the producers lose individual control over their labour and the means of production. They become subordinated to the pace of a machine or an assembly-line division of labour. They become *really* subsumed under capital (Marx, 1976a: 464–5, 486; 1976b: 1024; Morris, 1976: 300). Extrapolating from this analysis, it may be said that scope for variation in labour processes internal to a mode of production may be located in the forces of production at Moments A and B, and that this occurs within the limits of the class structure as defined by the relations of production.[7]

To sum up the argument so far, a labour process that is internal to a mode of production must involve homogeneity between the classes in it and in Moments A and C. Thus, if an economic system has a predominantly capitalist mode of production and, therefore, capitalist relations in Moments A and C, and there are some co-operative or simple commodity production enterprises in the system, then these latter must be characterised in terms of their own relations of possession/separation, distribution and utilisation, i.e. as external labour processes that articulate to the capitalist mode through a heterogeneous relations of production structure. There cannot be a non-capitalist labour process within a strictly defined capitalist relations of production structure. Only *capitalist* labour processes (including very particular variations) are admissible. (There may, however, be capitalist characteristics outside of the CMP, without these being sufficient to constitute the capitalist mode as such.) The relation of a (class) mode of production to its internal labour processes (including variations) will involve:

Forces of production		Relations of possession/separation	Relations of production
A.	technical co-operation in social production	→ Class x ⟷ Class y	←A. control of means of production
B.	internal division of labour	→ *Labour processes* Subsumption of x to y in the class relations in production (variations based on the forces of production)	←B. class exploitation
C.	entire product circulates between units (articulation between the labour processes of the mode)	→ *Relations of distribution/utilisation* Subsumption of B into C via system dynamics, where class relations of x are subordinate to y (variations located in degrees of subsumption)	←C. surplus part of the product between classes

In conclusion, in this section I have argued for criteria for what makes a labour process internal to a mode of production (and thereby also dealt more closely with what constitutes a mode). Within internal labour processes, I have examined the question of variation in terms of differing 'subsumption' of a labour process to Moments A and (through a system dynamic) Moment C of production. In the next section, I look at the articulation between modes of production and *external* labour processes.

Domination and subordination

The criteria for what constitute an internal labour process provide a negative designation for when labour processes – despite articulating to the mode of production – still remain external. The task remains to theorise the positive content of articulation between external labour processes and the mode, and what developments are likely from this. An initial problem is in distinguishing when an economic system involves an articulation of complete modes of production, and when it involves only an articulation of a mode with external labour processes and classes via heterogeneous relations of production. This involves the question of whether an 'external' labour process is actually internal to a different mode of production and therefore an aspect of the articulation of entire modes of production, or whether it is only part of a relation of production which is too heterogeneous to constitute a mode. (The detailed implications of this for development are discussed in chapters three and five.)

An articulation of two modes of production would require the existence of two distinct relations and forces of production combinations – each with its own relations of possession/separation, labour processes and relations of distribution/utilisation. There would appear to be few analytical problems when the interaction here is of a peripheral or *ad hoc* kind. The articulation between modes can, however, become a more complex interaction than simply juxtaposed coexistence. For example, Hindess and Hirst (1975: 161) speak about a subordinate mode as being dependent for its conditions of existence on other modes of production (referring here to American slavery articulated with the CMP). This raises the question, however, whether a dependent or subjected mode of production still constitutes a 'full' mode of production. Asad and Wolpe (1976: 492, 503–4) believe that a mode that is dependent on another for its reproduction is not a non-mode, but simply a subordinate mode. However, in my view, if modes of production are exclusive concepts and reproduction is one of the essential criteria for a mode, it is difficult to comprehend how an entire mode of production can be held to exist if it is reproduced by another. Such a case would appear to be an articulation of a subordinate relation of production with a mode of production.[8]

Historically, articulation between modes of production appears to have led to the undermining of one mode and its transformation into either the dominant mode or its reconstitution in a new form as an external heterogeneous relation of production. Webster (1978: 168, footnote 6) points to the latter in noting that while it is useful to distinguish features of a society that are not manifestly capitalist from the capitalist mode as such, it is questionable whether these features can still be seen as pre-capitalist if they are 'fully incorporated under the hegemony of the capitalist mode of production' (see also Cowen, 1981b: 123). Some writers have taken this up in a rather vague 'form-content' distinction. For example, Roseberry (1978: 47) speaks about pre-capitalist forms of labour process being maintained while their basis is altered. Mamdani (1977: 138) describes pre-capitalist relations and forms of production as being restructured with new content. This distinction becomes clearer when seen in terms of an articulation that imposes a new *system dynamic* on a pre-existing structure of production. One example is the way that a 'peasant' farm subsumed under a capitalist economic system changes its mode of functioning (Galeski, 1972: 22). For this reason, *inter alia*, the labour processes in such a situation are not part of independent modes of production 'in any scientific sense' (Joffe, 1980: 25). Some writers (e.g. Fransman and Davies, 1977: 297, footnote 4) use the term 'form of production' in order to stress the significant degree of dependence of an external production structure on a mode (see also Raikes, 1978: 321, footnote 23). However, this provides little more than an index of the consequences of articulation. If the implication is that a 'form' (unlike a mode) may develop new content (i.e. system dynamics), then the points above are pertinent.

Foster-Carter (1978: 228) holds that Rey's concept (1973) of relations of exploitation is helpful in conceptualising 'survivals' in this type of situation. It offers, he says, some precision for those who allow for the survival of pre-capitalist forms in 'indirect relations of production and exploitation' (i.e. in Moment B in my framework), but who react against the idea of entire modes co-existing. This does provide more specificity than the metaphorical 'form-content' view, although articulation also encompasses more than Moment B. It therefore needs to be located with an account of articulation of production structures at each of the different Moments of production, reproduction and system dynamics.

Some models of different types of articulation

A mode of production

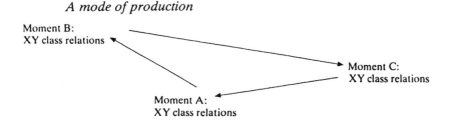

In this diagram, the same classes are present in each Moment of production, and the three form an integrated whole. Thus, relations in the labour process at B are congruent with the general class relations of possession and separation at A. In addition, the relations of distribution and utilisation at C follow the class divide in Moments A and B, and they in turn reinforce and perpetuate the possession/separation relations at A.

Articulation of two modes of production in an economic system

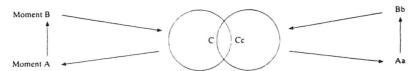

This diagram shows two distinct and autonomous modes of production that partially intersect at the point of their distribution relations. Different class relations exist in each at all Moments.

Articulation of a mode's internal labour processes

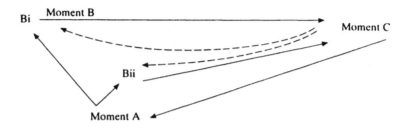

Labour processes (involving the same general class relations at A) articulate with each other through common and intersecting distribution relations at C. These labour processes are internal to the mode of production.

Articulation of an external labour process with a dominant mode of production, constituting a heterogeneous relation of production

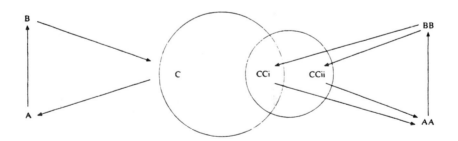

In the articulation with mode of production (A, B and C), the structure of AA, BB, CCi and CCii is constituted as a heterogeneous relation of production. This situation covers simple commodity producers whose distributive relations are wholly within the CMP. Its relations of possession/separation, in production and of utilisation remain non-capitalist.

Economic systems and social formations

Domination and subordination in articulation means that it is possible to characterise an economic system in terms of the dominant mode of production – as, for example, a capitalist economic system – whether this be at regional, national or international levels (Laclau, 1971: 33). Articulation within an economic system involves not merely different labour processes, but also a range of relations of possession/separation, distribution and utilisation (Godelier, 1972: 335). In other words, there are different levels at which the economic totality designated by economic system is effective – depending on the integration and intersection of the various Moments of each production structure. Another consideration is that an economic system also involves articulation between labour processes constituting sectors. These sectors may span several distinct forces of production structures (and therefore also the distinct relations of production structures that correspond to them). Thus, forces of production sectors defined by activity, size or product may involve relations which are part of several modes or heterogeneous relations of production.

Articulation 'on the ground' involves far more than economic factors, and here the concept of social formation is useful in analysing the added complexity. For some writers, the concept of 'social formation' is not very different from that of 'economic system' (e.g. Asad and Wolpe, 1976: 492, 504). However, the concept usually refers to more than this in that it designates the concrete conditions of existence of these economic forms (Hindess and Hirst, 1975: 13–14). In addition, although an economic system may exist at varying levels of territorial effectivity, 'social formation' tends to designate only the effective unit covered by a nation state (Poulantzas, 1978: 95). 'Social formation' takes the national economic system into account as a politico-spatially constituted system. In addition, the concept includes the entire social and political tableau of a national economic system, and not only where this pertains to the effective economic unit.

Articulation of modes of production within and across social formations involves both economic and extra-economic dimensions (Locke, 1976: 18, footnote 6).[9] There is some debate, however, as to the implications of this point for the scope of the concept of mode of production (see Sole, 1978: 41; 1977: 38). Thus, for Terray and Poulantzas, the concept includes political and ideological elements, but for Meillassoux and Balibar it covers only the economic (Mouzelis, 1979b: 175–6, footnote 51). For Muratorio (1980: 40, 57, footnote 2), extra-economic articulation indicates that the concept of mode of production itself includes the totality of social relations and human practices, which should therefore be seen as 'constitutive elements of the modes of production'.[10] In my view, the mode of production is better seen as determining the relations between its political, ideological and economic conditions of existence (Hindess and Hirst, 1975: 15).[11] Superstructural conditions of existence of a mode are thus never given in the abstract by a mode. Both these and the economic conditions are formed, modified and transformed at this level (see Morris, 1976: 308; Mouzelis, 1980: 364). Development policy often views articulation (not always recognising it by this name) in terms of the putative effects it should have at the superstructural level (see chapter five).

Economic transition

Articulation may result in destruction, absorption or qualitative restructuring of the weaker side in the relationship. However, while external articulation is an important factor, it is by no means the whole story of transition from the dominance of one mode to another. A significant part of economic change is the outcome of a mode's internal contradictions as distinct from its external dynamics. This genesis and development of new economic forms out of the old involves articulation among elements of the same mode of production.[12]

Balibar (1970) has theorised a concept of a 'transitional mode of production' to characterise internally determined transition from one mode to another (Hindess and Hirst, 1975: 264). For him, this describes a situation where the non-correspondence of the relations and the forces of production means that one side is transformed by the effect of the other. There are two basic problems with Balibar's efforts. In the first place, although he credibly tries to theorise the contradictions internal to the structures of a transitional situation, there is no explanation as to how these contradictions work themselves out in social transformation (Mouzelis, 1979b: 53). Secondly, Balibar does not explain how the correspondence of an ordinary mode of production can become the non-correspondence of a transitional one (Hindess and Hirst, 1975: 275; Mouzelis, 1979b: 52). The approach is thus unable to fully explain historical transition between modes of production.

An alternative approach to the problem is to do away with 'eternal' modes altogether and regard all modes as transitional. In one strand of Marxism, this view sees history as a more-or-less inevitable sequence of stages through the various modes of production, with the motor of the process being increases in productive capacity. The role of the relations of production is viewed as reactive and limited to accelerating or retarding the inevitable growth of this capacity, but still as ultimately swinging in behind this growth (see Stalin, 1940b, in Lecourt, 1977: 10; Cabral, 1969: 77; Barratt-Brown, 1976: 47, footnote 10; Marx, 1977a: preface). However, in my view, it is incorrect to posit that all modes of production teleologically develop productive capacity, or that this alleged phenomenon creates a structure of non-correspondence between forces and relations of production which then pulls the latter into line with the former. Firstly, not all modes of production involve an inexorable growth of productive capacity – the course of productive capacity (in whichever direction) itself needs to be explained. Secondly, and perhaps more importantly, not all transitions between modes of production are the result of relations of production 'catching up' with advanced means of production, as several writers have argued convincingly about the historical transition from feudalism to capitalism and from capitalism to socialism (Brenner, 1977: 78, 81; Sklair, 1979: 313).

I would argue that the point is to take account of tendencies and contradictions of a mode of production which may, though not necessarily, result in non-correspondence of economic structures. Such dislocations allow for *possible* outcomes wherein a degree of correspondence is re-established or created anew in a new mode of production. It is still necessary, however, to spell out the actual transforming agencies in these situations. Here, the reproduction and transformation of a mode of production has to be located in terms of the conditions of existence in a social formation, where, in my view, the real motor of change is primarily class struggle (in its various forms), occurring within the social structures and system dynamics of a particular concrete situation (see also Mouzelis, 1979b: 53; 1980: 367; Morris, 1976: 309). On this basis, it is possible to agree with Hindess and Hirst (1975: 202) that 'nothing in its concept prohibits the continued reproduction of a mode of production, and nothing in its concept requires that a mode of production transgress its own limits, i.e. dissolve itself'. The concepts of the various modes of production provide the basis for a qualitative differentiation of historical reality, but they do not constitute a theory of transition between a sequence of modes (1975: 7).

I would also follow Morris (1976: 297) who argues that despite the 'merging of features' in cases of transition, it is still possible to disentangle the web of relations sufficiently to specify the dominant mode of production. A question which still remains to be examined is when the turning point is reached. At what stage can the capitalist mode (or any other) be said to have emerged as dominant? (See Hindess and Hirst, 1975: 289.) Dobb's (historically applied) answer here is that 'one could only speak of the situation as being non-feudal if there were no longer a feudal ruling class with its particular source of income still surviving' (1962: 15; see also

Gallisot, 1975: 418).[13] Transition, seen in terms of class contradictions, can be identified as qualitative or quantitative according to whether the major terms of the contradiction – namely the classes involved – are changed or not. Inasmuch as classes can serve as indices of qualitative and quantitative transition, it is necessary to establish changes in class structure and class dominance clearly at all three Moments of production (and also at the level of political structures and consciousness).

Focusing on classes provides more than criteria for quantitative/qualitative assessment of economic change – it also enables us to analyse transition in terms of class formation, conflicts and alliances. Any concrete transition (e.g. following the Russian revolution) involves these class dynamics both within the dominant mode of production and in its relations of external articulation. The separation of internal and external dynamics is, of course, an abstraction performed in theory. In any empirical situation, *all* the class dynamics (including both those internal and external to the dominant mode of production) are part of the picture of economic change.[14] But if transition involves a complex and multiplex articulation bound up with class dynamics, this often escapes Third World development planners (see chapter five).

Surplus and economic development

The concepts of forces and relations of production of a mode of production, articulation between different economic elements in an economic system and transition provide a general framework for analysing development. On the basis of these, it is now possible to theorise the utilisation of surplus labour and its effect on development. Evidence from the Maoist experience in China suggests that a transformation of the relations of production coupled with a change in the forces of production can sometimes be sufficient to increase surplus labour and surplus product (Moore, 1969: 209; Nolan, 1976: 202, 217, footnote 18; Sklair, 1979: 317). Such advances are achieved by bringing unused items into production and by organisational measures such as rationalisation, co-operation and specialisation in the division of labour (Baran, 1962: 20; Hymer, 1972). However, while changes in the forces of production can lead to increased surplus labour and therefore to increased output, the relations of production may absorb this in increased consumption rather than use it in expanding productive capacity. What is vital for economic development is not only the *extent* of surplus labour (embodied in surplus product), but also its *use* – factors that are tied to the relations of production.

These issues have been theorised formally by Baran (1962: 22–4, 44), for whom the rate and direction of economic development depends on the size and mode of utilisation of economic surplus. 'Surplus' in his sense refers to the resources left over for investment in growth after the consumption of social groups and the renewal of the means of production and other items regarded as necessary in the social formation concerned (see also Heilbroner, 1981: 37; Arrighi and Saul, 1968: 287).[15] For Baran, 'potential surplus' is what *would* be available for economic development in a different organisation of the social formation. Hughes (1977: 217, 220) makes a further distinction within 'potential surplus' between 'hidden' and 'latent' surplus. 'Hidden' refers to items such as the consumption of the exploiting classes, luxuries, loan repayments, profit outflow and investment in prestige projects. 'Latent' surplus refers to what could be done with better methods of production, land-use and scale of production. In my conceptual schema, the category of 'hidden' surplus is bound up with the *relations of production* and – particularly at Moment C – the relations of distribution and utilisation. 'Latent' surplus refers primarily to re-organising the *forces of production*. Surplus for development may be increased by realising what was previously only *potential* surplus. This involves a change in the relations of production for releasing *hidden* potential, and a change in the forces of production for realising *latent* potential.

Ultimately, raising the productive capacity of an economic unit is premissed not merely on realising potential surplus and using actual surplus, but on these being geared towards exponential development of productive capacity. This means development not simply as a *quantitative* expansion of the extent of *existing* forces of production, but also as *qualitative* expansion by the introduction of advanced means of production. In Marx's writing (1971: 399), this issue is analysed in terms of the co-ordination of two departments of production. *Department I* concerns the production of *means of production*, while *Department II* concerns the production of *articles of consumption*. What is important for development is the expansion of productive capacity through surplus being deployed for expanding *Department I*. This perspective is useful for analysing what kind of productive labour counts towards development. In terms of the discussion of realised productive capacity in chapter one, the production of hidden surplus such as luxuries (and armaments) is productive labour because it involves the production of *material* items. But these items do not in themselves increase *productive capacity* and therefore can be reckoned as 'hidden surplus'. If one is talking about the production of *means of production* (for whatever purpose), then one is talking about the *use* of *actual* surplus, and hidden surplus does not enter the picture. This does not escape value considerations about the role of luxuries and armaments in development, but it does shift them to another plane.[16]

Focusing on the role of surplus in economic development draws attention to the political character of the process. Relations of utilisation are linked to the other wider relations at Moments A, B and C, and to the broader class structures and struggles. It is these that determine both the amount of surplus labour performed and appropriated, as well as what is done with it thereafter (Ziemann and Lanzensdörfer, 1977; Hughes, 1977: 218; Weeks, 1975: 99; Harrison, 1981: 331). Indeed, as will be discussed in chapter four, different classes even define development differently and likewise for the measures prescribed to achieve it (Dos Santos, 1969: 62).

The structure of the capitalist mode of production

I turn now to an analysis of the CMP in the light of the argument so far. The CMP is a mode of production in the sense that it is based on homogeneous relations of production, i.e. relations between the same classes at all three Moments of production. These Moments are integrated together in an interdependent whole, with particular system dynamics deriving from it. As far as internal articulation is concerned, the CMP's labour processes can be seen to be reproduced within the CMP, integrated with Moments A and C, and exhibiting the system dynamics of the whole.

To begin with Moment C, commodity exchange is a central invariant element of the CMP (Hindess and Hirst, 1975: 102).[17] Under capitalist relations of distribution and utilisation, the means of consumption, the means of production and labour-power must all be commodities and mobile on the market to a greater or lesser extent. These generalised commodity relations at Moment C are based on the CMP's particular class structure. From the vantage point of Moment A, this involves the separation of the direct producers from the means of production (leaving them in possession only of their labour-power), and the concentration of these means in the possession of a different class (Marx, 1972: 668).[18] Historical dispossession of the producers may be a necessary condition for capitalism at Moment A, but it is not sufficient unless it makes labour-power and means of production into circulating commodities to be bought and sold at Moment C (see Duggett, 1975: 165). A capitalist must thus be able to buy all production inputs on the market and assemble these under his control to constitute a capitalist labour process (Sohn-Rethal, 1979: 118–19).[19] Capitalism thus involves not only the market, but also the labour market (Friedmann, 1978: 80). In fact, 'only where wage-labour is its basis, does commodity production impose itself on society as a whole' (Marx, 1972: 733). The growth of proletarianisation – the supply of wage-labour – is therefore also the growth of the internal market and generalisation of commodity relations across the means of consumption (Dobb, 1962: 26).

Some dependency theorists have ignored the fact that it is not enough for a CMP labour process to be integrated into commodity circulation and that it should obtain its labour through this too. Frank (1969c), for example, sees capitalism simply as a system of production for profit on the market in which someone other than the direct producer realises the benefit. This view concentrates primarily on Moment C, and to a lesser extent B, and ignores how commoditisation at C is integrated with class relations at A. Wallerstein, however, explicitly tackles the issue within the dependency approach:

Capitalism ... means labour as a commodity to be sure. But in the era of agricultural capitalism, wage-labour is only one of the modes in which labour is recruited and recompensed in the labour market. Slavery, cash crop production ..., share-cropping, and tenancy are all alternative modes. (1974: 400)

This line of argument leads to designating these classes – as well as peasant petty commodity producers – as wage-labourers/proletarians (see also Amin, 1974: 26; Joffe, 1980: 24). This rather tortuous reasoning is clearly inadequate when seen against the more rigorous view of capitalism as a mode of production that combines specifically homogeneous, rather than heterogeneous, relations. A unit of production is only capitalist if, *inter alia*, it is integrated into a total commodity circulation system which in turn rests, as has been argued, on a structure of definite social class relations. If, in addition to being integrated into capitalist Moments A and C, these labour processes are reproduced predominantly by articulation with each other, and if they further exhibit CMP system dynamics, then they are internal to – and in fact constituent elements of – the CMP.

The context of capitalist commodity circulation integrating Moments A and C is exhibited in mobility of labour-power, money, means of production and wage-goods. This mobility in turn gives rise to competition as a *system dynamic*. It arises because the structure of generalised commodity exchange means that failure to exchange either labour-power or goods is a threat to each participant's continued existence. Survival of a capitalist enterprise under capitalism makes it imperative for it to try to win and maintain an edge over its rivals in the marketplace. In this way, the very class structure and relations of distribution (exchange) under capitalism constitute the root of competition and the corresponding system dynamic of commercialisation. These in turn underpin another system dynamic where the motive force of capitalist production is profit, and on a continuously expanded scale – i.e. the accumulation of capital. It is the case that the general formula for capital, $M \rightarrow M'$ (money advanced in order to make more money) covers not only productive capital, but also merchant and finance capital (Kay, 1975: 87; Bernstein, 1979b: 423). However, merchant and finance capital articulate with a whole range of labour processes and they exploit only in Moment C. For this reason, they constitute heterogeneous relations of production and are not an integral part of a mode of production. Productive capital is distinct from these other capitals because it combines the commodities of labour-power and means of production and organises them into a productive labour process (Bernstein, 1979a: 424).

Capitalist labour processes may vary in their mode of subsumption to the CMP. Workers may be only formally subsumed if their work operations are independent of each other. Formal subsumption may also characterise workers in a piece-work or putting-out system.[20] Under real subsumption, the workers become 'collective labourers' and the capitalist – who under formal subsumption often takes a direct part in the labour process – tends now to distance himself (Marx, 1972: 312–14). None of this variation – contra Berle and Means (1932) – changes the mechanism of exploitation, nor the capitalist features at all Moments of production, reproduction and system dynamics. Such variations in capitalist subsumption are highly relevant when analysing whether various rural classes and their labour processes are capitalist or not (see chapter five).

For Marx, capitalist exploitation consists in the fact that labour-power can produce value greater than its own. The difference between its value as paid for by the capitalist and the value of its output constitutes a surplus labour expended by the producer, embodied in commodities as a surplus value.[21] Marx (1972: 299) further identified two forms of exploitation under capitalism. While absolute surplus value involves more surplus through more work, 'relative surplus value' involves more surplus through more productive work (Fine, 1978). This latter form involves two ways of increasing surplus labour-time: firstly, increasing the surplus labour of *one set* of producers relative to the others and, secondly, increasing the surplus labour relative to the necessary labour-time of *all* producers. The first way arises from mechanising production, such that the productivity level of the worker is raised, enabling him to produce more in a given time.[22] By selling above the individual value, i.e. at the average value, the capitalist realises the difference in value as a surplus relative to other capitalists producing at the average social productivity. In contrast to this kind of relative surplus value, which pertains only to advanced labour processes, the second type affects the entire CMP. It derives from the way that greater productive capacity in sectors producing wage-goods reduces the labour-time necessary to produce the value of the wage. Reduction of necessary labour-time means the expansion of surplus labour-time – potentially a key factor for economic development. While all capitalist-employed wage-labour can produce absolute surplus value, not all such labour contributes to relative surplus value exploitation.[23] Agriculture, unlike armaments and luxuries, is fundamental to relative surplus value and in this way (as well as others) to economic development (see the discussion on the Agrarian Question, chapter four).

The internal widening and deepening of capitalism is described by Marx as the expanded reproduction of the mode (1972: chapter twenty-four; Amin, 1974: 2, 190). As the expansion proceeds, the size of individual capitals increases and the vertical and horizontal division of labour within each of them grows accordingly. In Marx's terms, this is the phenomenon of concentration of capital, alongside which is centralisation – a drop in the number of effective units of production (Marx, 1972: chapter twenty-five, section 2). Centralisation comes about through the merging, take-over or elimination of existing enterprises by others. Monopoly is the consequence of this, and it is effective primarily at Moment A, though it also often has implications at Moment B and Moment C. The expanded reproduction of capitalism involves a process of *capital accumulation* (Marx, 1972: chapter four). This accumulation depends on the *rate of profit* which determines the speed of possible expansion of each capital. Yet, while capital accumulation involves the development of capitalism, this is not the same thing as capitalist development, i.e. capitalist development of productive capacity. For example, accumulation may be in Marx's 'Department II' (the production of means of consumption). The *means of production* in these kinds of capitalist enterprise must certainly be included in an inventory of the productive forces constituting capitalism's productive capacity. But the *products* of these enterprises are a different question. Where these products help to reduce necessary labour and therefore to increase relative surplus labour, they *may* increase productive capacity, especially in 'Department I' – 'the production of means of production'. Items such as luxuries or armaments do not have this significance because they do not contribute to relative surplus value and thence to an increase in relative surplus labour. Against this background, let us now investigate the detailed relationship between capitalist *development* (of productive capacity) and capitalist *accumulation*.

The capitalist mode of production and the use of surplus

Capitalist labour processes (as opposed to the capitalist *mode of production*) can and do exist at low levels of mechanisation and small size of establishment (Ennew et al., 1977: 303; Marx, 1976b: 1034). What, then, is the connection between capitalism and development, given that capitalism involves expanded – rather than simple – reproduction? The nature of the CMP requires that profit is re-invested and the field of capitalist production be expanded, either through the enlargement of given enterprises or the setting up of new enterprises. Another form of capitalist expansion is transformation – through articulation – of non-capitalist units of production, but whichever kind of expansion is involved, it clearly need not be in exponentially developing the means of production as opposed to the quantitative extension of existing production. The expansion can even be through heterogeneous relations of production such as merchant, finance or landed capital.

Nonetheless, capitalism has tended historically to use its surpluses to create the means for generating further surplus, i.e. to transform its wealth into new and better means of production (Heilbroner, 1981: 37). One explanation for this – common to modernisation-school writers – is a voluntarist account which rests ultimately on a conception of *homo economicus*. It focuses on acquisitive and 'maximising' economic motivation. Capitalism is seen as a system which rewards hard work and innovative risktaking, and unleashes these drives in such a way as to optimise economic growth. But this assumes that capitalist ideas pre-exist, and in fact give rise to a capitalist social structure, whereas such ideas themselves need to be explained in terms, *inter alia*, of their structural context.[24] The *homo economicus* view errs by attributing a universal character and primary causal significance to an isolated aspect of the capitalist superstructure. In addition, it is evident that the rationale of capitalist production is not reducible to the consumption demands of the capitalist. Capitalism involves buying in order to sell (i.e. starting with money in order to make more money), not selling one commodity in order to obtain a different one (see Marx, 1976b: 1030). At the level of the system, the profit rationale exists independently of the motivation of the capitalist (which is not to dismiss the importance of capitalist ideology and capitalists' motivations).

A second explanation about why the CMP tends to develop productive capacity is based on the ability of the capitalist enterprise to reap the benefits of co-operation and division of labour (see, for example, Marx, 1972: 714; Hymer, 1972: 41; Sweezy, 1976; Adam Smith, 1937). Historically, by owning all the inputs of production, the capitalist was able to assemble them in one place – thereby increasing productivity and enabling machinery to be used. However, this situation is not unique to capitalism and, more fundamentally, the question of economic development is not simply productivity, but why this should be continuously expanded through the production and adoption of new means of production. It is necessary to explain the CMP's use of surplus for re-investment.

A third explanation emphasises the role of competition in the CMP, and holds that this explains increasing mechanisation of production (see Mamdani, 1977: 145; Furtado, 1964: 36; Howard, 1980: 65). Dynamism is not located in capitalist units of production taken separately, but derives from the effect of the whole system on the parts. An isolated capitalist unit in a non-capitalist context may have only simple and not expanded reproduction – but, this approach argues, this is not possible within the CMP as a whole. In this view, competition is crucial to the engine of capitalist development because it involves the 'stick of bankruptcy' and the 'carrot of extra-profits' to enforce investment and technological progress (Baran, 1962: 73; Dobb, 1951: 57).

There is value in this third approach, but how does the cost-cutting pressure of competition lead to continual growth in productive capacity? Measures to keep abreast of competition can include – other than adopting advanced means of production – expansion through the extension of existing methods and means of production without this including technological change.[25] In addition, capitalists may gain a competitive – albeit limited – edge by cost cutting through increased absolute surplus-value exploitation rather than by the introduction of advanced means of production (Marx, 1976a: 534; 1972: chapter ten; Fine, 1978: 92). In fact, historically, the finite and contested extent of absolute surplus value exploitation has meant that it has been advantageous for capitalists to cut costs by mechanising production (Habakkuk, 1967, cited in Hindess and Hirst, 1975: 334, footnote 59). However, the adoption of advanced means of production not only saves labour (and enables new tasks to be performed) – it can also increase both the productivity per labourer and the speed of production. While there is not space to go into this here, there are convincing arguments that both effects help to raise rates of profit and therefore capitalist accumulation as a whole (see Kautsky, 1976: 16; Friedmann, 1979: 181, footnote 14; Tribe, 1977: 78; Kay, 1975: 138–9, 145; also Sohn-Rethal, 1979: 148).[26]

This theorisation, which relates the economically progressive character of the CMP to competition which in turn rests on the articulation of capitalist relations and forces of production and the corresponding class structure, should not obscure the existence of capitalist collaboration. Collusion, price-fixing and monopoly (or oligopoly, strictly speaking) come about precisely in response to competition and may well have adverse effects on development (Fransman and Davies, 1977: 293, 296, footnote 42). Thus, monopolisation reduces competition as a structural imperative for the development and adoption of enhanced means and methods of production at Moment B. It also means that with a small number of firms of very large size, the costs of entry into competition are high (Baran, 1962: 76–7, 83). Monopolies may also often undermine the productive capacity of a given economic unit such as where (e.g., Ireland, Wales) they move production away, in search of greater profits elsewhere, or into less developmentally productive and even parasitic realms. Another countertendency to development exhibited by the CMP lies in the essentially unplanned character of Moment C. Baran (1962: 39) thus holds that waste and irrationality (i.e. 'hidden surplus' – see above) – rather than being fortuitous blemishes – relate to the very essence of capitalism. Crises of capitalist overproduction or failed investment lead to bankruptcies and to retardation or reversal of development (Dobb, 1951: 61; Beckman, 1980: 55).

To complete the analysis of how the social structure and system processes of the CMP have consequences for the development and underdevelopment of productive capacity, I turn now to the significance of the capitalist state.

Capitalist development and the state

Capitalism at the level of a social formation (rather than simply as a mode of production) cannot be analysed without taking into account its superstructural conditions of existence, especially the state. Indeed, the state stands out as being of major significance for not only the CMP, but also often as the locus of articulation between this mode and other economic forms. This is certainly the case with the colonial and post-colonial capitalist states (Mamdani, 1977: 143).[27]

The state is part of the superstructure in the base–superstructure abstraction, and it is conceptually distinct from the economic structure of relations and forces of production. This structural distinction also has a materiality in real social formations, notwithstanding the way that each capitalist state is closely integrated with economic structures and processes. This is the very basic form of the capitalist state and it continues despite changes in government, the differences in degree of involvement in the relations of production and variations within the state structure itself (Wolpe, 1980b: 401, 403; Wolfe, 1974: 149–50). Within the limits of capitalist relations of production, the state generally *promotes* capitalist exploitation, but does not do the exploiting directly: this is done by the capitalist class – with the aid of the state, to be sure, but not *through* the medium of the state (Holloway and Picciotto, 1977: 96). This does not preclude the capitalist state from becoming involved in production and exploitation and developing an economic apparatus for this purpose, as in the case of state capital. However, state capital is only *capital* in so far as it still exists within a context of capitalist system dynamics and capitalist relations at all three Moments of production in the social formation concerned. Where state capital develops to the point of supplanting, for example, private capitalist relations of possession/separation and capitalist processes such as competition, then the dominant mode of production is no longer capitalist in the sense defined in this monograph. Because of all this, the existence of state capital does not mean that the state has become a class. Under capitalism, the bureaucracy and the army only become a class by creating an independent base in the economy. State aid can be – and in many cases, especially in post-colonial contexts, often is – used to this end. But until such an independent base is achieved, state functionaries are not a class – although some of them may be in the process of becoming such. In the interim, they receive surplus and direct it through their state-based relations with production-based class(es) (Mamdani, 1977: 287–8).

The changes in the basic form of the capitalist state are bound up with the changing functions it has been made to perform, as described in the following brief and generalised sketch. Historically, an interventionist form of state has been a precondition for the economic instance of a capitalist social formation to come to the fore in reproducing capitalist relations of production. Once established, these relations of production can be reproduced – in comparison to other class modes of production – *relatively* independently of the state (Wolfe, 1974: 152–3). Similarly, once CMP domination over other external modes and elements of production is established, exchange at the economic level perpetuates the relationship, enabling neo-colonial capitalism to function without coercive control being primary (Dupré and Rey, 1973: 159). All this said, however, the state is still essential to guarantee – at the very least – exchange and exploitation through upholding private property ownership (Wolfe, 1974: 153; Holloway and Picciotto, 1977: 87; Burton and Carlen, 1979: 41; Heilbroner, 1981: 39).[28] More than this, the capitalist state may act not only to establish and help extend the CMP within a social formation, but do this specifically against foreign capitalist and non-capitalist classes (e.g. through protectionism, colonialism and imperialism) (see Kaplan, 1977: 112; cited by Jessop, 1982: 113).

Among the state's enduring economic and political roles, 'valorisation' and 'domination' can be distinguished (cf. Burton and Carlen, 1979: 36).

The two roles buttress one another, although they are effective on society at various levels. The object (albeit sometimes indirectly) of valorisation is primarily the forces of production; that of domination the relations of production. It can be noted that these functions may be retrogressive as well as progressive in terms of developing productive capacity. In addition, it would be wrong to see these functions as a result of the state being simply an instrument of external political forces, or of its own autonomous agency – it involves an uneasy combination of both these factors (Jessop, 1982: 61; Burton and Carlen, 1979: 40, 43; Wolpe, 1980b: 401–2; Hindess and Hirst, 1975: 36; Herring, 1981: 143, 146).

State economic activities vary in form, degree, agency and timing – depending, *inter alia*, on the degree of international competition, the outcome of class struggles and the stage of capitalist development (Murray, 1971: 118). In fact, the capitalist state is not inherently necessary for most economic functions. It may take them on, for example, because of concrete class struggles and strategies where classes and fractions seek the aid of the state to further their economic interests. The state may also take over activities that are unprofitable to capital at a given juncture, or which are unreliably secured by private enterprise despite being essential to the whole system (see Mamdani, 1977: 12).[29] One associated economic activity relevant to this monograph is the way that state development programmes may end up subsidising private capital (and, to a lesser extent, 'kulaks' or settler tenants), rather than expanding productive capacity. As will be discussed in chapter five, the capitalist state has also had a significant involvement in agricultural production in the Third World, either through the creation of detailed conditions for capitalist investment, or taking a direct part in various development strategies.

3 Capitalism and underdevelopment

Centre and periphery in the international capitalist system

Having looked in detail in the previous chapter at the CMP and its relation to labour processes, I now turn to the relation of the CMP to the international economy. The dependency approach is to conflate the two units. Thus, the dependence of diverse producers on the market is seen to link them together as participants in a global CMP (see Wallerstein, 1974: 77; Frank, 1969a, 1969b). Clearly, however, this view detracts from the particularities of the *articulation* of capitalist production with external *non*-capitalist relations. Differences between the 'trees', so to speak, are hidden by their intertwined foliage.[1] The dependency approach cannot properly explain why – if it is the CMP that characterises First and Third World alike – the two are so different economically (Roxborough, 1976: 119–20). As Dos Santos (1969: 75) asks about the Third World, 'is it a particular case of capitalism, a completely different mode of production, or a system in transition towards capitalism?'

Indeed, such have been the differences between developed and under-developed social formations that some writers have seen the latter as exhibiting a mode of production *sui generis*. Thus, if the one extreme is to identify the international capitalist economy with the capitalist mode of production, its mirror opposite locates modes of production at the same unit of analysis as social formations. For example, a concept of a 'colonial mode of production' has been advocated to cover certain Third World social formations (Alavi, 1975; Cardoso, 1976; Banaji, 1972; see also Biermann and Kössler, 1980). However, as Roxborough (1976) warns, this type of approach can lead to an uncontrolled proliferation of modes of production.[2] It becomes difficult to see similarities between relations of production in different social formations – i.e. which 'trees' are of the same 'species'. The concept of a colonial mode certainly emphasises the difference and specificity of the Third World, but at the cost of obscuring its similarity to the First World (namely the CMP dominant in both). In addition, the stress on the parts (social formations with unique modes of

57

production), independently of the whole (the international capitalist system), gives us nothing about the relations between the parts. This is to 'see the trees without the wood'. Yet, many writers have argued convincingly that Third World economies are better seen as parts of the First World (see Ehrensaft, 1971; Foster-Carter, 1978: 230; Mouzelis, 1979b: 34; Amin, 1974: 289). The challenge is to capture the way in which social formations are meaningful units in a wider integrated international economic system and why, if Third World economies are 'appendages' of the capitalist First World, they generally remain different – i.e. underdeveloped instead of developed.

The different national economies in the international capitalist system are characterised in large part by three features. Firstly, there are the specific class forces and state in each social formation which, *inter alia*, play a major role in enabling one part of the international capitalist mode of production to dominate other parts – resulting in metropolitan and colonial characteristics (Kaplan, 1977: 97–8; Mamdani, 1977: 108). Secondly, there are different articulations within the CMP – within and between each social formation. In this regard, many writers observe that 'capitalism at the periphery' is based on a foreign market, while 'capitalism at the centre' rests more securely on a national market. Thirdly, there is the extent of articulation of the CMP with external non-capitalist elements in each situation. While the CMP at the centre tends towards exclusivity, at the periphery it is one of several important relations of production, albeit the predominant one (Amin, 1974: 5, 38; Furtado, 1964: 36; Marx, 1974: 5, 38; Obregon, 1974: 394–8).

These points lead towards making the useful distinction between the CMP and capitalism. Capitalism – at both the centre and the periphery – refers to an *economic system* dominated by the CMP, notwithstanding important structural differences between central and peripheral capitalist economic systems. The three factors noted above are sufficiently different in First and Third worlds to constitute two qualitatively different types of *economic system: capitalism at the centre* and *capitalism at the periphery*. These two units of analysis exist as economic sub-systems within a wider unit, namely the international capitalist economic system. It is worthwhile pointing out here that it is precisely the issues of class forces, internal CMP articulation and CMP-external articulation that dependency theory tends to overlook.[3]

The transformation of non-capitalist production

Articulation within the international capitalist system needs to be analysed in terms of the different contributions made by the various sides in the articulation (see Taylor, 1979 in Mouzelis, 1980: 362). Taking first the CMP side, it may be asked why this mode of production has even come historically to articulate with other economic forms. While Bradby (1975: 127) is correct to reject any general theory to explain this, one can still describe some characteristics and processes involved in extensive capitalist expansion and the associated articulation. Thus, the spread of capitalism can be identified, following Halliday (1979: 104), in terms of the development of commodity relations in production inputs and outputs, the growth of a home market with commodity exchange between agriculture and industry, and the growth of a capitalist class structure. Applying the terminology of my argument, Halliday's points encompass Moment C (distribution and utilisation) and Moment A (possession and separation). To this analysis we can add the need for capitalist relations in the labour process (Moment B) as well as the system dynamic of competition, and the associated dynamic of commercialisation, and the reproduction of these relations. These factors apply to both the genesis of the CMP and its subsequent articulation as a fully fledged mode of production with non-capitalist economic elements.

Historically, the elements which were to constitute the CMP inevitably involved articulation with non-capitalist structures for supplies and markets. Subsequent transition towards the dominance of the CMP involved the expansion of commodity production and exchange between capitalist units, and the development of the internal capitalist market to pre-eminence in the central economic systems (Hindess and Hirst, 1975: 305). In the process, the CMP introduced its own labour processes or transformed existing non-capitalist ones. This has largely been through industrial capital investment in, and joint ventures with, other economic structures, although finance capital may also play a part here (see Palloix, 1973). As regards the periphery, such articulation is described in the Leninist theory of imperialism as the export of capital in the era of monopoly capitalism (see Lenin, 1964). While both theory and data in Lenin's view are controversial (see Gallagher and Robinson, 1953; Fieldhouse, 1967; Emmanuel, 1972b), it is not necessary to enter the debate here except to say that, historically, the CMP has shown a tendency to articulate with non-capitalist structures through extensive investment. The character of the CMP has been crucial in all this articulation – for example, at the periphery it was monopolistic right from the start and of a commercial rather than industrial bias. Much peripheral articulation was also indirect, occurring primarily through the state.

Turning now to the non-capitalist side of articulation, many non-capitalist modes of production tend to be passive, non-initiating partners in articulation, especially when they have only *simple*, and not *expanded*, reproduction, and therefore lack a tendency to expansion (Terray, 1974: 334). In addition, pre-capitalist modes of production have often been incompatible with the CMP, particularly with commodity exchange and expanded reproduction (Luxemburg, 1951; Bradby, 1975: 127–8; Fried-mann, 1979: 175). Above all, however, what affects the articulation from the non-capitalist side – just as from the capitalist – is whether its classes find the articulation to be in or against their interests.

If these are some of the features that both capitalist and non-capitalist sides bring to articulation, it is worth looking at how such a relationship may see the CMP transform and incorporate external economic forms, bearing in mind the criteria for identifying when a labour process becomes part of a mode of production as discussed in the previous chapter. In assessing the process of capitalist transformation, the follow-ing dynamics can be identified: monetarisation, commoditisation, com-mercialisation, proletarianisation and capitalist class formation. *Monetarisation* refers to the spread of money as the universal medium of exchange and measure of value. *Commoditisation* is the production for exchange and the corresponding circulation of commodities. Monetar-isation and commoditisation serve to integrate the reproduction of a labour process within the CMP at Moment C. *Commercialisation* in my argument refers to the operational principle of increasing profit as an end in itself and this covers the absorption of non-capitalist labour processes into the CMP's system dynamics. Involving Moment A, *proletarian-isation* is the creation of a class dependent on selling labour-power to survive, usually through dispossessing producers.[4] The other side of this is the concentration of the means of production in a separate class able to hire labour and set production in motion, i.e. the *formation of a capitalist class*. When the relations in production (Moment B) correspond to these class relations and to this system dynamic and reproductive context (i.e. with all five elements of transformation noted above), the transformation is total.

It should be noted that none of these five processes leads inevitably to total capitalist transformation. Commoditisation may mean that the structure of Moment C in the non-capitalist production relation gets progressively undermined, but it may also increase the independence of non-capitalist producers, thereby blocking further development of capi-talist relations (see chapter five). Monetarisation extends the commodity circuit (and indeed, in the form of taxes, it forces economic structures into this circuit) (Bernstein, 1978: 423–4). However, in the form of usury, it represents a subsumption of producers to capital which does not inher-ently require the separation of the producer from the means of produc-tion (Howard, 1980: 73; Joffe, 1980: 23). Regarding commercialisation,

the CMP's system process of competition may force non-capitalist producers to begin surplus generation on an increasing scale (Bryceson,
1980: 309). However, that this is not inevitable is shown by the fact that
much commodity production by feudal estates for a capitalist market
retained the consumption of use-values as its motive force (Banaji,
1976a: 312; see also Marx, 1976b: 1030). Non-capitalist structures may be
faced with pressures towards proletarianisation, but they may survive by
hiring labour-power out to (and in from) the CMP in peak seasons or
periods in the demographic cycle (see Friedmann, 1978: 79). On the
formation of a capitalist class, it can be noted that producers in non-
capitalist modes of production frequently end up – under transformation
– relating to already constituted capitalists. To a lesser extent, there is a
transformation of some non-capitalist producers into capitalists.
However, this type of transformation, even with deliberate attempts to
engineer it, has often failed in the Third World (see chapter five).

Nonetheless, to the extent that non-capitalist labour processes are
transformed in respect of the five elements analysed above, and therefore
in respect of their system dynamics, reproduction and class relations in
their Moments of production, they become integrated components of the
CMP. While the overall tendency of the CMP's external articulation has
been towards comprehensive, if uneven, transformation at the centres, it
has been, as I will now argue, rather different at the periphery.

Articulation in peripheral capitalism

Capitalist transformation of non-capitalist structures does not occur
thoroughly, unambiguously or universally, and non-capitalist production
elements remain as an organic component of the international capitalist
system (Mandel, 1975: 365; see also Williams, 1977: 290; Kollontai, 1970:
4). Their presence rests on a number of intertwined factors which can be
separated only analytically. Firstly, there is the fact of the *limited development of the CMP* at the periphery – especially in agriculture. A
second factor is where transformation has been prevented by the CMP's
own partial *conservation* of non-capitalist relations, sometimes by design,
sometimes by effect. Thirdly, remnants of pre-capitalist production survive through successful economic and political *resistance* to CMP articulation. A fourth factor is where non-capitalist relations actually grow and
flourish in the interstices of a capitalist economic system or are even
deliberately created by that system.

Elaborating on the limited development of the CMP at the periphery, it
is evident that the disruption of the pre-capitalist modes of production as
full *modes* does not mean an automatic and immediate generalisation of

the CMP (Mamdani, 1977: 141; Kay, 1981; 487; Amin, 1974: 380).[5] Compared to the centres, the CMP has had a shorter history at the periphery, and it has also sometimes articulated with modes of production that are more resilient than was the feudal mode (Amin, 1974: 14). In addition, unlike the centre, peripheral capitalist growth is characteristically and one-sidedly based on the external market. Consequently, CMP growth in the Third World is geared to the reproduction needs of the CMP in the First World and therefore lacks a tendency to become generalised locally (Taylor, 1979, cited in Mouzelis, 1980: 361–4). Indeed, transition to autocentric growth and to total transformation of non-capitalist relations is directly blocked by mechanisms such as monopoly, dependence, etc., discussed in the next section. The result is that in peripheral economic systems capitalist relations are not completely dominant at all three Moments of production and the CMP there often is not integrated into a properly cohesive mode of production.

Restricted in its spread, the CMP at the periphery nevertheless does have some relationship to non-capitalist elements there. The retardation of capitalist relations does not mean that *non*-capitalist economic structures retain their *pre*-capitalist functions and forms. The dependency school's rejection of the 'dual-economy' view of enclaves of capitalist development amidst undisturbed pre-capitalist forms is correct in this regard (Dos Santos, 1969: 75). Dependency theory is useful here in highlighting the linkages and the dominant-dependent character in the articulation between the CMP and non-capitalist structures. As Mouzelis (1979a: 351) is at pains to stress, articulation often involves strong negative linkages. In my view, these linkages are what constitute a peripheral capitalist economic system.[6] The situation is thus not a simple juxtaposition of capitalist and pre-capitalist elements and the latter are, strictly speaking, no longer *pre*-capitalist. However, contrary to dependency theory, neither are they *capitalist*. The insights of articulation perspective suggest that peripheral capitalism is characterised by a *variety* of relations of production, including *non*-capitalist elements externally articulated through heterogeneous relations to the CMP. It follows that one may therefore distinguish between dependency *within* the CMP (the peripheral capitalist relations on the central capitalist relations), and dependency 'across the board' of the underdeveloped social formation – i.e. including the dependency of non-capitalist relations on capitalist ones.

Against this background, I now consider the dynamics in peripheral articulation, including the controversy over whether the effect is conservation or dissolution of the non-capitalist elements. Several writers contend that the CMP at the periphery tends to develop through rather than against non-capitalist relations (see Frank, 1969a; Arrighi, 1971; Kay,

1975; Greussing and Kippenburg, 1975–6: 127; Halliday, 1979: 117; Mamdani, 1977: 138). This view tends to imply that it is the CMP itself which explains the persistence of these structures. This general idea has been rejected by other writers who hold that the CMP's inherent tendency is to dissolve and transform these structures completely into capitalist ones (Banaji, 1980: 514–15; Long and Richardson, 1978: 11). Against both positions, a number of valuable observations have been made from empirical analyses which show that CMP articulation contradictorily comprises destructive and conservative aspects. Whether any one prevails is an issue influenced by, *inter alia*, whether articulation occurs in the centre or at the periphery, and by the part played by the non-capitalist relations in articulation. Historically, under CMP articulation, many pre-capitalist forms have been undermined but at the same time perpetuated with new functions (Meillassoux, 1972: 103; Obregon, 1974: 399; Mamdani, 1977: 38). The resulting 'conservation–dissolution' (Bettelheim, 1972: 297) has not been conservation juxtaposed with dissolution, but a combined process (with possible emphases in either direction).[7] Indeed, a conservation emphasis in many cases has served the CMP where total transformation would have been counterproductive (see Wolpe, 1972, 1975).

Conservation and dissolution is also greatly affected by politics and the state. The state can represent the CMP and establish capitalist dominance even when the mode is not physically present (Mamdani, 1977: 147). However, 'conservation–dissolution' should not be seen simply as a function of the power of the CMP. As noted earlier, political and economic resistance of pre-capitalist classes has often played an important part in the persistence of non-capitalist production features. Producers ranging from French peasants to African agriculturalists have a long history of resisting articulation that threatens their control over production. Such resistance has often led to articulation being accompanied or preceded by violence, as in colonial domination (Rey, 1973, cited by Bradby, 1975: 147). The CMP's response to resistance has also often led to another dimension of conservation–dissolution whereby the dominant class in the CMP develops and supports allies within the pre-capitalist classes (Mamdani, 1977: 41; Ranger, 1968: 443; Kahn, 1978: 123). Indirect rule by a colonial state has been the main form here, and it has accompanied a parallel role by merchant capital in conservation–dissolution.[8]

If peripheral capitalist economic systems have seen an incomplete generalisation of the CMP, there has also been an expansion of dependent, and even new, production forms which result from the restructuring and subordination of former pre-capitalist relations (Kay, 1981: 487;

Obregon, 1974: 403; Tsoucalas, 1979: 126; Cliffe, 1977: 204). The CMP can also sometimes create economic forms *ex nihilo* (Laclau, 1971, cited by Foster-Carter, 1978: 213, 231–2). In this vein, feudalism in Latin America and slavery in North America have been called 'pseudo' modes of production created in the service of nascent European capitalism and hence distinct from true feudal and slave modes (Amin, 1974: 361).[9] The dependence of such non-capitalist forms on the CMP is evident in their articulation as heterogeneous production relations integrally bound up with and dependent on the CMP, despite retaining their distinct character. The state is often deeply involved in the creation of new, non-capitalist structures, which are often intended to be *transitional* forms. In fact, many develop unforeseen tendencies or have their development blocked in one way or another (see chapter five).

The extent of conservation tendencies and the persistence of non-capitalist relations of production at the periphery is substantially different to the CMP's articulation at the centre. The main reason for this difference has probably been the articulation between the CMP at the centre and the CMP at the periphery, i.e. internal articulation within the CMP on an international scale. The next section examines this through the phenomena of monopoly, extroversion and dependence.

Underdevelopment and the role of monopoly and extroversion

A large number of writers hold that development and underdevelopment are not sequential stages of growth but opposite faces of the same coin (see Datoo and Gray, 1979: 249; Bernstein, 1978: 25; Mamdani, 1977: 6). By this, they mean that the two concepts are related not merely *logically* and *semantically* (as discussed in chapter one), but that there is also a real interdependence as part of a *single* process producing 'development' at one pole and 'underdevelopment' at the other.[10] It follows within this perspective that the First and Third worlds are not separate independent entities heading in the same direction, and neither are their respective characteristics the result of factors indigenous to each. This conception has produced a useful theoretical distinction between 'undeveloped' and 'underdeveloped'. Here, 'undeveloped' refers to a pristine, indigenous and original condition. On this understanding, there is clearly no real interdependence between the *un*developed character of one unit, and the developing character of another. '*Under*developed', however, is based on the transitive verb, 'to underdevelop' (Brett, 1973: 18; Leys, 1975: xiv; Berger and Mohr, 1975: 21; Bernstein, 1978: 25; Harris, 1975b: 6). The productive capacity of an economic unit may thus be actively underdeveloped by exogenous agencies and forces, and hence be in the process of underdeveloping. This position is very different to that of modernisation theory which regards underdevelopment as 'development *manqué*' (Fitzgerald, 1983: 14).

The significance of this interpretation within the context of an international capitalist system is that economic units at the periphery are on a qualitatively different trajectory to the developed capitalist units – precisely because of their links to the latter (Mouzelis, 1979b: 34). There is some validity in this viewpoint, but two important qualifications must be made (both of which are elaborated upon below). Firstly, the contribution of non-capitalist elements to underdevelopment at the periphery also needs to be appreciated. Secondly, if *underdevelopment* is created (in part) by (capitalist) *development*, it does not follow that *development* can only occur at the expense of *underdevelopment*. I reject the 'zero-sum' argument that the expansion of productive capacity in one unit is only possible through its reduction elsewhere. Bearing in mind these points, I now consider how the CMP does contribute to underdevelopment, or at least blocked development, beginning with monopoly competition by the centre.

Monopoly and underdevelopment

For Warren (1973) and Cardoso (1972), the expansion of capitalism foments industrialisation – whereas for Frank (1969a) and Baran (1962), it stunts it (Evans, 1977: 43). In my view, the general situation is neither one nor the other, but a complex and uneven process that in a contradictory way combines aspects of both. However, as far as the stunting effect goes, it is clear that monopoly competition has indeed been an obstacle to an indigenous process of peripheral industrialisation, hampering the development of both the CMP and non-CMP at the periphery, and sometimes even causing underdevelopment in the form of regression of productive capacity (see Mouzelis, 1980: 362–3; Mamdani, 1977: 108, 142, 145; Mandel, 1968, cited by Sutcliffe, 1972; Wallerstein, 1971: 380; Baran, 1962: 295, 312, 336, 340; Cardoso, 1967: 192; Cliffe, 1977: 197; Kay, 1981: 494; Dos Santos, 1969: 63; Frank, 1969c; Barratt-Brown, 1976: 262).[11]

While in the past the West benefited from exporting manufactured goods, Third World countries today cannot compete on international markets (and often even on their *own home markets*) in terms of manufacturing because of the competition from imports or products assembled locally by metropolitan companies (Szentes, 1971: 31). Amin (1974: 156, 235) also points out that imports (besides destroying traditional industry) further smother fledgeling industries because they cancel the accelerator effect. Part of the anti-development picture is that besides advantages such as scale, productivity and access to credit and expertise, the monopoly sector tends to secure its position by constituting itself as a 'formal' sector which wins tariff privileges and protections, state contracts, duty-free imports, investment credit, licensing and so on (Weeks, 1975: 89; Mamdani, 1977: 88; Davies, 1977: 66). With the expansion of indigenous capitalist development significantly blocked, local capital tends mainly to move into the export, tertiary and light industry sectors. In this way, local industry (including non-capitalist) does not compete with foreign industry, but complements it (Amin, 1974: 147, 170; Kahn, 1978: 124). Indigenous development of productive capacity at the periphery via petty commodity or small capitalist production tends to take place within the limits of monopoly competition from the centre and is therefore subservient and prescribed development (Amin, 1974: 147) (see the discussion below about 'growth without development').

It is not necessary for capitalist development at the periphery to proceed via indigenous capitalists: foreign capital *could* in theory do just as well if, after destroying local craft industries, it created generalised capitalist industry (Ferner, 1979: 280). But, in addition to being restricted, much of the foreign capitalist investment at the periphery has tended to be in production for the external market in limited products such as exotic goods, minerals and agriculture (Amin, 1974: 161). Central competition tends to disadvantage even central capital with regard to establishing other types of industry at the periphery. While cheap wage levels have led to capital transferring some operations to the periphery, the shift has tended to be in light industry and final-assembly stages of production based on unskilled labour. Heavier and more complex production is still generally located in, or at least geared towards, the metropolitan CMP. Most importantly, the development of advanced technological means of production, and therefore of productive capacity over time, continues in the centre.

The historical dominance of the central CMP involves not only monopoly, but also a peripheral economic system characterised by *dependence* on the metropolitan economic system. This structure underlies and perpetuates underdevelopment in a way that is distinct from the effect of monopoly competition *per se*.

Dependence and extroversion

At the heart of the dependent character of underdeveloped economic systems is *extroversion*: the external orientation of the relations and forces of production of underdeveloped economic systems. It derives from the peripheral systems being originally constituted by merchant capital articulating with peripheral producers through heterogeneous relations of production which bound them to external economic interests (see Kay, 1975: 103). In central capitalism, production units expanded gradually and many eventually became exporters, while at the periphery, production was (and often still is) restructured or introduced from the start to produce for export (Amin, 1974: 175). Thus, 'while capitalism generates commodity production, underdeveloped capitalism general-ises commodity production for the *metropolitan market*' (Mamdani, 1977: 144; see also O'Brien, 1975: 18; Baran, 1962: 335; Le Brun, 1973: 279). The underdeveloped economy is thus an externally oriented 'part-economy' subordinated to metropolitan capitalism and, as part of this (as will be discussed below), it is a distorted, disarticulated entity (Amin, 1974: 17; Foster-Carter, 1978: 230; Shivji, 1977: 213; Beckford, 1969: 119).

The dependence associated with extroversion is something experi-enced not only by the CMP at the periphery, but also by non-capitalist production there. To the extent that this latter loses its own reproduction and becomes dependent on exchange articulations with the CMP, it loses its character as a mode of production, or as even a homogeneous relation of production. It becomes a heterogeneous relation through its articu-lation with capitalist classes. Extroversion is a structure where the re-lationships are characterised by a dependence operational through Moment C. There is no integrated circuit of distribution but rather a dependent integration into Moment C of the central capitalist economic system. This integration rests on, and reinforces, the international div-ision of labour in the world market (Harris, 1975b: 6). Thus, under-developed social formations have characteristically specialised in unprocessed primary product exports (Lall, 1975; Szentes, 1971: 20–3). To a large extent, other forms of dependence – financial, technological and social – with potentially equally negative significance for develop-ment – rest on this trade dependence and the extroversion that underpins it (Amin, 1974: 35–6, 170, 294–5; Williams, 1981a; O'Brien, 1975: 18; Lall, 1975; Frank, 1979a; Maré, 1977; Mouzelis, 1980: 363; Arrighi, 1977: 172; Arrighi and Saul, 1968: 290–1; Baran, 1962: 144; Le Brun, 1973: 384; Wallman, 1976; 103, 106).

Dependent growth and growth without development

Ironically, being the creations of the CMP (of the centre), monopoly, dependence and extroversion are an obstacle to both local and metropoli-tan capitalist development at the periphery – and indeed probably to the development of productive capacity *per se* there. Dependent capitalist growth in this context does not usually count as development, especially in the light of two more structural characteristics of the periphery, namely *disarticulation* and *unevenness*. To demonstrate this, a short detour into the limits of 'dependence' in explaining underdevelopment is useful. For a number of writers, dependence is the central, if not the only, distinction between development and underdevelopment. Dos Santos (1969: 60) goes as far as arguing that the term 'dependent societies' is a better characterisation than 'underdeveloped societies'. When it comes to defining 'development', these writers tend to see it primarily in opposition to dependence and therefore as the capacity for autonomous and self-sustained growth (Amin, 1974: 393; Rodney, 1977: 108; Arrighi and Saul, 1973: 293; Sutcliffe, 1972: 174–6; Girvan and Jefferson, 1968: 342). But this implies that underdevelopment is a deviation from a norm of *independent* development, and many critics dispute that this norm exists – or has ever existed. They argue that First World capitalist units developed precisely through their exploitative interconnection with units in the Third World. If this is (in part) the case (and the history of capitalist development bears this out), then 'development' as implying an 'own bootstraps' economy – as opposed to 'underdevelopment' signifying a dependent economy – is not particularly useful. This is brought home by Legassick (1976: 437), who asks if *any* capitalist development is ever autonomous.[12] If development itself therefore turns out to be dependent, then why does it differ from underdevelopment – given that this latter is also dependent?

In defence of 'dependence' as an identifying feature of underdevelopment and thereby as demarcating it from development, it has been argued that 'the platitude that all countries are interrelated and dependent on each other does not mean that there are not different types and degrees of dependence' (Mouzelis, 1980: 360; see also O'Brien, 1975: 24). The issue is held to be *relative* economic independence (Berger, 1976: 248–9). This defence is clearly correct in one sense, but it is also limited to reducing the differences between development and underdevelopment to the quantitative criterion of the extent of dependence. To go further than this, we need to examine if and how, distinct from degrees of dependence, peripheral capitalist economic systems remain qualitatively distinct economic units with their own structural specificity and with an autonomy which cannot be wholly explained by their relationship to each other. This is where other features are vital for understanding the issues. In the case of capitalist *underdevelopment* these include disarticulation, surplus transfer and class structure, while for capitalist *development* they include the mobility of factors of production, competition, an internal market, an integrated class structure with homogeneous capitalist relations of production and (see chapter four) resolution of (or capacity to bypass) the Agrarian Question.

Such a multi-faceted perspective makes it possible to assess the character of dependent growth in a context of underdevelopment. As Cardoso (1972) has observed, dependence, monopoly capitalism and 'dependent development' (in the terminology of this monograph – 'growth') have not been contradictory phenomena (O'Brien, 1975: 19). This perspective is countered by some writers (e.g. Warren, 1973), for whom growth through investment by foreign capital represents the end of underdevelopment. In addition, it is claimed that action by local classes and the peripheral state may overcome the problems of dependent growth (Amin, 1974: 390; Mamdani, 1977: 288). Warren (1973) argues that in the post-independence context of *multi-lateralisation* of dependence, Third World states have a degree of leverage previously denied them (see also Mafeje, 1977: 417). According to Evans (1977: 44, 63), these factors – which he accuses Baran and Frank of underestimating – allow for some measure of genuine expansion of national productive capacity in peripheral economic systems, as in Brazil. The evidence, however, suggests that such growth is fickle and fluctuating (see Fröbel et al., 1980: *passim*; Barratt-Brown, 1976: 272, footnote 6; Taylor, 1979, cited by Mouzelis, 1980: 364). As Dos Santos (1969: 73) also notes, one side can expand through self-impulsion, while the other side – being dependent – can only expand as a reflection of the first. And while it is true that Japan and, more recently, South Korea have, with vital state involvement, been able to absorb foreign capital and improve on foreign technology to their own national advantage, this is not the case with Brazil, which remains fundamentally dependent on international exchange, financial dependence and balance of payments factors (Amin, 1974: 384).

I would therefore tend to argue that, despite the efforts of peripheral states, dependence generally has not been transformed by growth. Indeed, according to Kay, industrialisation 'is now such an integrated part of underdevelopment that it can no longer be regarded as its solution' (1975: 125–6). In the Frankian outlook, this *dependent growth* is the 'development of underdevelopment'. In my view, such an assessment is broadly correct, although I prefer to use the term *growth without development* (see below). I also prefer to reach this judgement not simply on the basis of identifying continuing dependence, but on showing qualitatively why such growth tends not to constitute development and, in this regard, the concepts of extroversion and disarticulation are highly relevant. Regarding extroversion, the expansion of the means of production in a peripheral unit often constitutes not the enhancement of *its* own productive capacity, but rather that of *another* economic unit within the overall structure that links the two together. Thus, growth in both developed *and* underdeveloped units *is* development for the former, while for the underdeveloped units, it is often *growth without development*.[13] As Bernstein (1978: 16) argues, 'growth' in an underdeveloped economy is a quantitative extension of the existing structures, while 'development' (i.e. of productive capacity) involves qualitatively different economic (and non-economic) structures (see also Baran, 1962: 292). It is true that quantity *may* develop into quality – i.e. growth into development – but unless such transition occurs, especially at the level of structures, the distinction remains valid. Modernisation theory fails to understand the possibility of growth without development because it operates with the wrong units of analysis. It takes the distinction between units such as national economies as primary, and thereby leaves out the overarching structure of the all-important whole.[14]

The *dependent* character of growth in underdeveloped economies is bound up with the *extroversion* of the peripheral economic systems. However, it is because of the *disarticulation* and *unevenness* in these economic systems that such growth does not constitute even *dependent development*. Thus, not only do peripheral economies have *dependent growth*, but this growth is also, and distinctively, *growth without development*. Disarticulation, the obverse of extroversion, is the failure of an economy to gear its resources to its domestic market and indigenous economic needs due to a lack of sectoral or industrial integration in its internal linkages (Szentes, 1971: 9; Shivji, 1977: 213; Amin, 1974: 16–18, 263–7, 292). Adjusted to external factors, different branches of the economy do not develop in conformity with each other, and the resulting unevenness is evident in extreme imbalances and inequalities in productivity between sectors (Mouzelis, 1980: 361; Amin, 1974: 393).

Extroversion on its own does not preclude growth from counting as development of productive capacity but, in conjunction with disarticulation, this usually seems to be the result.[15] Looked at more closely, it is clear that growth in an externally oriented economy can reinforce rather than change internal sectoral disarticulation (Leys, 1975: 14, 17–18). The structural context means that growth tends not to have any integrating economic effect (Amin, 1974: 18–19; Seidman, 1978: 14). Disarticulation means the absence of an internal market except for the limited area of import substitution (Szentes, 1971: 20–30; Baran, 1962: 335–6; Sutcliffe, 1972: 186). It also means that there is minimal diffusion and the development of one sector has little mobilising effect on the rest. This is why for the CMP, as it exists at the centre, growth *is* development (it has an integrating effect), while at the periphery it is not necessarily so. The same *unevenness* in productivity between sectors applies to the whole economy – including the non-capitalist structures. In contrast, in a developed capitalist economic system, high productivity in one sector tends to diffuse through the economy due to competition and the tendency towards equalising wage and profit rates. The system is an integrated coherent whole with complementary sectors. For these reasons, the phrase 'the development of underdevelopment' is misleading. Dependent growth does not mean a *reduction* of productive capacity (although, as I have shown, it also does not mean *expansion* of capacity in the context of disarticulation and unevenness). Dependent growth in a disarticulated economy usually means *growth without development*.

Levels of the economy and surplus transfer

Pursuing the analysis of factors contributing to underdevelopment at the periphery, let us consider three levels of the economy and their relation to the formal/informal sector, *growth without development* and surplus outflow. According to Obregon (1974), an underdeveloped economy can be seen in terms of the monopoly capitalist, the competitive capitalist and the non-capitalist marginal levels. The dominant monopoly level is characteristically an extension of the CMP at the centre. The competitive level occurs in areas not yet encroached on by the monopoly level. It consists of small capitalist traders, farmers and artisans and their wage-labourers. The marginal level in turn operates within areas not yet taken over by the competitive level, and comprises the lumpenproletariat, petty commodity producers and the reserve army of labour (Legassick and Wolpe, 1976: 92).[16]

The formal/informal sector model is not identical to these three levels. It is defined institutionally rather than by relations of production, with the division between its parts being set by a superstructure of political, moral and legal relations (see Davies, 1977: 56–9; International Labour Organisation, 1972: 68). Unlike the marginal level, the informal sector includes not only non-capitalist relations, but also wage-labour and incipient capitalists (Leys, 1973: 427; Davies, 1977: 66). The 'informal sector' therefore spans *both* the marginal and, at least partially, the competitive levels. This may be diagrammatically represented as follows·

LEVELS	SECTORS
Monopoly	Formal
Competitive	
Marginal	Informal

For many development theorists, the informal sector makes a positive contribution to the development of the formal sector and also serves as the 'Cinderella of future growth' (Leys, 1973: 425; Black, 1977; International Labour Organisation, 1972; Davies, 1977: 69). This perspective can be assessed by using Obregon's model to analyse the role of the capitalist and non-capitalist (i.e. marginal) levels within the informal sector in relation to growth in the competitive and monopoly levels of the formal sector. Marxism holds that people who are marginal to the CMP can be conducive to capitalist expansion by serving as a reserve army of labour and keeping wages down (see Marx, 1972: chapter twenty-five, section 4). While this *may* be true of the history of developed capitalist countries, in the context of underdevelopment, things have worked out somewhat differently. Marginal people at the periphery do not generally serve as a reserve army for the high-skill, capital-intensive dominant monopoly level.[17] As regards the competitive level, its restricted scope means that only a portion of the marginal community acts as a floating and intermittently employed reserve. Most marginalised people are compelled, however, to resort to limited non-capitalist activity for survival. Indeed, marginal (i.e. non-capitalist) economic structures have grown spectacularly in many peripheral economic systems (Tsoucalas, 1979: 126; Muratorio, 1980: 39). Obregon's model reveals that much of this does not constitute development, but is rather subordinated to the operation of the monopoly level which both excludes labour from itself and limits the expansion of the competitive level. The growth of the marginal pole is an instance of *growth without development* – economic movement within the terms of the structures of underdevelopment, and which fails to transform these terms.

Obregon's model is also useful for drawing attention to the different levels through which surplus can flow. Despite the limited reserve army role of the marginal level regarding the competitive, a subsidy in the form of non-capitalist-produced labour-power can be passed on to the competitive capitalist level of the formal sector (Bernstein, 1979a: 423, 426–7; Wolpe, 1975: 224; Joffe, 1980: 18). So significant is this and other forms of surplus flow, that several writers have stressed them as the central factor in underdevelopment (see Frank, 1969a; Dos Santos, 1969: 75; Amin, 1974: 136, 178). In my view, surplus outflow is but one of the factors, and while it is a distinct and multi-faceted dynamic, it probably could not function without the others. Among the problems in assessing this dynamic is the difficulty in operationalising the concepts as well as the unresolved controversy about whether *non*-capitalist production can yield surplus *value* to capital. For the purposes of this monograph, however, I accept that there are diverse forms of transfer of surplus labour through the various levels of the peripheral economy to the CMP at the centres. One form of this drainage, manifested at Moment C – i.e. in the relations of distribution, results from the geographical location of classes involved in exploitative relations (Arrighi, 1971: 3; Roxborough, 1976: 122). Foreign investment and loans are the clearest case of this type of surplus transfer (Harrison, 1981: 349: Goncharov, 1977: 182; Baran, 1962: 336; Sutcliffe, 1972; Mandel, 1968; Amin, 1974: 231). Such drainage is not solely from exploitation within the monopoly investment level of the CMP at the periphery. Mechanisms such as joint ventures with state capital (which originates from the competitive and marginal levels) and savings mean that surplus flows from the lowest to the highest level (and from there, outside) despite there being no direct production links between these levels (Cardoso, 1972, cited by Barratt-Brown, 1976: 269; Harrison, 1981: 348).

Surplus transfer through trade also occurs through commodity exchange between all levels within the peripheral economy, and between these and the capitalist centres, and is easily apparent in declining terms of trade (Long and Richardson, 1978: 177; Mouzelis, 1980: 362; 1979a: 351; Harrison, 1981: 343). Whether surplus also gets transferred through 'unequal exchange' is a complex and controversial issue not dealt with in this monograph for reasons of space (see, however, Emmanuel, 1972a; Amin, 1974: 55–84; Bettelheim, 1972; Friedmann, 1979: 174; Kitching, 1982: 167–70). However, it is clear that merchant capital, operating by monopoly control of exchange, underpins much surplus transfer via trade (Amin, 1974: 90; Baran, 1962; Frank, 1969a; Kay, 1975; Rodney, 1972; Dos Santos, 1969: 76–7). Dependence on exports and imports – i.e. on an extroverted economic system – can provide a base for a commercial class to exploit, even though dependency in itself does not automatically mean surplus extraction (Godelier, 1972: 349; Kay, 1975: 90–123; Harrison, 1981: 421). Finally, it may be noted that while spatial surplus flows operate between central and peripheral economic systems, these relationships are reproduced within economic systems as well and the urban bias tends to be reinforced by political means (Weeks, 1975: 95–6; Muntemba, 1978: 74; Kay, 1981: 496–7; Harrison, 1981: 135; Arrighi and Saul, 1968: 291).

Several factors contributing to thwarted development and, indeed, to the underdevelopment of productive capacity have now been elaborated: *monopoly* (the result of the system process of competition), *extroversion–dependence* and *disarticulation–unevenness* (which relate to the character of the forces of production) and the *three levels of the economy* and *surplus transfer* (which are linked to relations of production and exploitation). While these dynamics are significant, they also need to be related to the issues of class structure, struggle and politics.

Class and development–underdevelopment

Debate around the developmental role of class has focused on whether it is more or less significant than the structures and processes outlined above. Taking first those who stress structures and dynamics as primary, the dependency theorists loom large. For Dos Santos (1969: 78), dependence determines the limits and possibilities of actions and behaviour. Frank (1969a) goes further and sees classes as derivative of surplus outflow processes (see also Mamdani, 1977: 145; Amin, 1974: 383). In turn, this outflow and the role of the peripheral state are seen as being determined *primarily* by the dependent economic structure and the international division of labour, and only *secondarily* by classes that are formed in this context. Obregon's analysis (1974) of the classes in the competitive and marginal levels of the structure also fits into this perspective.

The opposite emphasis argues that classes are primary. For example, Ferner (1979: 270) says that while the phases of development are related to the international capitalist system, precise national forms depend on class dynamics (see also Dos Santos, 1969: 76). For Cardoso (1972, cited by O'Brien, 1975: 13), dependency is (simply) part of an internal system of social relations between classes (see also Kay, 1981: 498). And according to Luton (1976: 577) 'the satellite/metropole contradiction (i.e. the contradiction of unequal exchange) is a manifestation of the expropriation/appropriation contradiction (i.e. the class contradiction) in the sense that the former's existence is secondary to the operation of the latter'. Thus, in this perspective, the spatial 'conveyor belt' of surplus is composed of and dependent on class relations (Barnett, 1977: 23; Booth, 1975: 79). Among other writers within this perspective, Weeks (1975: 95) points to the role of class political power relations, arguing that surplus is channelled to where political power is greatest (see also Leys, 1975: 20–1; 1983: 33). In this light, surplus transfer and the underlying structure of dependence–extroversion need to be seen in terms of who creates and operates the system, including at the periphery itself (see O'Brien, 1975: 16; Berger, 1976: 68; Dos Santos, 1969: 78; Brenner, 1977: 27).

In my view, it is important to see the situation as dialectical and not to *counterpose* or *reduce* a peripheral economic system's structures and dynamics to class relations. I would agree with Arrighi (1971: 10) that it is necessary to invert Frank and see the class structure in the metropole–satellite structure as the *dominant* element in the relation of *mutual* determination of the two structures. Taking this further, I would add that it is important to distinguish clearly system dynamics from the structures of social relations and, within the latter, to distinguish the different types of relations. *Monopoly* grows out of the system dynamic of competition which derives from, but is not reducible to, a structure of capitalist class relations. Both *dependence–extroversion* and *disarticulation–unevenness* involve structures of social relations (within the forces of production). These are linked to the structure of class relations (e.g. merchant capital, imperialist investment), but they are definitely not synonymous with it. *Surplus outflow* based on geographical class location rests on (and reinforces) a particular structure of class relations. Surplus outflow based on merchant exploitation is a form of class exploitation based on a heterogeneous relations of production structure. In fact, it is only Obregon's *three levels of the underdeveloped economy* which are identical to class relations.

Yet, class is also a significant factor in underdevelopment (and development) in a way that is distinct from its links to the factors listed above. This can be shown by criticising the way that writers like Frank reduce the relevance of class struggle to its role in mercantile surplus flow. By seeing class only in terms of dependency structure and spatial surplus control, Frankians tend to conceive it in market, rather than production terms (Joffe, 1980: 6). For them, exploitation occurs at Moment C – and it is here that they see classes as being based. This is only true for merchant capitalists, but Frankians misunderstand this limited situation as the general essence of class relations and conclude that the general relationship between development and underdevelopment is a zero-sum one. Without wanting to reject everything in this view, it is important – as I will now argue – to understand that development is not simply a function of being at the receiving end of surplus transfer. In this regard, class is significant not only for the structure of underdevelopment and surplus transfer – but also for the vital issue of the *use* of surplus. Thus, it has been convincingly argued that mercantile exploitation was a factor in western capitalist development, but that the major causal factors were indigenous class relations (Berger, 1976: 71; Dobb, 1962: 23–30).[18] While foreign commerce enriched some areas at the expense of others, this was only instrumental for development if it was realised as means of production (Hymer, 1972: 40; Brenner, 1977: 85). Surplus transfer, therefore, may have been a necessary condition for development, but it certainly was not sufficient (Legassick, 1976: 479). As a quantitative issue, surplus transfer should not be isolated from qualitative questions, including what happens to the surplus that is not transferred out of the Third World (Mamdani, 1977: 7; Baran, 1962: 164; Amin, 1974: 9). Class struggles, as distinct from class structure (to which they are, of course, related), have their own particular effect on the use of surplus. For example, capitalists at the periphery are able to take advantage of exploiting by absolute surplus value methods because of the weakness of class struggle in limiting this avenue (see Fine, 1978: 92, 94).[19] As Kautsky (1976: 26) has noted, 'a holding where the workers can be driven to any limits does not require the latest technical equipment, as do holdings where the workers may impose limits on the intensity of their labour. The possibility of increasing the labour time of a given workforce is a serious obstacle to technical progress.' The weakness of the proletariat and the peasant classes is closely linked to the way in which they have formed in the context of underdevelopment, namely in the context of a diversity of relations of production, and therefore of classes and class fractions (Fine, 1978: 94). The problem of Third World development today is that in the context of an international capitalist system, organised class struggle limiting absolute surplus value tends to drive capital away rather than compel it to develop the means of production (Mouzelis, 1979b: 41).

Are capitalist or non-capitalist relations to blame for underdevelopment?

Any answer to the question of whether the CMP will ultimately develop the underdeveloped economies depends very much on where the 'blame' for underdevelopment is placed. Many writers have pointed fingers at non-capitalist relations. The argument discussed above ultimately lays the blame on weak class struggle at the periphery, in turn tracing this to the existence of non-capitalist relations and associated class heterogeneity. Other writers have also blamed non-capitalist relations, citing simply their persistence as low-productivity relations. Underdevelopment in their view is thus a lack of capitalist relations (Cliffe, 1977: 333; Kahn, 1978: 110). In another emphasis, Kaplan (1977: 103) speaks about feudal and peasant classes constituting an obstacle to capitalist development. And for Friedmann (1979: 174–5), what makes for development under capitalism is the mobility of factors of production and competition, both of which are restricted by the existence of pre-capitalist classes. This general outlook parallels 1950s development theory, which held that underdeveloped countries would progress towards development by eliminating the 'obstacles' of 'traditional societies', 'feudal residues', etc. However, as Dos Santos (1969: 58) points out, the existence of many pre-capitalist forms is not fundamentally due to their own persistence, but rather to the very process of underdevelopment. This squares with Obregon's theory of the CMP contributing to the existence of the marginal sector. In an entirely different view then, the issue is not so much the stubborn continuation of pre-capitalist classes and structures as the particular development of the peripheral CMP, which not only fails to absorb and transform them into capitalist relations but which sets up a process of conservation–dissolution. The blame for this phenomenon rests with the subordination of the peripheral CMP to the central CMP, and the related structure of the peripheral economic system and surplus outflow. To sum up this view, the obstacle to development is the lack of generalised capitalist relations at the periphery, whose cause in turn is nothing other than the CMP in the centre.

There is certainly much truth in this conclusion, but it would be wrong crudely to blame everything on the CMP (central or peripheral), leaving no autonomous role for non-capitalist elements in contributing to under-development. There is also no guarantee that an expansion of capitalist social relations in the context of monopoly competition, dependence–extroversion, etc. would actually enhance the productive capacity of the unit (Halliday, 1979: 105). It may well be that development at the periphery requires a complete restructuring of the class relations that transform *both* 'pre'-capitalist and existing capitalist relations as well as the three-tier character of the underdeveloped structure. In addition, the transformation of the forces of production, especially as regards extroverted-dependent and disarticulated-uneven relations would seem to be crucial. This implies radical change in relations with the CMP at the centre. Finally, the class relations and class struggle as such would need to be of a kind that would ensure productive use of available surplus. All this involves a transition to qualitatively new relations of production, and the issues this poses are transition through internal changes or transition through articulation with an external 'superior' mode of production. Class structure and struggles and the role of the state are crucial for both. Many development strategies certainly have tried to come up with pro-grammes for transition, often combining elements from capitalist and non-capitalist relations, in an attempt to circumvent or overcome the obstacles to raising productive capacity (see chapter five).

4   Rural development

Agriculture and development

All too often, rural development is seen as a self-contained phenomenon. However, from a holistic perspective, the pertinent issue is the role of the rural areas in the overall development of productive capacity. Clearly, there needs to be some kind of general balance between urban and rural development and in particular between industry and agriculture in development (as well as, of course, a balance between these and other areas of economic significance – energy, infrastructure, education, etc.). In the integrated international economy, this balance may well have to be measured within a unit that is wider than a single social formation where international trade may enable the need for agricultural development to be bypassed. For the purposes of conceptual discussion, I assume, however, that agriculture has a necessary role in developing the productive capacity of a social formation. This issue has been conceptualised as the 'Agrarian Question', and refers to the way in which agriculture relates to the needs of industry and the production of new means of production. Expanding upon points made by Beckford (1969: 142–3) and Halliday (1979: 126–34), agriculture's role in development includes providing food and raw materials, subsidising industrial development through surplus transfer, serving as a market for industry with regard to agrarian inputs and consumer manufactures and releasing labour-power for industrial development, or productively absorbing labour-power where industry is unable to do so.

Crucially significant in all this are the agrarian forces and relations of production as they relate to the labour process, surplus generation and transfer, distribution and consumption patterns and the progressive expansion of productive capacity in agriculture.[1] Agrarian productive capacity is particularly bound up with agrarian relations of production, and notably in the relationship between productivity and scale of production. 'For over a century, economists have concerned themselves with the question of which is best – the big or the small holding', wrote Kautsky in

1899 (1976: 2). The problem with this question is that it is almost impossible to answer in any general way (Mouzelis, 1975–6: 488). As I argue below, it needs to be rephrased in terms of the relations of production, encompassing the issues of when, under what social conditions and for whom large or small farms are more advantageous (Galeski, 1972: 182). The scale of production – a feature of Moment B (the labour process) – also needs to be seen in relation to Moments A and C (relations of possession and separation, distribution and utilisation). This issue is significant because much development theory believes that resolving the Agrarian Question requires going beyond what it assumes to be the limits of small-holding production based on family labour (Harrison, 1981: 92). The way forward has been seen to lie in the creation of large-scale capitalist or socialist farms. To investigate properly such claims, one has to examine what is actually meant by small- and large-scale farming. By analysing the scale question in terms of land, means of production and labour, it becomes clear that the issue depends almost wholly on the particular determinate agrarian relations and forces of production.

Taking first the relationship between land scale and agricultural productivity, one can consider the arguments that large-scale farming offers economies of scale, such as the use of modern machinery and scientific management, and cost-effectiveness through greater specialisation (Kautsky, 1976: 21–3; Baran, 1962: 23, 166, 275). Against this, increased scale may sometimes mean that production inputs can rise disproportionately to the output generated. In addition, small land-size does not preclude economies of scale in the use of means of production. This is evident if one places the means of production within the wider context of relations and forces of production – in particular at Moment C with regard to utilisation. There is no reason why fifty small plots each require their own plough, etc. when common means of production can be shared as, for example, in a moishav or co-operative model, or even mediated by a capitalist servicing organisation (see Halliday, 1979: 113; Muntemba, 1978: 64; Harris, 1980: 90). In view of these factors, one may conclude that land-size as such is not a fundamental determinant of agricultural productivity (Patnaik, 1979: 400; Kautsky, 1976: 33).

A different question to consider is how the scale of use of *labour-power* affects agrarian productivity. It has been argued that 'small' is better than 'big' with regard to utilisation of labour. 'One of the most passionate advocates of small cultivation, John Stuart Mill defines as its most important characteristic the untiring labour of its workers', wrote Kautsky (1976: 26). This characteristic is usually linked to family ownership and operation of small-sized farms. The basic argument here is that productivity on small farms is high because small family farms own or have an attachment to their land, and have a direct stake in raising productivity (Stavenhagen, 1964: 91; Buckley, 1981; Keddie, 1968: 168; Brietzke, 1976: 640). At the same time, this explanation for the hard work put in by small family farms is not the full story. In sub-Saharan Africa where there has been no feudal exploiting class generally, unlike Asia and Latin America, it is questionable whether private tenure *per se* will inspire increased production effort – contrary to the assumptions of many development planners (see Thomas, 1975: 39). As discussed in chapter one in regard to 'base and superstructure', labour productivity cannot be subjectivised. Indeed, there are strong coercive pressures affecting motivation and strong material factors conditioning and tempering it. Thus, as Friedmann writes:

the more 'commercial' behaviour of simple commodity producers relative to peasants stems not from motivational differences, but from the individualisation of each household which accelerates commoditisation, and the resulting transformation of communal and particularistic relations, both horizontal and vertical, into competitive and universalistic ones. (1979: 174; see also Galeski, 1972: 159–60)

The 'self-exploitation' of the family labour farm is frequently therefore not a voluntary or a natural feature, but the outcome of the need for money for tax or necessary goods for reproduction (Ennew et al., 1977: 304). The developmental significance may also be less rosy than assumed. An increase in labour-intensity on a family labour farm realises what would otherwise be *latent* surplus. But development of productive capacity is ultimately predicated on *decreasing* the labour time needed to produce an item by introducing advanced means of production (Cohen, 1978: 56). While an increase in family labour-time *in itself* may contribute to development, it does not count directly as development in the longer term. (This is not to rule out the possibility of the distinctly different situation of smallholders increasing their labour-time relatively through advanced means of production – see section entitled 'Peasants and simple commodity producers' below.) To the extent, therefore, that producer possession of the means of production may (due to ideological and structural factors) increase labour intensity absolutely, development of productive capacity via advanced means of production does not universally follow. In short, categorical claims about the developmental significance of family farms are clearly problematic.[2]

Agrarian social structure

Analysing how social relations develop in agriculture and what this means for development, requires an identification of the various distinct rural classes. Non-capitalist classes in agriculture are very often lumped together as 'peasants', even though this generic term disguises a large number of differences between them. 'Peasants' are also often defined primarily by the forces, rather than the relations, of production, and accordingly identified as having low productivity and as being partially integrated into the market. But there is no reason why a highly productive peasant should cease to be a peasant, nor why low productivity should be unique to peasants. The feature of semi-integration into the market defines producers only in terms of commodity exchange, and locates them negatively from the poles of full and no integration (Friedmann, 1979: 158, 166). While such differences at Moment C are important, they cannot be the sole point of focus in distinguishing classes.[3] In general analytical terms, I would follow Ennew et al. (1977: 296, 308) and argue that there is no peasant family labour farm in general, and that it is necessary to distribute the components of the diffuse category of the 'peasantry' into differing peasant and other classes. It should also be borne in mind that there is no concept of a 'peasant mode of production', but rather specific forms of agricultural production involving – in diverse ways – household production units which exist within a particular mode (or heterogeneous relation) of production (1977: 310). In addition, agriculturalists should also be seen in relation to urban groups and the state, and rural relationships in relation to the class structure of society as a whole (Hinton, 1973: 208; Cliffe, 1977: 219–20; Raikes, 1978: 285).[4]

There appear to be as many different ways of describing rural differentiation as there are writers. Allan (1949) uses criteria such as amount sold, and on this basis distinguishes between subsistence producers, smallholders and farmers. Brandt et al. (1973) use the method of cultivation as a criterion, and identify hoe cultivators, two-oxen plough users, and more-than-two-oxen plough users (Cliffe, 1978: 335–6). Some writers take a class approach and touch on features at all Moments of production, as well as reproduction and system dynamics (e.g. Post, 1977: 249; Sklair, 1979: 330). But often lacking is a clear theoretical overview that assists in linking the different elements together. There are also those writers who focus on class but take only one aspect in isolation. The limitations of this method merit some further discussion. For example, one approach focuses exclusively on *Moment* 4. Thus, Cabral (1969: 48) differentiates between rural classes on the basis of ownership of the means of production and, fundamentally, of land. The 1970 Tanzanian census goes further by dividing up agricultural classes in terms of *size* of holdings (Cliffe, 1978: 336; see also Byres' analysis of India, 1981: 425). However, land is obviously a very important means of production (especially in a non-industrial society), but it is not the only one. In addition, it is also capable of having a varying stratifying significance where, for example, topography and soil fertility vary (Leo, 1979: 267). As with income, land-size is also a purely quantitative indicator, and it does not give the structured relationships between the groups. Other writers (e.g. Howard, 1980: 72) study rural stratification primarily in terms of *Moment C* regarding the buying and selling of labour-power. Sometimes, however, this is done in isolation of the relations of possession/separation (Moment A), and looked at only in terms of exchange (Moment C). The problem is that without considering relations of possession, distribution and utilisation, evidence of exchange of labour between classes is not in itself a sufficient index for class differentiation (see Bernstein, 1979a: 431).[5]

Several writers have focused on the different systems of class *reproduction*. One emphasis here concentrates on how reproduction relates to the market. Friedmann (1979: 163) suggests, in effect, that the best way of conceptualising differences between rural groupings is through the way that the social relations at Moment C influence and restructure the relations in Moment B and Moment A. According to her, the development of the productive forces, the relation of agricultural households to markets and class relations 'all differ according to commoditisation or resistance to it'.[6] This focus on commoditisation is a useful concept for it enables us to distinguish, *inter alia*, agrarian capitalism and simple commodity production (the latter being completely commoditised with regard to inputs and outputs – but unlike the former, not for regular labour-power). Taken alone, however, commoditisation does not give us the differences between rural classes where relations are not commoditised, nor does it direct us to the issue of system dynamics and the extent to which classes may exhibit these differently.

A second emphasis of the 'reproduction' approach looks at the question of who does the labour. Awiti, for example, identifies as capitalists those producers who get their income solely from hiring labour to work their means of production (1973: 223, 231). He describes as petty capitalists those who receive only one-third of their income from hired-labour. 'Poor farmers' are those who have to sell their labour-power in order to survive – their reproduction being primarily dependent on relations with the possessing capitalist class. Similar approaches elsewhere by Steeves (1978: 124), Bernstein (1979b: 31–2), Galeski (1972: 15–18) and indeed Lenin's classic schema (1899, see 1960a) of farmer capitalists, middle peasants and poor peasants have led to similar conclusions. Clearly, this criterion of differing reproduction systems is useful in distinguishing certain rural classes. However, it misses the extent to which the entire structure gives rise to system dynamics which help to explain, for example, the differences between capitalists, simple commodity producers and landowners, as well as the similarities between capitalists and rich peasants (see below).

Rural classes in the international capitalist system

It is only a start to analyse classes in terms of all the Moments of production, reproduction and system dynamics. The entire socio-political structure is also relevant (Dias, 1978: 182). At the conceptual level, however, it is legitimate – and essential – to define distinct class categories using purely economic criteria. In this light, I now proceed to analyse the specificities of agricultural wage-labourers: share-croppers, feudal tenants and métayers; then between poor, middle and rich peasants; and finally between capitalist farmers, feudal landowners and simple commodity producers. The criteria used for highlighting the distinctions between them are i. different Moments of production, ii. reproduction and iii. system dynamics.

Starting with the producers, it is useful to distinguish *share-croppers* from their exploited counterparts in the CMP, i.e. proletarian wage-labourers. Like the latter, share-croppers are separated from the means of production, and only gain access to the means of production through another class which exploits them. Relations of possession/separation are thus insufficient to distinguish the two classes. It is also very difficult to distinguish these classes in Moment C, especially where payment of proletarians is in kind and lacks a visibly distinct form from the remuneration of share-croppers. It is thus necessary to look elsewhere than Moments A and C for the difference between these two classes. Here, we can turn to Moment B, focusing on the control of the means of production, where it is apparent that the share-cropper – unlike the proletarian – controls the means of production within the labour process (see Byres, 1981: 435). Going further, and taking reproduction – see in terms of the articulation of Moments A, B and C – into account as well, one can also note that while share-croppers are responsible for producing their own subsistence, proletarians depend on capitalists to pay them the value of their labour-power. A similar difference in reproduction distinguishes *feudal tenants* from proletarians (Morris, 1976: 100). There are shades of grey between feudal tenants and share croppers, but I would characterise the major distinction as being in system dynamics. While feudal tenant production is typically limited by its use-value to feudal lords, share-croppers' surplus crops are often destined for sale by their landowners.

The three classes described so far are also distinct from 'métayers'. The major point of difference is in Moment A. In métayage, a tenant supplies labour (including family labour) and part of the means of production. The landlord supplies the land and the rest of the working capital (see Marx, 1972: 694). The product is divided between the two. What the landlord gets is not pure rent – but partial capitalist surplus value (Hindess and Hirst, 1975: 337, footnote 183). (Where the tenant hires outside labour, not to supplement but to replace family labour, he becomes a capitalist producer paying rent to the landlord (1975: 245).) Métayage is a structure of relations similar in certain respects to those on certain development settlement schemes, but it is distinct from another system on many other schemes – that of piece-work wage-labour (see next chapter). Piece-wages appear as if the producer is paid for the products produced rather than the labour-power sold. However, following Marx's arguments, such payment may be understood as actually being for labour-time spent on the products (1972: 518). This flows from consideration of Moment A, where the piece-worker – unlike the métayer – is dependent on the capitalist advancing *all* the means of production. A piece-wage labour process involves *formal subsumption* in the sense that conditions at Moment A subsume producers to capitalist production, and the capitalist only controls Moment B indirectly through the piece-rate remuneration.

The difference between share-croppers, feudal tenants, métayers, and proletarians on the one hand, and the *poor peasantry* on the other, can now be examined. It lies in the last-named having partial access to some means of production and having partial control of the related labour process, while being unable to secure reproduction on this basis. As a result, poor peasants are compelled to articulate with a possessing class for survival. Often forced to become semi-proletarian, poor peasants are thus involved in a dual set of relations of production. They form an unstable class, pulled in various directions, and susceptible to transition into a single class relation – or to being maintained as a self-sustaining labour reserve for the CMP.

The *middle peasantry* is another distinct rural class. The primary difference between it and the poor peasantry lies in reproduction – middle peasants are capable of securing reproduction on the basis of their own means of production. This is not to say, however, that they are entirely self-sufficient: whether it be for labour, food or means of production, each middle-peasant household tends to articulate externally. This may involve both performing outside labour and selling commodities. It may become a structured articulation with different classes – thereby constituting a heterogeneous, and possibly exploitative, relation of production. The peculiar position of the middle peasantry in this situation and its possible development into other classes is analysed in more detail later in this chapter.

The differences between middle and *rich peasants* (also known as

'kulaks') can now be analysed. Regarding Moments A and B of production, these two classes – like agricultural capitalists – both possess and
control means of production. What distinguishes rich from middle (and
poor) peasants is not a quantitative issue such as income or size of means
of production, but the qualitative issue of exploitation. Rich peasants
often exploit poor (and middle) peasants by leasing them land, renting
out equipment, lending cash or hiring their labour (Standing, 1981: 204,
footnote 33). In contrast, middle peasants' production units are productive enough to ensure their reproduction, but insufficient for steady hiring
of labour (Galeski, 1972: 110). While rich peasants exploit labour, they
also take part productively in the labour process. Thus, as simultaneous
producers and exploitative owners of the means of production, they
combine features of both capital and labour and are sometimes called
petty bourgeois in consequence (see Duggett, 1975: 160). As discussed in
chapter one, this leads to dual and contradictory class practices.

I move now to the difference between the rich peasantry and *agricultural capitalists*. It has been argued that the distinction lies in Moment B:
that, unlike capitalist farmers, kulaks participate in the labour process
(see Mamdani, 1977: 10; Awiti, 1973: 231). However, it may be noted
that participation in the labour process is not *in itself* an indication of
non-capitalist relations. As discussed in chapter two, often corresponding
with formal subsumption of labour to capital, the capitalist frequently
takes part in production – without this altering the capitalist–proletarian
class relationship. It is therefore important to look at other factors if we
are to distinguish kulaks from capitalists. Some writers have drawn
attention to the differences in the extent of hiring labour as a way of
distinguishing kulak and capitalist classes. But in isolation of other factors, this is very problematic. For example, middle peasants may hire
labour at certain periods, but this does not necessarily make them either
capitalists or rich peasants.[7] The 'hiring of labour' criterion can also lead
to highly formal and artificial analysis, as with some writers who draw the
line between capitalists and kulaks by identifying differences in the
number of days hired (see Galeski, 1972: 18, 122; Patnaik, 1979: 376).
The problem with such quantitative assessments is that qualitative distinctions in relationships are difficult to perceive.

So far, we have looked at Moment B – at owner-participation and at
hired labour in the labour process – for criteria to distinguish kulaks and
capitalists. For Polly Hill (1963: 107), this is almost irrelevant: 'labour
employment is *not* the crux of the matter: many capitalist (*sic*) farmers
who over the generations have been accustomed to invest their surpluses
in the expansion of their businesses have never employed labourers'.
The similarity between this and Banaji's theorising (see chapter one) is

evident – there is a blurring of the distinctions in different Moments into the primacy of the overall dynamic and rationale of the production cycle. At the same time, it is true that to identify a capitalist labour process and therefore a capitalist class, it is important to examine the system dynamics of the whole – in this case, if production is geared to making profits and increasing capital accumulation rather than towards consumption. Hill (1963: 110) describes some farmers who hired workers as 'employers proper' because they were thus able to release themselves for management, but, at the same time, they did not reinvest in expanded reproduction (see also Howard, 1980: 160). In my view, even with continuous hiring of labour (i.e. with capitalist relations at Moment B), an 'employer proper' does not become a capitalist unless he exhibits a dynamic of capital accumulation.[8] What we have here is the distinction between the circuits of Commodity → Money → Commodity, and Money → Commodity → More Money → More Commodities → Still More Money → etc., as a distinction between non-capitalist and capitalist commodity production (Marx, 1972: chapter four; Banaji, 1976a: 315).

A possible objection to this distinction is evident in the argument by Raikes (1978: 319–20) that there is little difference between rich peasants and capitalist farmers in Africa since even the largest of the latter class have only a very short-term investment pattern. The implication of this is that rich peasants and capitalists are not distinct with regard to accumulation. Against this, however, while rich peasants may develop into capitalists with reproduction on an expanding scale, they remain distinct unless they accumulate enough to initiate and maintain a capitalist cycle of extended reproduction based on hired labour and with the purpose of accumulation – i.e. until they become proper capitalist farmers (Bernstein, 1977: 67, 75; 1979b: 31–2; Howard, 1980: 75–6). Kulaks may therefore be an unstable class, tending towards full participation in one, rather than two, relations of production, and in particular the capitalist one. At the periphery, however, this development has frequently been distorted or frustrated – with significant consequences for economic development (see next chapter).

The distinction between capitalists and *feudal landowners* is partially in terms of their differences in relations of distribution. However, feudal landownership does not preclude commodity exchange at the level of distribution and reproduction. The key differentiating factor lies instead in the relations of possession, methods of exploitation and relations of utilisation. Land as a non-reproducible commodity means that landowners are not subject to the system dynamic of competition in the same way that capitalists are. As a result, accumulation is not a structural imperative for feudal landowners' relations of utilisation.

Simple commodity producers are producers who possess the means of production and work without the intervention or claims of a class of non-producers who have ultimate possession of the means of production. The typical unit of production is the household with family management (Long and Richardson, 1978: 179). Middle peasants are also characterised by household possession of the means of production and family labour. Where simple commodity production differs is that it has a circulation of commodities in both directions – inputs and outputs of production (excepting regular labour), unlike middle peasants who are not as fully integrated into the commodity circuit (Friedmann, 1979: 161). A middle peasant, or a share-cropper, may have complete specialisation in cash crop production, but this is not simple commodity production if the inputs are not all commoditised – i.e. if they remain based on non-market ties (e.g. kinship) for land, non-family labour, means of production and credit.

Simple commodity production is commodity production by a family labour farm without capitalist wage-labour or profit. Market integration is aimed only at meeting the needs of *simple* (rather than expanded) reproduction – hence the term *simple* commodity producers (Bernstein, 1979a: 423–5; Hunt, 1979: 281, footnote 3; Friedmann, 1978: 80). This is notwithstanding the fact that simple commodity producers are still governed by competition which sets the average means of production and labour required for reproduction. Periodically, this labour has to come from outside, because of the demographic cycle of the simple commodity producing family (Friedmann, 1978: 76, 96). The tension here is between the forces and relations of production, and it means that simple commodity production needs to articulate with a labour supply from different relations of production.[9] For middle peasants, such ancillary labour is often obtained through non-market mechanisms. But simple commodity production involves commoditised inputs and hence a labour market. It therefore cannot exist independently of suitable relations of possession/separation which provide this, and the CMP is pre-eminently suited to this. Such hiring of labour is not equivalent to kulak or capitalist hiring, because it tends to be *periodic* hiring, unlike kulaks who hire external labour permanently, and it is different to capitalists who hire labour not to supplement their own labour, but to make money. Because their aim remains simple reproduction, the relations of utilisation are not capitalist relations even if the hired labour generates surplus value.

Having contrasted a range of agricultural classes, and shown how they can be distinguished by taking into account differences in Moments A, B and C of production, as well as differences in reproduction and system dynamics, I now look at some of their dynamics regarding the Agrarian Question.

Agrarian transition

Historically, resolution of the Agrarian Question has been bound up with the development of new agrarian classes. In terms of my theorisation of transition (see chapter two), this would involve a variety of changes in agrarian relations through either internal or external dynamics (or both). In the literature, however, the character of agrarian transition has often been taken to imply a *capitalist* transition. The term 'Agrarian Transition' is used to designate specifically the development of capitalism in agriculture in a context where an urban bourgeoisie is hegemonic and able to prevent a dominant rural class (whether capitalist or not) from blocking the movement of surplus to the industrial sector (Kay, 1981: 499; Taylor, 1984: 171). In this view, any strong agrarian class, such as big landowners or a big agrarian bourgeoisie, can be an obstacle to the growth of capitalism.[10] In much development theory, kulaks and middle peasants are seen as an obstacle to industrial capitalist development because they too are landed classes and therefore a problem for outside classes making demands on them (Williams, 1976: 170). There is some validity in this aspect of the Agrarian Transition model which highlights the fact that, far from being a technical issue, the Agrarian Question contains class political dynamics right at its centre.

According to the Agrarian Transition schema, the resolution of the Agrarian Question requires not only a dominant urban bourgeoisie, but also capitalist agriculture which is assumed to raise productivity to the level needed to create a surplus for industry. The implication is that where capitalist transformation in agriculture is absent or incomplete, the surplus is too low for industrial capital (Kay, 1981: 489). This view is flawed because *non*-capitalist relations in agriculture may produce adequate surplus for development (as in the case of simple commodity production, see next section). In addition, for the CMP (or any other relations) to develop productive capacity in agriculture, a wider context is needed with an articulation to industrial production that can supply the advanced means of production for agrarian development. In this regard, the hegemony of an urban bourgeoisie is not simply to extract surplus from agriculture: it also needs to contribute to its generation. In my view, agrarian capitalism is neither a *necessary* nor a *sufficient* condition for resolving the Agrarian Question.

These two elements of Agrarian Transition (as qualified above) are clearly very general and of limited relevance to the diverse, uneven and often stalled experiences of transition to agrarian capitalism (see, for example, the cases of Britain, as described by Mouzelis (1975–6: 75, 81–3) and Brazil, by de Oliveira (1972, cited by Goodman et al., 1984: 190)). However, one may still argue that there is value in the theory of Agrarian Transition, provided that it is recognised as an ideal-type highlighting two key problems that face a particularly *capitalist* resolution of the Agrarian Question, rather than as a model about real historical experience.

These observations enable us to avoid the errors of much analysis of rural differentiation, which assumes teleologically and erroneously that features such as inequality, wage-labour and dependence on the market indicate a process of Agrarian Transition, when in fact these characteristics may represent the *perpetuation* of non-capitalist producers in the context of an articulation with the CMP (see Williams, 1984: 3). In this regard, agrarian change in non-capitalist relations can be not so much a phase of *transition* as *conservation–dissolution* (see chapter three). In fact, *capitalist* agricultural transformation is not only not inevitable, it is also severely inhibited by specifically agrarian factors – notably the nature of agriculture, absolute rent and differential rent. So significant are these obstacles that one writer has felt it preferable to ask how capitalist agriculture emerged in cases where it did, rather than wonder why it has not done so in others (Williams, 1984: 60). By looking at these obstacles, one can place Agrarian Transition in context and highlight the conditions needed for it to be successful.

Taking first the character of agriculture and its negative significance for capitalist transition, one may note the influence of environmental, climatic and seasonal factors. These mean that agriculture is not conducive to organising and rationalising, unlike capitalist industry (see Cox, 1979: 38; Banaji, 1976a: 301). Absolute surplus value exploitation is more difficult than in capitalist industry because variables such as daylight and weather hinder the extension of labour-time. (The other side of this is that agricultural wage-labour is known for its *intensive* exploitation – which helps to explain why capitalist agriculture commonly suffers from a shortage of labour and, concomitantly, why strong political mechanisms have often been used to counter this (see Williams, 1984: 7–8).) The delayed character of production in agriculture is another obstacle to capitalism because returns on capital tend to materialise slowly, with a negative effect on the rate of profit (Baran, 1962: 166; Mann and Dickinson, 1978). In addition, low returns in relation to the high capital investment in agriculture discourage small and competitive capitalist investment in this branch (Mouzelis, 1975–6: 484; Amin and Vergopoulos, 1974; Thomas, 1975: 40–1). (This is one reason why state involvement in agriculture has occurred – the state is able to raise the necessary capital and to sustain low returns.) A further obstacle for capitalism in agriculture is that where land is fragmented, spatial centralisation may sometimes be a precondition for capitalist accumulation (Kautsky, 1976: 30–1; Marx, 1972: 715). Such consolidation can however be delayed or even prevented indefinitely by the very nature of land as a commodity – that is, by its immobility.

In addition to these obstacles, absolute and differential ground-rent are further impediments for agrarian capitalism. They affect the transfer of surplus from agriculture to industry, and the actual generation of this surplus and the development of agrarian capitalist relations *per se*. Absolute ground-rent derives from the relatively non-reproducible character of agricultural land in that this means of production can be monopolised comparatively more easily than industry and an absolute rent charged for its use. This is effectively an element of monopoly price depending on the control of the supply of land (Tribe, 1977: 77; Hindess and Hirst, 1975: 187, 295).[11] Absolute rent means that prices of agricultural produce may be above value, and through this may represent a surplus transfer into, rather than out of, agriculture. In my framework, absolute rent (outside of the feudal mode of production) is a heterogeneous relation of production spanning Moments A, B and C, which may articulate with the CMP (even in the form of the same person). However, its existence may be contrary to the development of capitalist relations as is evident in the way that absolute rent sustains a non-capitalist rationale. As it is, the fact that land is a relatively immobile and non-reproducible commodity weakens the system process of competition – with the effect of retarding agricultural development. Absolute rent, as a monopoly income, is unlike profit which requires saving and re-investment (Friedmann, 1979: 179). This rent can be spent entirely on consumption – an obvious limit on the development of production (Amin, 1974: 177, 195).

Differential ground-rent, based upon the differences in fertility of land under cultivation, may also impede agrarian capitalism (Marx, 1969: 17–18, 240). Average agricultural prices reflect the costs of the least fertile capitalist enterprise surviving in the market at any one juncture (Kautsky, 1976: 17, 19; Hindess and Hirst, 1975: 184, 293–4). By selling at this price goods which have been produced on land of better fertility, a surplus profit can be made. Because differential rent – unlike super-profit in industry – is relatively permanent, capitalist competition is less effective in agriculture than in industry.[12]

Despite the obstacles to the development of capitalism in agriculture, Marxist writers often draw from Lenin (1960b) and assume that agrarian capitalist classes grow inexorably out of non-capitalist classes, especially by way of a polarising middle peasantry (see Njonjo, 1981; Taylor, 1984). British colonial officials too have seen this as 'a normal step in the evolution of a country' (Kenya's Swynnerton Report – cited in Any-ang'Nyong'o, 1981: 115). However, this perspective ignores not only differences at the centre (between, for instance, the British, French and 'Prussian/Junker' routes to rural capitalism), but also the vast difference between the centre and the periphery. In the centre, agricultural capitalism has generally developed internally (if unevenly and in some cases haltingly) in each central social formation. At the periphery, external dynamics have played the major part. Although there are large variations in both cases, what is clear is that the development of capitalist relations in agriculture has generally been far slower than industry, even if in instances it preceded it. According to Galeski (1972: 28), capitalist farms have never developed anywhere on a massive scale except in the United States.[13] Although capitalist relations (often in the form of monopoly capital) are dominant and *tending* to exclusivity in much central agriculture, generally speaking this is taking place much later than industry (Buch-Hansen and Marcussen, 1982: 177). At the periphery, the situation is extremely varied and agrarian capitalism, while often predominant, is by no means generally prevalent.

With a view to the analysis of planned rural development at the periphery in the next chapter, I turn now to the agrarian transition models of the rich peasant road to capitalism and the alternative of simple commodity production.[14]

Peasants and simple commodity producers

The transformation – where it occurs – of middle peasants into rich peasants (kulaks) and, ultimately, farmer capitalists on the one hand, and into poor peasants and, ultimately, a proletarianised counterpart on the other, produces the class elements of the CMP, and fulfils one of the 'classic' requirements for resolution of the Agrarian Question. This 'rich peasant route' to capitalism in agriculture, as opposed to the 'Prussian' road, takes place from below. It has developed – in widely varying degrees – in Britain, the United States, Bolivia, Venezuela, Peru and Rwanda. This type of transition tends to presuppose that feudal estates have either not existed, or have been dismantled (through reform – as in Taiwan and South Korea, or revolution – as in Mexico). In such conditions, there are fewer obstacles for rich peasants to develop into capitalist farmers (Standing, 1981: 186–9; Dobb, 1962: 10; Banaji, 1976a: 317–18; Moore, 1969: 10–11, 39–40; Morris, 1976: 339, footnote 14; Hindess and Hirst, 1975: 245, 259; Kautsky, 1976: 44). In classical terms, once the rich peasantry has begun to transform itself by permanently hiring labour and by enlarging the commodity market, the remaining middle peasantry is affected by a new competitive environment and new social and technical needs. A middle peasant involved in the process of commodity exchange is vulnerable to market fluctuations and even to a 'simple reproduction squeeze' (Bernstein, 1978; Williams, 1981a: 34). The pressure is to keep in step with the market, producing more cheaply (thereby converting the family farm into an enterprise) and hiring labour and re-investing. Failure to do this means falling behind and losing independence to become a poor peasant increasingly dependent on selling labour-power and, eventually, land and other means of production too (Cooper, 1978: 158–9).[15] Which middle peasants become rich and which become poor is a consequence of existing inequalities, politics, the state and resistance. Family size and demographic cycles may also be significant (Chayanov, 1966; Hunt, 1979: 249).[16]

The rise of a rich peasantry and its growth into fully fledged capitalist farmers entails a major struggle against the obstacles to capitalisation in agriculture. However, where these are overcome (typically with state supplies of labour, subsidised production costs and guaranteed prices and markets – see Williams, 1984: 57), and where a supply of advanced means of production is available, there is every reason for farmer capitalists to raise productive capacity (see Amin, 1974: 155). The degree to which this feeds back into industry depends largely on the class political dynamics involved, and in particular on the second element of the Agrarian Transition model – the hegemony of the urban bourgeoisie.

Contrary to the classic schema, while participation in the market increases dependence on the CMP, it may also produce a relative independence, especially in cases where producers benefit from advanced CMP means of production, supply the market only to the extent that this benefits them, and retain the capacity to scale down commodity production without suffering accordingly. Thus, as an alternative to becoming rich peasants, middle peasants may develop into simple commodity producers sustaining a heterogeneous articulation with the CMP – and, in this manner, even resolve the Agrarian Question without requiring capitalist Agrarian Transition. While there are very different opinions about the status of simple commodity production (see Mouzelis, 1979b: 177, footnote 58; Marx, 1972: 166–7), one can certainly distinguish it from the petty commodity production by middle peasants or other classes. Simple commodity production comes into its own and constitutes a heterogeneous production relation when it articulates with economic elements that can supply its inputs as commodities – and as noted already in this chapter – the CMP is most suitable here. It is under these conditions in central capitalism that this form of production has been capable of developing productive capacity in agriculture.

Simple commodity production presupposes an independent household production unit. It therefore requires a break with bonds of servitude with landlords or state, and the separation of producers from each other – i.e. the dissolution of communal property rights, work organisation and distribution (Kahn, 1978: 113–14). In some respects, the rise of simple commodity production parallels the transformation of middle peasants into rich peasants. By participating in commodity production, a middle-peasant production unit often finds itself on a road which leads to the growing commoditisation of household reproduction and, ultimately, a shift from the market place to the market principle and from a domestic economy to a commercial enterprise (Post, 1977: 243; Galeski, 1972: 12). This requires that the household specialises, enlarges scale and produces more cheaply. However, unlike the classic scenario, the unit may be able to adapt and survive through simple commodity production. One reason for this is the 'self-exploiting' and 'tenacious' character of the family farm (Mouzelis, 1975–6: 482–4). Unlike capitalist production, simple commodity producers work for survival and not profit. Consequently, they often continue, despite low agricultural prices and high industrial prices, because of their capacity to let merchandise go to market at a price lower than a capitalist producer would have to charge. They can relinquish claims to value that would otherwise be due to them, and still reproduce themselves (Perelman, 1979: 120; Patnaik, 1979: 388; Kautsky, 1976: 35). In this regard, a simple commodity producer is similar to Kautsky's middle peasant who is the 'first to endure overwork and underconsumption under the pressure of competition' (1976: 40). Both forms of production also have a lower marginal cost than (time-waged) wage-labour because they dispense with the need for external supervision (see Marx, 1976a: 450, footnote 16). The ability of simple commodity producers to undercut capitalists is one reason why agriculture experiences a slower development of capitalist relations than other economic sectors (Galeski, 1972: 114, 158). The vulnerability of simple commodity producers in this situation is linked to their general weakness as a class, which in turn may reflect the atomised character of their production. They tend to lack the organisation to demand monopoly rent from capitalist purchasers – a factor that disadvantages them, but which contributes to the resolution of the Agrarian Question.

It has been argued that the lower production costs in simple commodity production provide a surplus transfer to capital (Perelman, 1979: 120). Controversy about whether this 'subsidy' is in fact surplus value need not detain us here.[17] I also leave aside the controversy about whether any such 'subsidy', i.e. appropriated surplus labour-time embodied in a product, is provided at all.[18] To the extent that some form of 'subsidy' may exist, it may initially be premissed on a relative increase in the intensity of the producers' labour. Ultimately, however, simple commodity producers cannot survive only by working harder; the key to their continued existence is their ability to mechanise. Indeed, it is largely through raising productivity that households have been able to retain their position in advanced capitalist economies (Friedmann, 1979: 159). The ability of industrial capitalism to meet the need of these producers for means of production and for supplementary labour is therefore most important. The use of hired labour and advanced means of production does not, however, mean an automatic transformation into capitalist status. The process involves an accumulation of means of production, rather than of capital (Goodman et al., 1984: 202). Related to this, simple commodity producers retain a simple reproduction momentum aimed at meeting household reproduction requirements and not at capital accumulation as an end in itself. Income goes on wages, household consumption and renewing the means of production (Friedmann, 1978: 80). Thus the 'incorporation' (Mouzelis, 1975–6: 485) of simple commodity production into the CMP, does not mean that this type of production therefore becomes an internal part of the CMP. Through its reproduction, it is articulated to capitalist relations at Moments A and B (labour) and Moment C (means of production inputs, agricultural produce outputs). But it also retains its own distinct relations at all three Moments, and does not share the CMP's system dynamics to the extent that a capitalist enterprise does. In terms of my framework (see chapter two), simple commodity production is an *external* labour process articulated to the CMP in a heterogeneous relation of production.

Having analysed the kulak–capitalist and simple commodity producer routes to resolving the Agrarian Question, it is worth qualifying the two trajectories. Peasant classes *may* polarise into farmer capitalist and rural proletariat; they *may* become simple commodity producers articulated to the CMP. However, it is also the case that middle peasants may 'continue to reproduce themselves as peasant households and maintain some degree of control over the disposal of their produce' (Williams, 1984: 60). This presupposes, however, successful opposition to the pressures to follow a different path – not least pressures from other classes opposed to the relative autonomy of middle peasants. It would be wrong, though, to see any of these options as mutually exclusive. Middle peasants articulated to the CMP may (even within the same middle-peasant household to an extent) exhibit aspects of all three of these options (as well as others) in varying and changing degrees. Finally, while countries of the centre have seen both rich peasants and simple commodity transitions which have helped resolve their Agrarian Questions, the peripheral situation has been different. There, middle peasants, kulaks and simple commodity producers (in formation or fully fledged) have not developed endogamously, but rather in response to, and sometimes at the behest of, an articulation with an external CMP, often via the peripheral state. Characteristically, these classes have been weak and their development not merely controlled and restricted but also not geared towards resolving the Agrarian Question. 'Rural development' as a conscious and deliberate policy has thus increasingly come to the fore and agrarian relations have been subjected to intensive social engineering.

Planned rural development

Development planning arises because allowing endogamous rural dynamics to unfold in their own way tends not to suit governments or capital. The Agrarian Question cannot thus be treated simply as an economic issue. The political response to it is always important, and particularly so when social classes and the state take it upon themselves to channel rural class formation in a particular direction. These agencies attempt to orchestrate an agrarian transition that corresponds to their interests, while typically presenting this as being in the interests of rural producers as well. 'Rural development' therefore characteristically refers not to the ongoing internal process of development in rural areas, but to planned agrarian change by outside agencies using the language of participation to legitimise the manipulation (Heyer et al., 1980: 1, 4; Seidman, 1978: 319).[19]

It is within this framework that specific development strategies are devised, whether their emphasis is towards additive planning, growth-centres, structural transformation or something else.[20] The selection and implementation of any such option is not a technical issue. It depends on the politics and ideology of planners. Perhaps the most basic ideological–political assumption in planned rural development is that rural classes 'must be developed' (Williams, 1976: 144).[21] Another nigh intrinsic assumption is that development means bureaucratically administered, large-scale commodity production with capital-intensive production (Wallace, 1981: 283; Williams, 1986b: 19). The form of development becomes all-important, and the content (i.e. the process of expanding productive capacity) is lost sight of. More explicit politics and ideology come into play in the choice, for example, between a free-market model, a technocratic model and a collectivist model (Lea and Chaudri, 1983b: 19; Proctor-Simms, 1978: 55). Political differences lie behind diametrically opposed development plans, such as the exclusion of kulaks from co-operatives in socialist agricultural plans or stimulating them as 'progressive farmers' in capitalist planning. Political assumptions about social structure affect whether a development plan stresses centralisation or decentralisation, and whether the emphasis in agrarian reform should be on redistribution of large-holdings to small farmers and the landless, on better use of means of production within existing tenure patterns, or on improving transport, communications and marketing facilities (Petras and La Porte, 1970: 232). Political orientation also influences whether land reform means an incremental increase in output within existing production relations on the assumption that landowners will become 'modernisers from above' or whether it means structural change and 'modernisation from below' (1970: 233–4).

How underdevelopment itself is explained affects the prescriptions recommended for it (Datoo and Gray, 1979: 257). For example, idealist premises tend to blame cultural factors for underdevelopment and accordingly emphasise the role of education in changing traditional beliefs and practices (e.g. Eisenstadt, 1968, cited by Berger, 1976: 55). Regional explanations and prescribed regional planning often imply incorrectly that problems originate – and can be solved – within that unit (Datoo and Gray, 1979: 257). Ideological and cultural premises influence development plans right down to the very form of specific projects – including what is seen as appropriate to people (Foster, 1969: 108–9). Thus, in Niger the choice of co-operatives derived from a romantic analysis of African society which failed to recognise the divisions in the rural social structure (Roberts, 1981: 213, 216). Similarly, land reforms frequently allot individual title to *men* only – even though women tend to work the plot (Harrison, 1981: 442; Seidman, 1978: 298; Muntemba, 1978: 83; Roberts, 1981: 217). Elitist assumptions that go into planning often result in inegalitarian growth-centre strategies being adopted. Colonial governments in Zambia and Kenya assumed that only a minority could be superior farmers, and accordingly devised highly unequal land reforms (Foster, 1969: 110; Leo, 1979: 632; Ruthenberg, 1966: 132). The mistake in this view has led one writer to conclude that 'most experts in rural development do not really know about whom they theorise' (Leo, 1979: 635). Flawed ideological assumptions by the colonial planners at the Gezira scheme in Sudan included the labour needs for tenants' plots, the hierarchical organisation of the scheme and the *homo economicus* belief that tenants would act to maximise their consumption by maximising production (Barnett, 1977: 170–205).

The ideology and politics of development planning are not free-floating, nor are they a self-sufficient explanation for development policy and practice. Development strategies are not a field within which governments make free choices between different means to the same ends. Different development ideologies and plans suit different social interests and social classes (Rudebeck, 1979: 30–1; Dos Santos, 1969: 62). Different classes even have contradictory definitions of development and different measures to achieve it. Although the capitalist state has a relative autonomy from classes (see chapter two), development plans at least in part reflect the political outcome of class struggles (Taylor, 1981: 384–5; Barnett, 1977: 6–15; Dobb, 1951: 80; Kollontai, 1970: 13; Bates, 1981: *passim*; Harrison, 1981: 331). And irrespective of how a development plan is drawn up and adopted, the most important decisions are often made in the implementation (Baran, 1952: 200). Further, every development plan inevitably affects the interests of all social classes and strata, because it entails the mobilisation and allocation of resources (Kollontai, 1970: 13). It is not surprising then that a necessary myth is created whereby rural development plans are constantly presented as being in the interests of all (Heyer et al., 1980: 3). Despite such ideological myths, however, the practice of rural development gives rise to an intense political struggle. Precisely because rural development is a particular type of intervention aimed at directing production in accordance with, *inter alia*, state and ruling class priorities (as well as fashions in international agencies), it is often correctly seen by rural classes as being against their interests (Dutkiewicz and Williams, 1987: 42). Far from being the lauded participants in development, they may well – as Williams (1986b) argues – become its adversaries.

The state and development at the periphery

Development planning at the periphery is intrinsically linked to the nature of the colonial and post-colonial state. The classic structural form of the colonial state has been described as being 'overdeveloped' in its bureaucracy and coercive apparatus (Alavi, 1972). This is attributed to its base being in a metropolitan structure and its representation of absentee capitalist dominance over almost all indigenous classes (Alavi, in Kaplan, 1977: 98–9; Mamdani, 1977: 148, 312; Cabral, 1969: 81). The colonial state undermined the pre-capitalist economy, and simultaneously devoted resources to military and unproductive expenditures while allying with inefficient pre-capitalist groups (Bernstein, 1979a: 423–4; Hymer, 1972: 51). In many cases it increased commodity relations in order to raise revenue and in this way contributed indirectly to developing the structures of a peripheral economic system (Bernstein, 1979a: 427). It was due only to political unrest and the Second World War that the colonial state took direct responsibility for promoting development and expanded its apparatus to control exports, imports and internal marketing (Dutkiewicz and Williams, 1987: 41). Yet, the strategy neglected the modernisation of the means of production as a means to generate revenue (Kay, 1975: 106; Seidman, 1978: 301; Lea and Chaudri, 1983b: 8; Birnberg and Resnick, 1975). At the same time, the state also directly and indirectly continued to thwart the development of an indigenous capitalist class (Amin, 1974: 363–6).

If the colonial state was an agent of underdevelopment, it is less clear whether the post-colonial state has a negative or positive significance for development (Alavi, 1972: 75; Leys, 1976). In fact, to explain this, one has to look at the broader class dynamics (Ziemann and Lanzensdörfer, 1977). This stricture is relevant to Baran who argues that in underdeveloped countries, 'it is only the state that is in a position to mobilise the surplus potentially present in the economic system and to employ it for the expansion of the nation's productive facilities' (1962: 223; see also Dobb, 1962: 33). To move beyond such rosy platitudes, one needs to take account of the interests and capacities of the classes linked to the peripheral state. Thus, as Bernstein (1979a: 433) argues, the economic role of the post-colonial state

has to be located in relation to the possibilities (and contradictions) of accumulation by the ruling classes which have formed since independence, whether they are reproduced and seek to accumulate on the basis of individual or state property (or some combination . . .), and in various alliances with international capitals.

Given the colonial context described above, an indigenous bourgeoisie (in Africa especially) was often not in any position to lead the struggle against colonialism nor to inherit state power after independence (Cabral, 1969: 57–8). This situation, combined with the weakness of the proletariat and the peasant classes, has seen the petty bourgeoisie – usually assumed by Marxists to be a lesser political force than other classes – come to the fore in much of the Third World. The absence of strong economically based ruling classes has placed a large amount of autonomy on this governing class. Indeed, this governing group has often tried to develop itself as a bourgeoisie by using the post-colonial state not only to erect the necessary conditions (infrastructure, credit, etc.) that would benefit private capital, but also as a basis for its own immediate accumulation of funds. Conditions have favoured this situation in some respects. Capitalist development can occur without a national bourgeoisie if *other* local classes can use the state and international capital to this end (Ferner, 1979: 280). While a colony is tied to its metropole, an independent country responds to a wider world economy (Mamdani,

1977: 48, 222; Barratt-Brown, 1976: 273, 278; Warren, 1973: 138–9; Evans, 1977: 44–63).

Nowhere in Africa, however, does it seem that these possibilities have been successfully exploited to generate a fully fledged national bourgeoisie with an interest in and capacity for development. The historical formation of the governing petty bourgeoisie and its associated class character is an important factor here. This class's aspiration under colonialism was not to change the structure of underdevelopment, nor to develop national production, but to be promoted within the existing structure (Hymer, 1972: 58; Mamdani, 1977: 221–3, 315; Barratt-Brown, 1976: 256). And the role of the post-colonial state in economic development remains prominent in part precisely because of the failure of local petty bourgeois and bourgeois classes to use it to enable them successfully to develop privately (Amin, 1974: 372; Woddis, 1977: 276).[22] Against this backdrop, the overdeveloped features of the colonial state have in fact proliferated. There is a hypertrophy of administrative activities and development planning as evidenced in the growth and direction of public spending (Amin, 1974: 197). This development is due in part to public expectations and the corresponding institutionalised developmental role of the peripheral state, and is therefore relatively autonomous of class control motives. However, it is also due to bourgeois and petty bourgeois groups trying to widen their access to state resources and extending state control over the producers of these resources (see next chapter). Related to this is the internal character of the post-colonial state – namely inefficient, corrupt, wasteful and overly bureaucratic. The same dominant interests have also meant that the post-colonial state has tended to devote considerable resources to combating political instability and promoting territorial unity and governmental legitimacy – at the expense of development (Harrison, 1981: 384; Saul, 1974). While these may be preconditions for development, they are not in themselves a productive use of resources.

The issues raised above have been the subject of a lively debate about the developmental significance of Kenyan capitalists and the Kenyan state. A number of issues are confused in the debate, arising from the conflation of four different points:

i.   the political and developmental character of Kenyan capitalists (comprador or national);
ii. the (broader) issue of the development of capitalist relations in Kenya;
iii. the development of productive capacity in Kenya;
iv. the role of the Kenyan state in development.

Kaplinsky has criticised what he sees as Leys' (1978) emphasis on i. and what he regards as the implied conclusion that there is an indigenous national bourgeoisie successfully using the state for development in Kenya. He attempts to shift attention to the issue of iii., where he argues that indigenous industrial accumulation by local capital is flawed due to its being based on an alliance with foreign capital that has only *temporarily* located production in the low-wage periphery (1980: 104). In response, Leys has argued that his evidence showed merely African entry into manufacturing and that he was not characterising this as an indigenous industrial bourgeoisie (1980: 109). Yet, it does appear that for Leys, if Kenyan capitalists are not quite a 'national bourgeoisie', they are still part of a situation where Kenya is developing. This is evident in his criticism of Kaplinsky and dependency theory for minimising peripheral development: 'when the fact of such development cannot be denied, it is decried as inegalitarian, unbalanced, anti-popular; and when this is admitted, it is finally dismissed as being at most short-lived and illusory' (1980: 112). The nub of the issue is thus the character of this 'development', and how Kenyan capitalists and the state relate to it.

One pointer to analysing this is provided by Beckman's intervention in the debate. Like Kaplinsky, Beckman appears to have doubts about whether Kenya's growth amounts to development *per se*. He focuses attention on ii., arguing effectively that capitalist relations (as distinct from the issue of national development) are not in contradiction with imperialism (1980: 57). He points out that close links between domestic capital (private and state) and foreign capital (i.e. i.) are compatible with the low employment and non-integrating character of Kenyan growth (i.e. compatible with a *negative* interpretation of iii.) (1980: 54). What Leys has done, it would seem, is to have merged i. and ii., linked these to iv. (the state), and then to have deduced iii. as positive productive capacity from this. But his is an erroneous operation, however, because attention to iii. in Kenya does not show positive productive capacity, no matter that there are African capitalists, capitalist relations and an active state.

In my view, these four distinct elements must not be conflated with each other. Each is significant, and I therefore disagree with Godfrey (1982: 274) who scorns element i. by trivialising it as concerning the nationality of capitalists' passports. However, he is correct in noting that rather than a national bourgeoisie, Kenya has a local bourgeoisie within a [dominant] international system of production (1982: 289). I would argue that Kenya's bourgeoisie is not 'national' in that despite its use of the state, it is still unable to develop Kenya's productive capacity because of its subservient place in the international capitalist system. In this perspective, issues i. and ii. are linked to show clearly that the result is not a positive interpretation of iii.

Kitching has made a valuable contribution by arguing that the Kenyan state is not an agent of either international or local capital (or fractions of either), but a site of struggle which results in contradictory outcomes; and that the state itself fractures into contending forces in this struggle (1985: 132). In my view, Kenyan capitalists certainly are a factor in these struggles, and they have a contradictory significance for productive capacity in Kenya. While this is not the place for a full analysis of the Kenyan state, the general points that emerge here are pertinent for understanding the role of rural development planning at the periphery. The Kenyan debate highlights that the peripheral state, indigenous capitalists and their politics, capitalist relations and development are not intrinsically connected phenomena. State development planning may therefore accommodate the interests of indigenous capitalists (and the capitalist aspirations of a petty bourgeoisie) and/or the interests of international capital – but these are not necessarily geared towards, or realised in, developing national productive capacity. Some development plans may concentrate on one of these four objectives, others on more than one, and some may combine all aspects. In the end, the developmental significance of the peripheral state and its social base is ambiguous and variegated, and to analyse this empirically requires keeping distinct the different issues of class politics, production relations, productive capacity and the state.[23]

To draw together the conclusions in this section, I have argued that the overdeveloped character of the colonial and post-colonial state has contributed to underdeveloping productive capacity in the Third World. The colonial authorities inhibited the development of indigenous capitalist relations, while the governing petty bourgeoisie post-independence has used the state to try to develop these relations. However, in the case of Kenya, this has not been sufficient to develop the productive capacity of the country as a whole. The developmental character of the peripheral state is consequently ambiguous and partial, rather than wholly negative or wholly positive. At the same time, it is clear that the development of the interests of the petty bourgeoisie through the state has not been the same as development as such. Instead, their interests and relations have developed dependently in conjunction with international capital, indeed internalising its domination thereby. In this context, development planning at the periphery has often been undertaken with political rather than developmental goals in mind, and this may be counterproductive to development. Generally speaking, both pre- and post-independence, rural development in the Third World has often concerned not an integrated national development strategy and the Agrarian Question but, first and foremost, issues of political strategy. Indeed, in some instances, rural social engineering has taken place for political reasons which have a negative influence on the development of productive capacity (see next chapter).

Rural development strategies in tropical Africa

The countries of tropical Africa have shared similar colonial and neo-colonial experiences and are therefore a useful source for looking at development strategies. Kenya is cited most frequently here because of the pervasive external intervention into its agriculture (Heyer, 1981: 90; Carlsen, 1980: 11). Development schemes in tropical Africa have varied in terms of rationale, time and type, but common to many has been the role of developing not so much national productive capacity, as the interests of governments, international capital and (post-independence) a local bourgeois/petty bourgeois class. Rural development planning in most of the examples here may emanate from the state, but it is also interlinked with the demands and capacities of private (usually inter-national) capital. The shortage of state funds and technical/managerial skills ensures a major role for foreign involvement in development pro-grammes. This often leads to an alliance where the state organises the political, ideological and administrative conditions for rural intervention while capital organises the technical and financial means for this (Bern-stein, 1979a: 433–4). State financial involvement (via budget grants, shares or loans) also often benefits private capital (see next chapter), and even state-owned schemes are frequently controlled by international capital (Raikes, 1978: 317). In such cases, although control of Moment A is formally vested in governments, in reality the international firms pos-sess most of the means of production and, to a greater or lesser extent, control Moments B and C as well.

The capacity of international capital and local ruling classes for appro-priating and accumulating is closely related to the development of com-modity production. Thus, governments and capital in many cases introduced wholly capitalist relations of production through plantations and settler agriculture. Prior to World War II, the production of cash crops in tropical Africa was dominated by these two forms of capitalist farming, which benefited from state support as well as from state action against rival non-capitalist farmers (Muntemba, 1978: 61; Dinham and Hines, 1983: 49). But agrarian capitalism nevertheless still failed to spread across agriculture. Among other factors, there was not an across-the-board separation of local producers from their means of production and their transformation into fulltime wage-labourers. In addition, there has generally not been a powerful indigenous class with wealth and means of production to be able to hire fulltime wage-labourers in tropical Africa. A further factor, however, is that state and capital have themselves spurned plantations and even settler capitalism in some instances where peasants were already developing cheap export production (Williams, 1985: 145). Indeed, one strategy of planned development which differs from plantations and settler agriculture is that aimed at the 'peasantisation' of pre-capitalist producers. Taxation, land and education policies played an important part here in raising the cash needs of pre-capitalist producers and compelling a degree of commoditisation of agricultural produce and labour-power. In parts of East Africa, colonial merchant companies supported the development of African commodity production – even against settler capitalist farms (Mamdani, 1977: 60; Van Zwanenberg, 1974: 445; Williams, 1984: 16). Accordingly, state development plans often have aimed to increase and control commodity production by indigenous farmers who, in much of tropical Africa, are the bulk of the population and today earn a significant portion of foreign exchange (Bernstein, 1979a: 433; Hill, 1977: 25; Heyer et al., 1981b: 5).

In this context, tropical Africa has seen the use of the 'progressive' or 'master' farmer development strategy by both the colonial and post-colonial state. The aim here has been to increase output through upgrading agricultural methods and diffusing improved means of production. Associated projects have ranged from extension services, teaching agriculture in the schools and the provision of roads and railways. Growth-centred features are evident where a particular programme (for example, extension advice) is aimed at selected areas and farmers reckoned to have developmental potential (Coulson, 1981: 58; Williams, 1985: 153). A more transformative approach has seen land reform strategies – as in Kenya under the Swynnerton Plan which involved registering title to land, and the consolidation of scattered plots. Credit schemes are also often part of 'master farmer' development strategies, representing an intervention that tries to raise productive capacity by facilitating the acquisition of improved means of production. Bates (1981: 109) sees it as a paradox that African governments *subsidise* production through credit, at the same time as *taxing* farm output. In fact, this is quite logical: in order to tax output, it is necessary first to ensure that there is production.

To the limited extent that the 'progressive farmer' approach has raised rural productivity (see next chapter), this strategy characteristically has benefited a minority of farmers, assisting their development into middle peasants, simple commodity producers and kulaks. However, while the goal has been to supply bureaucrats and the class/es they represent with peasant surplus, it is difficult to secure this when the producers graduate into a rich peasantry engaged in private accumulation (Raikes, 1978: 299, 314; Williams, 1984: 59). An independent rich peasantry is difficult to tax, its economic power gives it control over local decision-making bodies and it can set the terms of supply of produce or refuse to supply altogether (Heyer et al., 1980: 5). Such bargaining power represents a problem for state and capitalist industry intent on resolving the Agrarian Question (Williams, 1981a: 34). Consequently, the growth of relatively autonomous rich peasant producers is often seen as needing to be contained if not thwarted (Buch-Hansen and Marcussen, 1982: 18). Governments have thus tried to stop middle peasants and simple commodity producers from developing into kulaks, as well as attempted to block the development of kulaks into farmer capitalists (Heyer, 1981: 92). The same social forces that in some cases helped to prevent the full and generalised proletarianisation of African producers as desired by settler capital, and which then helped to develop middle peasants and set a stratum on the road to kulak or simple commodity producer status, have also sometimes acted to freeze this very trajectory.

Thus, crop authorities place restrictions on volumes and prices of marketed produce and on what should and should not be grown how, when and where (Raikes, 1978: 295–6; Mamdani, 1977: 142; Muntemba, 1978: 60). Indigenous capital has been excluded from investment in marketing. Control of Moment C, relations of distribution, has been exercised through the institutions of marketing boards and co-operatives. Contrary to their original purpose of benefiting producers, these institutions have provided a mechanism for appropriating peasant surplus labour through unequal exchange (Bernstein, 1979a: 434; Bates, 1981: 12–14; Kitching, 1980: 414, 416–17). In this way, marketing boards can actually run counter to development. While in Kenya tea and coffee boards did play a role in encouraging output, in Nigeria they taxed produce to the extent of threatening existing production and marketing levels (Williams, 1981b: 49). Co-operatives similarly have found favour with governments for their use as an instrument of public administration (Williams, 1981a: 25; Heyer et al., 1981b: 5–6). It may be noted that because such controls typically involve only the level of the market, they are not always wholly effective. Farmers resist by smuggling, hoarding, switching crops or even withdrawing from the market in the face of low prices (as in the case of small-scale coffee growers in Kenya) (Bates, 1981: 82).

In contrast, contract farming and rural settlement schemes provide for tighter control of production (Heyer et al., 1981b: 8). Contract farming by smallholders typically represents a joint strategy by capital and the state for intervening in production through a contractually enforced heterogeneous relation of production which transforms producers into outgrowers. The focus here is on richer farmers producing cash crops for agro-industries. In Kenya, there is a growing number of such producers tied to multi-national firms through credits that have to be paid for in produce (Dinham and Hines, 1983: 92; O'Keefe, 1984: 162).[24] On capital's side, contract farming is often a strategy of vertical integration to supply processing plants (Raikes, 1978: 286, 307; Goodman et al., 1984: 209). To this end, it is (like many settlement schemes) often combined with a nucleus estate, as in the case of Kenya's Mumias sugar scheme. The company at Mumias does much of the mechanised work, and also supplies fertiliser and transport to mills. These services are given on credit and deducted (plus 8 per cent interest) at harvest (Mulaa, 1981: 89, 91). While outgrowers have often been successfully productive, the nucleus estate also means that the enterprise is not totally dependent on them (Williams, 1981a: 25; Dinham and Hines, 1983: 86).

Settlement schemes characteristically involve changes in land tenure and, correspondingly, producer control of this key means of production is typically weakened, if not wholly excluded. Such schemes enable outside control over all Moments of production and especially over Moment B concerning the timing, quality and use of inputs, as well as Moment C concerning payment systems and channels for distribution. The total control facilitates comprehensive measures (Raikes, 1978: 308; Heyer et al., 1981b: 8; Williams, 1981a: 24; Cliffe, 1978: 337). It has thus been argued that the aim of development schemes is:

to generate the development of an undifferentiated middle peasantry, producing high-grade export crops under controlled and increasingly technically advanced methods of production and to avoid the uncontrollable aspects of rich peasant differentiation. (Cowen, 1976, quoted by Raikes, 1978: 286)

While producers under other forms of intervention are – up to a point – capable of withdrawing into subsistence, agricultural settlement schemes eliminate this possibility (Hill, 1977: 27). For example, in Kenya's million acre settlement project begun in 1962, settlers became tied into controlled commodity production through their need to generate cash to repay the state loans received to buy land on the scheme. Elsewhere, settlement schemes (often combined with irrigation) have involved a package of tight production and marketing controls where settlers only have tenure on the basis of performance. There may also be a package of incentives such as housing, health care and schooling. Typically on settlement schemes, the authorities run a capitalist nucleus estate to provide transport, processing and marketing facilities and labour for extra work

on settlers' plots (Heyer et al., 1980: 9; Heyer, 1981: 107). The role of
international capital in such schemes is often to control production
through management and consultant advice, with the state taking responsibility for most other things (Buch-Hansen and Marcussen, 1982:
35). Although direct financial investment is absent, companies are still
able to influence and control the choice of particular cash crops, and the
markets that these are sold in (Dinham and Hines, 1983: 158). The
strategy also enables companies to glean surplus through supplying advanced means of production such as fertilisers and machinery (see Heyer
et al., 1981b: 8).

The diverse rural development strategies discussed above, as well as
other strategies such as moishavim (see Halliday, 1979: 113), may be
exhibited in a given social formation both singly and in combined form.
Thus, Nigeria's third development plan (1975–80) included setting up
large irrigation projects, supplying extension and inputs to capitalist and
progressive farmers, promoting high-yielding crops and bypassing peasants with state companies (Williams, 1985: 153–5; see also Riddell's
recommendations for Zimbabwe as discussed by Williams, 1982). All
these may share the goal of facilitating either governmental or commercial (or both) exploitation and control over rural producers. But one
important factor limits this: as will be discussed in the next chapter, many
strategies are too unviable to realise such objectives.

5   Social structure and failed development

The social structure of progressive farmers and outgrowers

Development projects serve as a catalyst of class formation, the generation of class interests and the emergence of class-motivated activity (Steeves, 1978: 124). However, to elucidate the class character of 'progressive farmers', outgrowers and settlement scheme tenants is a complex issue, as is evident in a debate concerning the extent to which African and other agriculturalists are peasant or proletarian in character.

On the one side of the debate, Njonjo notes that almost 50 per cent of income to smallholders in Kenya's central province comes from wages and remittances. He asks whether this class is therefore a peasantry or a proletariat with patches of land (1981: 37). His judgement tends towards the proletarian characterisation, and it has come under fire for ignoring both the smallholders' domestic labour process and the question of ownership of land (Gutto, 1981: 44). Indeed, different conclusions have been reached by taking these two considerations into account. With regard to the *domestic labour process*, O'Keefe (1984: 160) argues that this precludes proletarian status, even though in the village he studied, 44 per cent of smallholders depended on off-farm sources for more than half their income. While O'Keefe rejects calling these producers 'farmers' (likening them instead to a 'lumpen rural proletariat-cum-peasantry' functioning as a labour pool for capitalism), he stops short at calling this class a proletariat proper, reasoning that its members take part in wage-labour for the purpose of supporting their own rural family-based labour process. With regard to *land ownership*, Amin (1974: 30) argues in general terms that the possession of land means that rural producers who sell their labour-power cannot be full proletarians; instead he characterises them as semi-proletarians. Taylor (1984: 184) similarly finds it significant that Egyptian rural producers retain some control of land and concludes that this stops them from being a proletariat.

If, in the light of these considerations, and contra Njonjo, smallholders are not a true proletariat, to what extent are they then poor or middle peasants? Analysing the Kenyan case, Cowen (1981b: 124, 139) sees rural producers not only as *not* proletarians, but as actually resisting proletarianisation. He argues that they are a regenerated peasantry formed by workers who are able to withdraw from wage-labour as wage remittances become increasingly secondary to income from their own production.[1] Yet, as Cowen also observes, such peasants' production is not solely for direct consumption, but also for commodity exchange in the capitalist market. For this reason, these producers 'do not escape either the circuit of capital or the capital/labour relation' (Cowen, 1981a: 69). In Cowen's view, no less than other places of production, the smallholding is now subject to the control of capital. Although he stops short of saying that peasants participating in the 'capital/labour relations' are proletarians, it is exactly this scenario which has led Brazilian writers (amongst others) to describe the modernised family farm as a new form of capitalist relations, with the new peasant as a worker for capital – i.e. as a proletarian (Goodman et al., 1984: 194). In other words, the debate comes full circle to Njonjo's conclusions (albeit for different reasons). And indeed, as with Njonjo, this perspective may be criticised for missing the fact that the rural labour process itself is not capitalist. The approach focuses on the whole relation, but neglects the heterogeneous character of the parts.

  The problem with the peasant/proletarian debate outlined above is the implicit blanket categorisation involved. It is little wonder that there are such different positions, when not only is a range of producers being analysed, but the diversity of relations engaged in by any single rural producer is also not adequately appreciated. Njonjo's peasants are proletarians through their off-farm production; Cowen's are subjected to capital through their on-farm production. In an attempt to conceptualise the on-farm relations, Williams (1981a: 31–2) argues that most smallholders lie somewhere between being independent producers (outside the market) and 'outworkers' (i.e. piece-workers) for capital. He suggests defining the diverse groups in between these two extremes in terms of their varying incorporation into 'circuits' of capital. I would agree with this suggestion, adding that this could also encompass their off-farm production. At the same time, this method risks overstressing the *articulation* between the smallholders and the CMP at the expense of evaluating the specificity of the non-capitalist features in their domestic production. Furthermore, I would emphasise that, following my argument in this monograph, the circuit of capital does not render everything in it capitalist (as Cowen and the Brazilians mentioned above would have it). As I will now attempt to demonstrate, by analysing producers in terms of all three Moments of production, reproduction and system dynamics, it becomes possible to cut through much of the debate about the class character of rural producers.

There is little problem in analysing properly capitalist and proletarian classes as on plantations, settler farms and on company/state-owned estates. It is also relatively uncomplicated to assess tenants who share-crop, and pay rent to a landowner (see Williams, 1984: 17–18). But it is much more complex to try to analyse those rural producers convention-ally described as 'progressive farmers', outgrowers and settler tenants. 'Progressive farmers' are in fact made up of several distinct (though also overlapping) classes and cannot be attributed any single class character. Historically, 'progressive farmer' initiatives have contributed to the 'peasantisation' of pre-capitalist producers and even to the generation of simple commodity producers. Generally, the emphasis has been on fos-tering a middle peasantry involved in petty commodity production – a process which just as often contributes to the development of rich and poor peasants (see below). Progressive farmer strategies may involve land reform to develop peasant relations of production, as well as the promotion of advanced means and methods of production. Producers are induced to rely more heavily on the market and the bureaucracy for supplies and services (Heyer et al., 1980: 9). Where these inputs are acquired through credit, 'progressive farmer' producers are often subject to exploitation by their creditors, and this applies to outgrowers and settler tenants as well.[2] For Roseberry (1978), this relation means that many 'peasant' producers are actually proletarians. But this assessment ignores the fact that production relations remain non-capitalist at both Moment A and Moment B. In my view, the articulation between peasants (and again this applies to outgrowers and settler tenants) and creditors constitutes a heterogeneous relation of production. It is not necessarily the dominant relations among the many they participate in, and neither does it obliterate the existence or significance of their other relations.

'Progressive farmer' strategies may encourage the growth of middle peasants into simple commodity producers with commoditisation of both inputs and outputs of production. Hill (1970: 21–9) observed this de-velopment in Ghana, although she incorrectly characterised the pro-ducers as rural capitalists because of their commercial behaviour and treatment of land as an investment, while ignoring the fact that they did not hire labour. In many cases, however, commoditisation has not de-veloped to this extent. Figures for Kenya in the late 1970s show that more than 50 per cent of smallholder production was used for household consumption (Carlsen, 1980: 37). While this average statistic conceals substantial variations, it does imply that as far as *reproduction* goes, many smallholders were far from having a full simple commodity producer

status. Most appear to be rich or (decreasingly) middle peasants strug-
gling against becoming poor peasants or proletarians. Thus, middle level
smallholders involved in cash cropping, but who hire labour neither in
nor out in significant quantities, have been a 'rapidly eroding group' in
Kenya (Kitching, 1980: 374, 406–7). A detailed analysis by Carlsen (1980:
191) points to growing differentiation into rich and poor rural households. The development of rich peasants into farmer capitalists is,
however, as discussed in general in chapter four, often blocked by means
of marketing boards and monopolies operated by the very same agencies
that promoted middle peasant and kulak commodity production in the
first place. In contrast, transformation from middle to poor peasant status
faces far fewer obstacles. This development reduces rural producers'
relations to commoditisation to selling their labour-power. Contrary to
Njonjo, while this status implies certain proletarian characteristics, it
depends, *inter alia*, on the significance of this labour as to whether the
producer is wholly proletarian. And this in turn varies according to what
other relations the producer is involved in, and what the wage-labour
means for household reproduction. These remarks enable us to interpret
a survey of 7,000 farmers in Kenya which found that non-farm cash
income exceeded farm cash income, and in fact was the main means of
repaying loans made to farmers entering settlement schemes (Kitching,
1980: 357). These producers (or at least some members of their households) therefore shared both some proletarian characteristics and some
peasant characteristics. However, there was substantial variation in the
latter which affected the significance of the former. Thus, the survey
found that at the higher levels, off-farm income was used to buy land and
labour and it facilitated capital investment. Paid employment at lower
levels served to take the strain off peasant household subsistence. In
comparison to 'progressive farmer' strategies, outgrower (contract
farmer) strategies restructure class relations much more clearly because
they intervene more extensively in the labour process (usually via control
of Moments A and C). What this means in terms of the class character of
outgrowers, and how it may combine different features normally characteristic of the various disparate classes, may be examined by looking in
turn at proletarian, capitalist, landlord and simple commodity producer
characteristics. Taking first the issue of outgrowers' proletarian features,
it has been said that in many schemes multi-national companies control
the production of plantation crops by smallholders under conditions
which, according to Heyer et al. (1980: 8), come near to relegating the
producers to the position of wage-labourers. There are indeed similarities
between outgrowers and proletarians which, for the purposes of expo-
sition, may be analysed in the order of Moments B, C and A. Concerning

Moment B, the operations of the outgrowers are closely controlled (Currie and Ray, 1987: 95). This has obvious parallels with a capitalist labour process. At Moment C, outgrowers also resemble proletarians in that they have no control over the class relations of distribution and utilisation. For example, at Mumias the scheme has a monopsony on buying cane (Williams, 1984: 17–18). The producers become indebted to the company and have little scope for negotiating the price. Linking this to the conditions at Moment B, it has been argued that 'the idea that the farmer "sold" his/her crop becomes something of an illusion' and that what is actually being paid is 'tantamount to a wage' (Currie and Ray, 1987: 95).[3] Outgrowers may also be similar to proletarians at Moment A, where – as at Mumias – their entry to or exclusion from the scheme is out of their hands. The fact that they do possess the land may not in fact be meaningful given their reliance on other means of production supplied by the contractors, and given their lack of control in Moments B and C.[4]

Against the view that outgrowers are in effect proletarians, it has been claimed that they are not really subsumed to capital at Moment B because they are not congregated together into mechanised and socialised production (Bernstein, 1979a: 432). Yet, such a situation does not preclude capitalist relations of production. Formal subsumption may be capitalist without transforming the labour process (Cowen, 1981b: 126; see chapter two). It is therefore not significant if outgrowers' relations in production are not underpinned by the forces of production to the same extent as real subsumption in the CMP. Another, more valid, argument against the outgrower/proletarian equation points out that for the capitalist investor, contract farming means precisely not having to enter a direct capital–wage relationship (Buch-Hansen and Marcussen, 1982: 18). It is true that this in itself does not preclude the possibility of an *indirect* capital–labour relationship, as with piece-work proletarians. Both outgrowers and piece-workers may retain some control at Moment B, the labour process. As discussed in chapter four, piece-work involves wage-labour because the means of production are supplied by the capitalist (Dobb, 1962: 22–3; Marx, 1972: 520). However, unlike piece-worker proletarians, the point about outgrower farming is that the major risk is transferred from state and capital to the producer (see Buch-Hansen and Marcussen, 1982: 18; Currie and Ray, 1987: 94). This difference is bolstered when outgrowers produce their own household subsistence – which means that, unlike proletarians, their reproduction is not wholly dependent on what capital pays.

A further argument against seeing outgrowers as proletarians might be that their land ownership is not merely formal. This view would contradict claims by Williams (1985: 171) who argues that outgrowers often supply little more than their own labour-power to production. In my view, the fact that outgrowers supply land as well as labour-power is what distinguishes them from settler tenants. It is significant that possession often constitutes an obstacle to control by capital and state, and this is one reason why both agencies may try to alter tenure and make it conditional on subordination to them (see the case of settler tenants in the next section). In cases where land ownership is meaningful in terms of producer control over other Moments of production, I would hold that the outgrowers may be better described as potential simple commodity producers (see below). Where land ownership is nominal, however, they may indeed resemble proletarians taking part in a capitalist relation of production. Yet what may be true for some of the parts (proletarian), is not true for the whole of outgrowers' class character. It would be reductionist to describe outgrowers as capitalist given that their production relations (concerning payment and land), and their reproduction, may be quite separate and distinct from proletarians. What is more, outgrowers may exhibit *proto-capitalist* and *landlord* characteristics. I now consider this dimension.

Dealing firstly with landlord characteristics, it has been argued that outgrowers in Mumias with legal ownership at Moment A receive the equivalent of land rent (Buch-Hansen and Marcussen, 1982: 30; Heyer, 1981: 115). In my view, where outgrowers supply land but do not work it, they are clearly landlords, receiving rent. I would argue that at Mumias, it is a case of renting land where, for example, the outgrower fails to undertake the work and the company uses its own labour to plant, fertilise and weed (Buch-Hansen and Marcussen, 1982: 31). If the outgrower hires outside labour on the basis of his possession of land, then this places him in semi-capitalist relations at Moment A. Where outgrowers supply land but depend on other means of production from capitalists to work it, then (in some respects) they resemble the general structure of métayage. As such, they produce surplus value for capital as part of the relation of dependence on the means of production supplied by capital.

The significance of labour hiring may be examined as part of investigating whether outgrowers exhibit capitalist characteristics. Like their counterparts on settlement schemes, some outgrowers may resemble capitalists in hiring labour. However, this needs careful qualification. At Mumias, one study found that 90 per cent of participants hired labour for weeding (Buch-Hansen and Marcussen, 1982: 31). Another study says that 46 per cent hired labour, and that 36 per cent depended exclusively on hired labour (Mulaa, 1981: 97). The extent to which this is capitalist depends on its role in the reproduction of the enterprise (is it central?), and on the system dynamic in the hiring (is it part of capital accumulation?).[5]

Analysis of Moment C shows that in terms of relations of utilisation, some capitalist features are evident among a stratum of outgrowers. It is the case that at Mumias all major activity is carried out by the company, and this limits the opportunities for outgrowers to develop into capitalists. Though some farmers have fifty acres under cane, employ labour and receive high returns, they are unable to invest in agriculture (Mulaa, 1981: 92). At the same time there is a small capitalist farmer stratum where a capitalist rationality and investment pattern is developing among 10–15 per cent of outgrowers who have high incomes (also from other occupations), and who invest to accumulate, especially in circulation but also in agriculture (Buch-Hansen and Marcussen, 1982: 33). There is also a middle group of outgrowers whose level of reproduction has risen with income from cash crops and who produce with a mix of family and wage-labour. This group appears to be a middle peasant group with limited similarities to capitalists.

Some outgrowers may resemble neither proletarians nor capitalists, but simple commodity producers, as with Kenya's contract tea farmers. Regarding Moment A, it appears at first sight that outgrowers differ from simple commodity producers in that, aside from land, they possess no means of production. However, some outgrowers do actually acquire these means in the course of their production. In Kenya, the Tea Development Authority (KTDA) licences growers, and administers a credit and fertiliser scheme funded by international groups and the Kenyan government. Growers also receive plants and materials from the KTDA. However, they pay for all the services, with the charges deducted as a standard levy on the monthly payment they receive (Blume, 1971: 88, 101). All of these would seem to buttress simple commodity producer status as regards possession of means of production. At the same time, these producers do not have altogether unqualified possession. The Tea Act gives the KTDA legal rights to take over neglected outgrower land (Buch-Hansen and Marcussen, 1982: 24). With tree cash crops in general (which take a long time to yield), Blume (1971: 213) argues that 'pressure can be exerted directly through control of production materials and credit securities'. This is true, but it remains compatible with simple commodity producer status.

Concerning Moment B, it has been noted that simple commodity producers are more difficult to control than contract farmers, and 'legal regulations have to be created so that disciplinary measures can be enforced' (Blume, 1971: 58, 93, 100). In Kenya, a law called the Tea Cultivation Order sets out rules amounting to directives for production under close supervision. Lists are drawn up of problem growers, who are warned in writing a few times and may ultimately be fined. Up to a point, however, this is not inconsistent with simple commodity producer status. At Moment C, in addition to buying inputs, simple commodity producer status means selling most of the produce. In the case of the KTDA producers, however, many farmers devote only a small sector of their land to tea and cultivate subsistence crops on much of the remainder (Buch-Hensen and Marcussen, 1982: 18; Blume, 1971: 88–102). This precludes them from full simple commodity producer status and suggests that they are also involved in middle peasant relations.

'Progressive farmers' and outgrowers, almost irrespective of their multi-class character, fit into the category of 'new production forms' created by articulation within peripheral capitalism. Production by these largely non-capitalist producers should be seen as *external* non-capitalist labour processes articulating with the CMP (often indirectly through the state). The total relation does not involve the same classes at all three Moments of production. Such non-capitalist relations cannot be reproduced independently of the CMP, nor do they have definite *system dynamics*. As a result, in terms of the criteria advanced in chapter two, they are not a *mode of production* articulating with the CMP. At the same time, however, they are not an *internal* part of the CMP. They constitute heterogeneous relations of production articulated to it, and sharing certain of its features in respect of different Moments of production, reproduction and system dynamics.

In consequence, one may conclude that progressive farmers and outgrowers are neither wholly proletarian or capitalist. In addition to being class-differentiated among themselves, in many cases they also combine (in varying degrees) both characteristics – as well as others such as simple commodity producer, landlord and middle peasant features. It would appear that the best way to understand their class status is to recognise them as participants in *at least* two (interactive) heterogeneous relations of production. To the extent that, for example, their articulation with one side such as capital may predominate, they would constitute a more definite class, with a single and homogeneous general character. In such a case, one could speak of their participation in the capitalist mode of production as their primary relation of production (see Cohen, 1981: 100). This is a matter of conflict and struggle, amongst other things, and is linked to the dynamics of domination and subordination in articulation.

The social structure of settler tenants

Settler tenants, like progressive farmers and outgrowers, combine proletarian and capitalist features in their various relations of production and cannot be conceptualised as being simply one or the other. Some writers, however, argue that such producers should be seen as proletarians exploited by state or private capital. The claim is based on similar features shared by the scheme settlers and wage-labourers such as their mutual lack of control, their insecurity and their remuneration. It is true that at Moment A, agricultural settlement schemes typically create a new group of agricultural producers who are dependent on the government and bureaucracy for the right of access to means of production – including land (Hill, 1977: 26).[6] According to Wallace (1981: 286), the most absolute form of control of rural producers is through ownership of land. This can be seen at Sudan's Gezira scheme where tenants have access to land on an annual lease, renewable only if their performance is satisfactory (Barnett, 1981: 150, 313). Likewise, South Africa's Ciskei bantustan schemes specify that 'tenure is subject to performance' (Proctor-Simms, 1978: 72). Settlers on Tanzanian schemes can be expelled for breaching cultivation rules (Raikes, 1978: 307–8). Like proletarians, at Moment A settlers only have access to means of production through (state or private) capital.[7]

Settlers' lack of control at Moment A tends to mean that they also lack control of Moment B. At settlement schemes in Sudan, western Nigeria and Tanzania, the manager has *de facto* control (Raikes, 1978: 307; Barnett, 1975: 194; Hill, 1977: 30; Seidman, 1978: 325). Settlements on newly developed land with irrigation lend themselves 'to production under close supervision' (Blume, 1971: 219). On many schemes, producers are not only controlled by management, but are also really subsumed at Moment B by having to depend on the timing and inputs of fellow settlers and/or the scheme's management services (including the nucleus estate). Government control of land, water and other inputs characteristically means that tenants have to obey a set of production rules concerning the type of crop grown, the timing and quality of their activities, and over the use of purchased inputs, choice of sales outlets and systems of payment (Williams, 1984: 16–18; 1986a: 3; Bernstein, 1979a: 428; Raikes, 1978: 286, 307; Barnet, 1977). For example, irrigation rules at Kenya's Tana River irrigation scheme licence settlers for only a year at a time, and they ban sub-letting or labour hiring without permission. They also stipulate that 'a licensee shall cultivate his holding to the satisfaction of, and in accordance with the crop rotation laid down by, the manager, and shall comply with all instructions given by the manager relating to the cultivation and irrigation of his holding' (Blume 1971: 143). Producers can also be prosecuted and finally have their licence withdrawn. Cliffe and Cunningham (1972: 26) describe these conditions as resembling landlord-tenant relations – which may be so, although I would hesitate to designate producers here as *feudal* tenants, given that – unlike the feudal case – scheme settlers usually have no significant means of production of their own. Barnett (1977: 72, 77) concludes that, due to their limited area of decision-making and their lack of choice, the Gezira tenants resemble industrial wage-earners. They 'seem like a herd of landless labourers signing on each year to get a dhurra crop and the pocket money and loans' (1977: 122).

As regards settlers' position in Moment C, they tend to have little say over the distribution or utilisation of surplus. At Gezira, the board has a monopsony on the sale of cotton (Williams, 1984: 16). As with out-growers, this control over distribution is easier when the firm or state has a monopoly on necessary processing facilities for sugar, tea and tobacco (Williams, 1985: 170). As regards the form of remuneration at Moment C, settlers are also in a similar position to wage-labourers. According to Barnett (1975: 194; 1977: 169), while the Gezira tenants were not in-tended to be workers in the sense of being wage-earners, the *basis* of their remuneration implied this because while they contributed a few basic tools, their main input was labour-power. Remuneration also needs to be looked at in terms of its relation to reproduction, the value of labour-power and control of surplus distribution. On one Mozambican co-operative, members were paid advances on a regular weekly/monthly basis:

Formally these were an advance installment of the final distribution of the co-operative's net revenue to its members. In fact, however, the amount paid was calculated as an hourly rate set at a level to attract labour to the co-operative in competition with the state farms and the rate bore no relation to the co-operative's expected net revenue. (Harris 1980: 347)

In addition, the amounts distributed were determined by the co-oper-ative leadership and government officials rather than all co-operative members, leading Harris (1980: 347) to argue that elements of a wage-system existed there. Similar features exist in many settlement schemes' payment systems. In Tanzania, the development schemes were con-sidered by most settlers to be government farms 'with considerable justification, since control of their incomes was entirely in the hands of the manager, who could decide how the gross receipts should be divided between loan repayment, scheme investment and settler incomes' (Raikes, 1978: 308).

To evaluate the points above, it can be noted that the argument for settlement tenants as proletarians implies that there are capitalist relations on the development schemes. Regarding Moment A, it is clear that these producers are similar to proletarians in their separation from means of production. At Moment B on these schemes, settler tenants share in varying degrees similarities with proletarians regarding their lack of control over the labour process even if (as with piece-workers) there is not real subsumption of labour. Concerning Moment C, the designation of settlers as proletarians may be legitimate in terms of an analysis of piece-wages, i.e. where their incomes come not from the produce they generate, but from the *de facto* exchange of labour-power. (On western Nigerian schemes, settlers explicitly receive hourly or piece-rates for their labour (Hill, 1977: 291).)

However, the issue of settler tenants' status as proletarians also needs to be examined in terms of relations of reproduction, and it is here that certain non-proletarian features may become evident. On many schemes, settlers reproduce themselves to a greater or lesser extent through their own production activities on food plots, and in this they are distinct from proletarians. They are also distinct in that they may also exhibit capitalist characteristics. This question is raised by settlers' relations of utilisation which may involve buying in labour-power to supplement, or in some cases replace, their family labour on the tenancy even though, unlike capitalists, they lack possession of the means of production at Moment A. Barnett (1977: 36, 58, 177; 1975: 195), for example, argues that because tenants hire outside labour, they cannot be seen as pure proletarians. To see to what extent they are semi-capitalists, however, it is important to consider the extent to which hiring accords with a CMP system dynamic of accumulation. Some settlement schemes, such as co-operatives, may become an agency for monetary accumulation provided that members receive enough (Harris, 1980: 345). However, monetary accumulation is only capitalist if it is invested in buying and combining labour-power and means of production under exclusive control with the aim of producing more surplus so as to expand the process (1980: 346). The scope for capitalist agricultural accumulation is strictly limited on many development schemes. At Gezira, this control exercised by management limits settlers' standard of living and causes their production to stagnate (Barnett, 1977: 169–71, 180). Tanzanian schemes, for example, have fixed acreage and enforced rules to keep individual producers in line with quality controls and technical criteria (Raikes, 1978: 286, 314). Controls aimed at the production of export crops also limit the diversification of activities. Aspirant capitalists often have to look elsewhere to invest their money.

Relations of distribution, in particular the form of remuneration of settlers, are also pertinent to the question of settler tenants' class characteristics. Gezira tenants may be regarded to some extent as shareholders in that they receive 40 per cent of the project's income. But, in fact, this percentage is based on a traditional Sudanese share-cropping model, rather than a capitalist one. The share is not controlled by settlers as investment capital because they do not possess it in the first place. It represents rather a fluctuating return on their labour-power inputs and, in effect on the value of their labour-power, i.e. a type of piece-wage (O'Brien, 1984: 122). Settler income at the Ciskei Keiskammahoek scheme is labelled 'profit' by the project managers, with the implication that settlers are no different from capitalist farmers participating in capitalist accumulation through a co-operative scheme. However, on closer inspection, it emerges that

the 'profit' the settlers obtain through their participation in the scheme is regarded [by management] as part of the operating costs. The difference between income and operation costs i.e. profit . . . will go to the Ciskei government. The settlers may therefore be regarded as wage-earners rather than joint owners of the enterprise. (PADRI, 1979: 12)

From all this, it can be seen that settler tenants share some similarities with proletarians in so far as they lack control at Moments A and B and often receive effective wage remuneration at Moment C. On the other hand, they also exhibit some capitalist features to the extent that they begin accumulating. In conclusion, one can say that, as with many other rural classes, settler tenants are involved in an admixture of relations of production. As participants in multiple relations (including relations off-scheme too), it is difficult to attribute a single class character to them except in that their practices may consistently combine the practices of these diverse relations. Even so, their class character is likely to be contradictory – as with several other social classes (see chapter two).

The economic failure of progressive farmer strategies

Planned rural development in peripheral social formations has generally fallen short of financial viability, let alone contributed to raising national productive capacity. Tropical Africa has seen the failure of 'progressive farmer' development, while outgrower and settler tenant strategies there have fared little better. Part of the problem is that development planning at the periphery is almost intrinsically flawed. The fact that agriculture is not wholly susceptible to state planning and control is compounded by the fact that planning in the Third World is not a well-developed productive force (Kollontai, 1970: 5; Seidman, 1978: 296). Thus, in Kenya there has been a dire lack of research behind development schemes.[8] The character of the peripheral state is such that planners themselves are not necessarily willing or able to put aside political and ideological considerations in favour of designing economically effective programmes. Many projects are more about developing the political power of the state and/or sections of the petty bourgeoisie and bourgeoisie than about development (see section on politics and rural development below). Furthermore, the policies and measures used to implement a plan may often distort its structure and developmental intentions. Members of bourgeois and petty bourgeois classes at the periphery use the state to channel surplus to their *own* ultimate benefit (Harrison, 1981: 369; Williams, 1981a: 28). This reflects a 'soft state' where, despite its 'overdeveloped' and hyper-trophied structure, it is 'soft' on protocols, bureaucratic impartiality, accountability, etc. – at least as regards the privileged classes (Myrdal, 1968; Seidman, 1978: 383). This feature allows for 'absolute surplus' to be converted into 'hidden surplus' such as where investment finance is channelled into private consumption through bribery and corruption. Such 'soft development' in tropical Africa has seen planning achieve little success in either its private or public sector aims (Seidman, 1978: 286–7). Instead, throughout the region, state-imposed controls and limits on agricultural development have been instituted. Rather than developing endogamously out of middle peasant production, petty and simple commodity production was managed from the start. In Uganda, the colonial state tried to prevent production relations from developing into capitalist ones through banning land sales (Mamdani, 1977: 60, 142). In Kenya, middle peasants and simple commodity producers were suppressed initially as a threat to settler production. While these were later deliberately encouraged, industrial interests, trading companies and the colonial and post-colonial state all tried to regulate what was produced, how it was produced, the prices paid and the marketing arrangements. Immediate organisation of production remained in the hands of the producers, but it became increasingly determined by extroverted and disarticulated market relations and measures such as cultivation laws, credit and extension services (Bernstein, 1979a: 427).

State marketing boards have especially inhibited 'progressive farmer' development. Far from stimulating increased productivity, they have been notoriously inefficient (for examples in Kenya, see IDS, 1975: 18–24; for Tanzania, see Coulson, 1981: 67–8). Even exceptional cases such as tea production schemes in Kenya have nonetheless involved dependent and limited growth aimed at the external market, and also operated more akin to an outgrower system than a marketing board (Raikes, 1978: 308). Acting as monopolies, boards have passed the costs of their weakness and corruption on to the farmers (Bates, 1981: 27). It is sometimes even worse when co-operatives have acted as marketing boards: Kenya's 'progressive' coffee farmers who developed under the Swynnerton Plan in the 1950s were forced into government-controlled co-operatives which often had monopolies on marketing. The effect was that these growers received 20 per cent less of the world market price than large plantations which sold directly to the state board (Bates, 1981: 28; Cowen, 1981b: 137).

In addition to these factors, Third World development planning is also undermined or thwarted by the broader structures and processes of underdevelopment. An illustration of this may be seen in the Kenya of the 1960s. At the time, the planned development of 'progressive farmers' seemed to have some success. But, on closer inspection it is evident that this was both caused and constrained by the country's peripheral economic system. The Kenyan 'progressive farmer' development strategies saw a flourishing of smallholding production after colonial restrictions on African cultivation of cash crops were lifted and African access to land expanded (Carlsen, 1980: 218; Williams, 1984: 9).[9] Ruthenberg (1966: 37, 100) argues that the rise in marketed output was related to government rural development policy, but significantly he also notes that the increase cannot be seen solely as the consequence of public inputs. Indeed, the growth of rural commodity production depended ultimately on economic articulation with the CMP. In particular, it was made possible by remittances of wage-earners to non-capitalist production processes (Kitching, 1980: 3).[10] In addition to supplying finance, the CMP also provided a market for agricultural commodities (Heyer, 1981: 117). That this articulation was probably more important a determinant than state development policy is suggested by the failure of a government credit programme in the 1960s. This programme, despite being substantial and generous, was unable to change the fact that the low monetary returns in relation to labour-time spent served to dissuade smallholders from growing cotton (Kitching, 1980: 319).

However, if increased smallholding production in Kenya was thus dependent on the CMP for its existence, it drew little in the way of technological innovation (Ruthenberg, 1966: 134; Carlsen, 1980: 76, 83). Producers expanded the area under cash crops instead of adopting advanced means of production to facilitate higher yields (Dinham and Hines, 1983: 1870). Kitching claims that there was a 'massively expanded programme of research' into hybrid crops, fertilisers, insecticides and planting practices. For him, this was 'a prime factor in raising the productivity of physical labour power on smallholdings', and it 'represented a powerful intervention by the state into production on smallholdings'

(1980: 381). However, more convincing evidence points to the conclusion that few technological advances were involved in (or evolved out of) the expansion of commodity production. Most rural households were actually untouched by Kenya's 'agrarian revolution', continuing instead to farm as before for basic food crops and pasturage (Buch-Hansen and Marcussen, 1982: 20; Ruthenberg, 1966: 120; Kitching, 1980: 324, 329). The continuation of 'progressive farmer'-type strategies in the 1970s had little or no effect on production (Williams, 1981a: 31). According to Buch-Hansen and Marcussen, by the mid 1970s, 'progressive farmer' development in Kenya had reached its limits in terms of both land availability and the productivity of family labour (1982: 20).

The failure of Kenyan middle peasants to develop into successful simple commodity producers reflects not only the character of the state, but also the structure of underdevelopment. The Kenyan smallholders, as producers at the periphery of the international capitalist system, evidently articulate very differently with the CMP in comparison with their counterparts in the centre (Mouzelis, 1975–6: 487–8). In the latter case, simple commodity production develops by increasing its productivity and establishing positive complementarity with industry. Technical progress in the CMP is diffused to the simple commodity producers. At the periphery, however, disarticulation–unevenness and dependence–extroversion means that the dynamism and high productivity of the CMP at the centre tends not to get transferred to small commodity producers. The relative immobility of labour, incomplete commoditisation of household reproduction and the absence of competition have meant that there is little pressure to reinvest in agriculture. In consequence, there is a large productivity and income gap between the rural commodity producers and large-scale capitalist farms (Mouzelis, 1979b: 81; 1979a: 353). Thus, at the periphery, simple commodity production by middle peasants has not become their primary relation of production, but rather co-exists – in partial form – with various other relations (Friedmann, 1979: 178).[11] Simple commodity production at the periphery has thus widely failed to consolidate and develop itself and its own productivity (Kahn, 1978: 124; Amin, 1974: 147). Its development has been constrained and unable to provide an answer to the Agrarian Question.

The same failure is evident in the development of a class of kulaks and, out of this, a class of farmer capitalists. While African co-operatives and marketing boards have channelled surplus away from peasant producers, frequently this has been to kulaks who have dominated these bodies (see Raikes, 1978: 297; Seidman, 1978: 324–5; Cliffe, 1977: 213–15; Harris, 1980: 344). Often merged with the local bureaucracy, kulaks are able to interpret national policy and programmes in their own interests (Feldman, 1975: 176; Raikes, 1978: 302; Kitching, 1982: 345; Brietzke, 1976: 658). An example of what tends to happen may be seen in the Ugandan co-operatives, described by one writer as the 'organisational vehicle' of an advancing bourgeoisie (Mamdani, 1977: 199). They served as a means of accumulation for the rich who controlled the committees and the use of surplus funds. The post-colonial state not only gave the co-operatives control of allocation of 75 per cent of all crops, but continually channelled funds into them. These funds ultimately came from the marketing boards – in other words, surplus was transferred to the kulaks from the middle and poor peasants. The state tractor-hire service, which ran at a loss (i.e. subsidising its users) was only available for large lands (1977: 230–6). In this way, then, 'progressive farmer' development strategies can assist the rise of a kulak class. And yet, despite such 'aid', kulaks in tropical Africa by and large have not developed themselves into a powerful class of farmer capitalists. A noticeable feature of the progressive farmer strategy has been its inability to change the obstacles facing the development of capitalist farming: the cost of labour-power and the lack of full command over it (due to incomplete proletarianisation), the international determination of price and quality of produce and the exclusion of private producers from the processing of crops (Cowen, 1981b: 140; for Kenya, see Ruthenberg, 1966: 27). In Ghana, government subsidisation became vital for capitalist rice farming to continue in the face of the disappearance of cheap labour and land (Williams, 1984: 11). Likewise, Nigerian capitalist grain farmers require government subsidies to survive (Dutkiewicz and Williams, 1987: 652). The one strategy in Kenya which did develop an African capitalist farming class involved state credits that enabled well-off African state employees to simply replace white capitalists with black ones – a form of development which hardly amounts to an expansion of capitalist farming or to a revolutionising of production (Carlsen, 1980: 80; Williams, 1984: 9). On the contrary, the result at the time was an estimated reduction of productive capacity by a third (Ruthenberg, 1966: 96).

The obvious question is why, despite their access to the state, kulaks have generally failed to develop either productive capacity or themselves as farmer capitalists. The answer to this is partially in the character of the post-colonial state and the associated planning process (see above). It also lies with the fact that the benefits available to kulaks may not necessarily compensate for the losses they sustain in surplus appropriated from them. Their privileges are often only relative to middle and poor peasants and do not change their overall status as losers. However, perhaps the key part of the picture is the class behaviour of kulaks. There is a tendency among kulaks to amass wealth rather than capital (Mamdani, 1977: 307). Thus, in the Sukuma area of Tanzania, kulaks accumulated wealth quantitatively in cattle stocks rather than in improving the quality of their animals. Instead of development, the outcome was underdevelopment resulting from overgrazing (Cliffe, 1977: 213). In other cases, consumption took precedence over saving – so that even in Ghana, Polly Hill's productive farmer 'capitalists' (*sic*) used their income for funerals, celebrations and housing (Hill, 1963: 111). In Ghana and Tanzania, the incomplete institution of private property dissuaded rich peasants from becoming rural capitalists, and their class relations were constrained into money-lending (Howard, 1980: 72; Awiti, 1973: 231). In some cases, kulaks have invested surpluses in enlarging their land (Hill, 1963: 110). But, in many other places, such as the Tanzanian highlands, high population density and customary obstacles to the transfer of land have limited this (Raikes, 1978: 300).[12] Accumulation is also channelled into bribery, the acquisition of licences and securing local trading monopolies (Raikes, 1978: 317). On some of Kenya's low-density settlement schemes, just under half the settlers are part-timers, hiring others to work their farms (Ruthenberg, 1966: 73). Many of these do not have enough capital to invest on their farms, and for some the plot is reduced to a land insurance policy.

Such behaviour is a logical response by kulaks and farmer capitalists to the obstacles they face in trying to accumulate in agriculture (Raikes, 1978: 319–20, footnote 7). Understandably, many prefer to expand out of farming to avoid the risks of specialisation in an extroverted and disarticulated market (see Long and Richardson, 1978: 191, 205, footnote 7). Investing their surplus in trade and transport activities often yields better returns than farming (Bernstein, 1979a: 442; Woddis, 1977: 267; Hill, 1963: 111; Kitching, 1980: 27). These activities may well enhance the national economic system, yet, if they occur at the expense of developing production, their contribution to development becomes questionable. In Kenya, kulaks' failure to invest in agriculture has been partly explained by the relatively easier, less risky and more profitable opportunities opened up with 'Kenyanisation' policies after independence and also by the restrictions on land transfer and crop quotas in the 1960s (Carlsen, 1980: 83, 90). By the late 1970s, some kulaks were buying and renting more land, as well as improving it and investing in long-term crops. But there was still very little investment in farm equipment, and most savings still went into non-farm business (1980: 188, 191). Kenyan kulaks have also found that bureaucratic jobs have been more remunerative than small-scale farming, and one-third of them have moved into these spheres, becoming absentee landlords (Leo, 1979: 635–6; Ruthenberg, 1966: 73). To acquire bureaucratic jobs, Kenyan kulaks – like their counterparts in Ghana and Tanzania – have invested in education (Howard, 1980: 196–7; Hill, 1963: 111; Raikes, 1978: 300; Williams, 1984: 15). Alongside these factors, kulak investment in small-scale industrial production in tropical Africa is often unviable because of competition from imported goods (Howard, 1980: 76; Muntemba, 1978: 75). State marketing board monopolies have blocked private bourgeois development in the area of marketing and processing (Heyer, 1981: 104). All this squares with Mamdani's comment (1977: 145, 166) that underdeveloped capitalism means the primacy of commerce, and the investment of agricultural surpluses in exchange rather than production.

Summing up, then, one can note that African kulaks, while often aspirant capitalists, have generally failed to become actual capitalists and, in particular, farmer capitalists. Both their capacity and their propensity to participate in one relation of production rather than several is low. Accordingly, they operate as semi-capitalist farmers who exploit labour-power, rent out machines, serve as local merchants and moneylenders and deal in crops, retail business and transport (Bernstein, 1979a: 431). The roles of landlords, merchants and usurers have been discussed in earlier chapters and it is clear that such modes of utilising surplus do not develop productive capacity (at least not directly). Capitalist agriculture at the periphery has thus been stunted: kulaks emerging from middle peasant and simple commodity production have proceeded no further. It appears then that the 'progressive farmer' development route, with associated possibilities of simple commodity production, rich peasant and capitalist outcomes has not been a solution to the Agrarian Question in tropical Africa at least. On the contrary, the peripheral state and the structures and processes of underdevelopment have interacted with the formation of these classes in such a way as to inhibit them from fulfilling any such historical role and to divert them away from agriculture as a potential base for national development.[13]

The poor record of settlement and outgrower schemes

Settlement and outgrower schemes, like progressive farmer strategies, are aimed at developing rural commodity producers who will generate surplus (for the state and capital). But they, too, often do not realise this goal. The familiar factors of the backwardness of planning and the structures and dynamics of a peripheral economic system play their part. For example, in Uganda in 1966 there were thirty-seven group farm schemes involving 3,500 members, but a slump in the cotton market cut the number to thirty farms with 1,800 members (Seidman, 1977: 164). Although the Gezira scheme is financially successful, it too is exposed to the instability of the world market (Barnett, 1977: 15). As I will argue below, the character of the state and the specific social structure of settlement schemes have also contributed significantly to their failure. Outgrower schemes have been less negative in narrow economic terms, but still of ambiguous significance for national development.

Dealing firstly with settlement schemes, their failure in Africa is legend (see e.g. Heyer et al., 1980: 8; Williams, 1985: 152–3; Forrest, 1981: 233; Bates, 1981: 48; de Villiers, 1977: 108). One typical characteristic has been the way that they constitute a seemingly indefinite drain on re-sources – as is evident in countries as diverse as Mali, Kenya and Senegal (Grove, 1979: 156; Thomas, 1975: 38; Blume, 1971: 147, 162). In one notorious example, the western Nigerian farm settlement scheme ab-sorbed 50 per cent of total capital spending on agriculture between 1962–8, but 'by any criterion, these schemes failed' (Bates, 1981: 47). The cost of setting up 1,200 settlers represented 75 per cent of the total agriculture budget for the region – money which could have gone on extension services for non-settlement producers. The settlements were 'not merely self-contained failures, but also had a deleterious effect on the larger economic picture' (Hill, 1977: 28, 30). In Nigeria's Kano River irrigation project, people downstream lost their dry season farms due to the ending of river flooding. By 1980, there had been a loss of 20,000 hectares of cultivatable land compared to a gain of only 1,000 hectares of newly irrigated land (Wallace, 1980: 65). Another feature of settlement schemes is the way that some end up supporting settler tenants while still losing money. In Zambia, the 'returns to state agencies are such that the schemes are more a form of subsidisation to selected settlers rather than a form of surplus extraction' (Cliffe, 1978: 336–7). Settlers on the western Nigerian schemes were expected to develop into a rural bourgeoisie who would buy their enterprises over fifteen years. In fact, however, pro-ductivity was so low that settlers could not hope to become viable, let alone independent. They became instead a public sector salariat sup-ported by the government – a privileged stratum in the public sector with better income and benefits than the government's agricultural field staff (Hill, 1977: 228, 30; for Tanzania, see Raikes, 1978: 308; for Kenya, see Ruthenberg, 1966: 74, 148).

The reasons for commercial failure are often linked to the character of the peripheral state, in terms of which the schemes are typically over capitalised, badly or under planned and poorly managed (Hill, 1977: 25, 32). In terms of *over capitalisation*, Uganda's Mubuku pilot irrigation project and its replicas are a good example of heavy overheads preventing commercial viability (Seidman, 1977: 163). Irrigation schemes are so hugely expensive that the outlay simply cannot be matched by the value of the crops grown (Ruthenberg, 1966: 101; Williams, 1984: 44; 1986b: 15; Peel, 1982: 21; Hill, 1977: 32). Even non-irrigated tenant schemes incur costs for equipment, spares, repairs, housing and social facilities and salaries of officials, managers and technicians (see Williams, 1976a: 168).[14] Donors and governments often favour relatively capital-intensive projects and, in general, nearly all so-called 'transformation' programmes require a large-scale capital expenditure (Peel, 1982: 21). The effect has been to render 'peasant production more expensive without bringing significant improvements in the peasants' standard of living [or in their productivity]' (Heyer et al., 1980: 8). Thus, at the Kano River project, the expense of labour, seeds, water, tractors and fertilisers raised the cost of farming so dramatically that many farmers could not meet their financial or labour demands and were forced to leave land fallow or to rent it to others with a larger land and labour base (Wallace, 1980: 67).

In terms of *underplanning*, many Tanzanian schemes were planned to have modern cultivation methods producing maximum yields per acre, even though this was not the most relevant measure of improved farming in (relatively) land-abundant Tanzania (Raikes, 1978: 298; Coulson, 1981: 53–4, 82). Consultants and project managements often plan on the assumption that family labour can meet new-style farming demands. But, on the Niger agriculture project this would have meant that each settler would have had to do the equivalent of 408 days' work in six weeks (Forrest, 1981: 233). Planning is also often based on flawed economic and political assumptions which contribute to unviability. Loan repayment on the Kenyan million acre settlement scheme was treated by the Kenyan government (pre- and post-independence) as more important than the welfare of settlers or the successful long-term development of the scheme (Harbeson, 1971: 248). This meant special favours for low-density settlers who were expected to become 'progressive farmers', able to repay loans for the land although in fact the high-density farmers proved to be the better performers. In terms of *management and administration*, irrigation schemes are 'appallingly inefficient' (Williams, 1984: 46). Uganda demonstrates how inadequate management of schemes, beginning with the colonial managers' inability to establish an effective working relationship with scheme participants, can get schemes into decline. Poor management on Ugandan settlement schemes led to a wastage of resources: tractors were idle except when planting and the charge to settlers hardly covered half of the recurrent costs (Seidman, 1977: 164–5).

Turning now to the significance of the *social structure* of settlement schemes for their economic performance, the class character of settlers can be considered. Settlers' *capitalist* characteristics are based on them being in a position to set production in motion and extract surplus labour from employees. Indeed, this may be made necessary by their articulation with the state or capital – in which they themselves may be exploited. But while this situation serves to keep production going, it is constrained by the settlers' low potential to develop productive capacity. For example, Tanzanian schemes have been of fixed land size and they do not allow for expanding production (Raikes, 1978: 308). Such limits on monetary accumulation may limit settlers' motivation to 'satisficing', rather than maximising incomes and therefore adversely affect output on the schemes (Barnett, 1977: 71). 'Satisficing' behaviour at Gezira is linked by Barnett to the fact that settlers there can only vary the type of labour input and the cropping input on a fixed size of land. Also, tenants lacked a clear appreciation of the relation between effort and reward because of the system of arrears payment and fluctuations of income caused by the world market (1977: 75, 171). Because capitalist development is blocked by the size of the tenancy, and because crop choice is restricted, some tenants in Gezira and in Uganda have concentrated on their food plots rather than the cotton which they have to cultivate in order to occupy the tenancy (Barnett, 1977: 107, 113; Seidman, 1977: 164). It is true that a stratum of tenants may develop their interests outside of agriculture such as at Gezira, where some retain their tenancy but no longer work it personally because of their involvement in shops, lorries or usury (Raikes, 1978: 286; Barnett, 1977: 174; 1975: 196). In some instances, participants have used schemes as stepping stones to becoming a private rich peasantry (Raikes, 1978: 308, 314). Although this is not conducive to the development of the projects, it may have some positive effect on production in the social formation as a whole.

With regard to the *proletarian* characteristics, an important factor influencing development is settlers' position at Moment A where they typically do not own the land or the means of production. At the Kano River project, this meant that farmers had little commitment to the project, displayed little initiative on it and preferred to invest money outside it (Wallace, 1981: 289). It is small wonder, comments Seidman (1978: 325), that the attitudes of many settlers correspond to those of paid labourers. 'Peasants regard state-managed settlements and co-operatives as "government farms" and consider work on these schemes as work for the government and subsistence allowances to settlers as low wages' (Williams, 1976a: 168).[15] The settlers' position at Moment A gives rise to an ideology that is counterproductive to development. For example, on many Ghanaian schemes in the 1960s the 'public sector peasantry', with public sector employee status, worked 'civil service hours' – which meant that productivity was below that of private peasants (Hill, 1977: 33). On the Niger agriculture project, settlers resented the authoritarian management and lacked incentives under the share-cropping arrangements (Forrest, 1981: 233). While this particular attitude by producers has not stopped capital in other places from developing productive capacity, it does not serve to stimulate settlers to do this on many development schemes. Where there are, however, incentives, the hierarchical control of settlers does help maintain a level of productivity. For example, at Kenya's irrigated rice settlement scheme at Mwea, high output is linked to the fact that '[t]enants are willing to follow the orders of the Settlement Officers because their income is high and disobedience leads to eviction' (Ruthenberg, 1966: 61).

Settlers at Moment B are frequently under real subsumption to the state or private capital controlling the schemes. This may increase productivity in that the socialised labour process imposes a form of production discipline.[16] At the Mwea scheme, 'mechanical cultivation has made possible a degree of planning and discipline and extension unthought of in the past ... (and) produced an atmosphere in which strict discipline can be enforced without opposition' (Giglioli, 1965, quoted by Ruthenberg, 1966: 58). With regard to Moment C at Mwea, the scheme's control of rice marketing makes it comparatively easy to collect payment for water. Mwea's relative success in yields, however, is not the whole picture. According to Ruthenberg (1966: 60), the scheme has still not introduced sound farming practices nor significantly increased marketed production. It appears that proletarian characteristics on such settlement schemes, in the absence of other capitalist features such as productive accumulation by the scheme owners (state or private capital), are evidently insufficient conditions for exponential development.

In contrast to the failure of most settlement schemes, outgrower schemes seem to have achieved a degree of economic profitability as well as providing smallholders with some means of production (Heyer et al., 1981b: 8; Buch-Hansen and Marcussen, 1982: 17). One reason for this would appear to be the comparatively shallower involvement by agencies of the overdeveloped state in this form of production. Instead, with capital – internationally linked capital in most cases – at the forefront, outgrower schemes tend to be better planned and managed than state settlement schemes. (State-run outgrower schemes are often inefficient: the KTDA is specifically noted as an exception to this (Blume, 1971: 200).) Among the factors contributing to outgrower viability is the social structure of the enterprise. In this regard, much depends on the degree of articulation with, and integration into, outgrower relations on the part of the rural household. Within this, what is almost as significant is the specific and varying class characteristics exhibited by the household.

Regarding proletarian features of outgrowers at Moment B, it has been noted that these facilitate stringent control over the labour process. Thus, at Kenya's Mumias scheme, field supervisors monitor farmers' work and the efficiency of the whole scheme is attributed by officials to the centralised management there (Mulaa, 1981: 91, 92). At Moment C, outgrowers, like proletarians, often have no control over distribution or utilisation, and little capacity to lower their level of exploitation or to keep surplus within agriculture. Unlike an independent landed farming class, outgrowers are therefore not an obstacle to the Agrarian Question. Turning to Moment A, to the varying extent that possession of land has significance, and therefore to the extent that outgrowers have métayage features, this can be conducive to productivity. On the one hand, it sustains a motivational ideology that outgrowers are working for themselves on their own land, even if there is little to show for it and minimal control over the labour process. On the other hand, it may also mean that outgrowers' reproduction is partially secured through their own independent efforts. This reduces the contribution required by capital to maintain the producers' labour-power and, indeed, may be deliberately fostered for this very purpose (see Blume, 1971: 29, 200; Dinham and Hines, 1983: 27).

To the degree that a stratum of outgrowers acquires its own means of production (in addition to land), and thereby approaches simple commodity producer status, this aspect of social structure also helps explain the relative success of this form of development. Proto-capitalist characteristics may similarly characterise a stratum of outgrowers, and again this could well prove positive from an economic standpoint.

Yet, there are also limits to the outgrower strategy and its record must be qualified when evaluated in terms of the Agrarian Question and the development of productive capacity in the social formation. To a large extent, outgrower schemes exhibit the classic features of extroversion and disarticulation. Thus, even where they are operated by state institutions, they still tend to integrate vertically with the international capitalist economy, supplying its processing plants and markets (Goodman et al., 1984: 209). There are typically few links with local agriculture while, at the same time, there is often an increase in dependence on imported materials and foreign credits (Dinham and Hines, 1983: 50; Blume, 1971: 101; Buch-Hansen and Marcussen, 1982: 23). As part of the 'formal sector', many schemes have solicited the help of discriminatory state-imposed licensing and marketing arrangements that put small non-scheme farmers out of business. The system dynamics and social structure of outgrower production – while coercing producers into increased output – also forces many participants themselves to go to the wall (O'Keefe, 1984: 162). Tight control at Mumias facilitates efficient centralised management but, by the same token, it restricts the development of rural capitalists because all major activities are carried out by the company (Mulaa, 1981: 92–3).

Despite these problems, governments continue to persist in promoting both settlement and outgrower strategies. This is not so much because of their need to respond to the Agrarian Question through rural development, nor because of ineptitude, but in large part because of the power of the ideology of development which sees progress as commodity production, bureaucratic control and advanced technology – all introduced from the outside (Williams, 1986b: 19). A further factor is that the drain that this 'development' puts on state funds may constitute a surplus gain for capital in its capacity as management/marketing agent and input supplier of unviable public projects. In addition, if development schemes do not always yield income for the state, there are still certainly *political* pay-offs.

Rural politics and development

Agricultural schemes and peripheral rural development often reveal more about political control than about the economics of agricultural development (Hill, 1977: 38). For example, in the view of one consultant,

there is a tendency to decide on or evaluate rural programmes or projects on purely economic grounds. This is invalid, especially in southern Africa where one of the most urgent requirements is to win the support of rural communities . . . [P]ositive rural development is one of the best bulwarks against communism and one of the best means of border defence. (Proctor-Simms, 1978: 57)

Such statements make a number of assumptions about the character and significance of rural class politics and the significance of rural development in relation to them. As one writer points out, 'in all ages in all countries, reactionaries, liberals and radicals have painted their own portraits of small rural folk to suit their own theories' (Moore, 1969: 117). Some have characterised the middle peasantry as being involved in a defensive struggle, others see it as offensive (Lieberson, 1981: 37). While one perspective views peasants as both radical and conservative – depending on the principle of their security (Joshi, 1981: 69) another believes that radicalism is less likely than reaction (Charlesworth, 1980: 261). What is clear is that rural class struggles can often take on major political significance (Harrison, 1981: 116; Stavenhagen, 1964: 95; Marx, 1977b; Duggett, 1975: 169). While the entire rural community can act as a social force, sometimes its internal differentiation needs to be given priority of account (Galeski, 1972: 118). Overarching peasant consciousness is conceivable primarily insofar as differentiation within the peasantry is secondary to their common characteristics and their common interests *vis-à-vis* other groups and the state (Hobsbawm, 1973: 7). Conflict between rural classes, such as between tenants and landlords, or between kulaks and poor peasants may not always be the primary focus of contradiction, but it is still significant for rural class politics.

The potency of rural classes as political forces varies with each class. Historically, most rural classes experienced – albeit unequally – disadvantages such as illiteracy and ties to seasons, with the result that peasant movements were usually only conglomerations of local and regional revolts into a momentary unity (Hobsbawm, 1973: 9, 12; see also Marx, 1965: 66, cited by Duggett, 1975: 171). Regarding the political potency of the middle peasantry, Marx (1977b) argued that although these producers live in similar conditions, they lack relations with one another. Middle peasants therefore have a low 'classness' because what they have in common is, paradoxically, a way of life that divides them (Duggett, 1975: 172; Gallisot, 1975: 427). Therefore, according to Marx, 'they are consequently incapable of enforcing their class interests in their own name ... They cannot represent themselves, they must be represented' (1977b: 170–1). It can be argued that the relative economic independence of the middle peasantry enables this class to be the most militant of the whole peasantry (Alavi, 1973; Charlesworth, 1980: 261). However, this autonomy is only relative to the rich and poor peasantry, and the ties to the land in fact allow it only minimal tactical freedom. In many instances, middle peasants – certainly those who become the object of development initiatives – are also caught up in economic articulations and obligations with other classes (1980: 265).

Many of the above generalisations derive from western history and have to be modified in the case of the Third World today. As Cliffe (1977: 197) reminds us, the African peasantry has arisen as part of an articulation with a fully fledged capitalist domination imposed from outside, which extends (in various forms) over the entire gamut of rural class relations. Unlike their historical counterparts in the West, African peasants are linked to a world system via their varying forms of integration into a world market (which, *inter alia*, makes agricultural crises more national in scope), and in many cases via a centralised state (Friedmann, 1979: 178). This makes rural class politics a crucial factor in the politics of any Third World social formation today. Certainly in Africa, writers like Fanon (see Caute, 1975), and to a lesser extent Arrighi and Saul (1970), have dismissed the urban proletariat as a labour aristocracy and focused their political attention on rural classes. It is thus only to be expected that development planning should be affected by this consideration, and that almost every regime, of whatever class nature, has a distinct interest in rural stability and production (Herring, 1981: 132).[17] This is especially the case at the periphery where governments often represent an ambitious, though weak and frustrated, bourgeoisie and petty bourgeoisie trying to use the state for their own development. What is remarkable, however, is that the political interest in stability seems to take prominence over an economic interest in so many cases. The Agrarian Question, to the extent that a plan is even constructed with an eye to it, is treated mainly as an economic means to a political end. One consequence of this is that in practice the economic sense of 'development' is lost sight of, and the concept really does come to have a primarily political meaning (see chapter one).

The politics of planned rural development are most evident in the case of land reform. This development strategy is often justified in terms of eliminating pre-capitalist structural obstacles to development. At the same time, however, it is also 'typically the model utilised by governments seeking to defuse rural unrest and rationalise agricultural production, but unwilling or unable to mount a full-scale confrontation with the landlord [or peasantry classes]' (Herring, 1981: 134). Land reform has thus aimed at eliminating real or possible revolutionary threats from discontented rural classes, and at creating groupings in the rural areas that will support the government in power (Halliday, 1979: 134). The effect of United States-backed land reform in Japan, South Korea and Taiwan was to create a politically conservative class of peasant proprietors' as well as to raise food output (Buckley, 1981: 54). South Vietnam and China showed that the failure to achieve proper land reform could produce an explosion (Halliday, 1979: 123). After the 1961 Cuban revolution, the United States-backed 'Alliance for Progress' pushed for land reform to counter agrarian unrest in Latin America (Harrison, 1981: 117). This was part of a general economic development package designed as 'an antitoxin to halt the spread of communism' and which has been applied in countries ranging from Thailand and the Philippines to El Salvador (Buckley, 1981: 78; *Time*, 1981: 27; Krinks, 1983: 108–9).[18] The role of political considerations in planned rural development is also evident with regard to sensitivities over the use of land by plantations. For the Third World state as entrepreneur, plantations are an obvious form of development, but they require large land areas to be acquired and this is often precluded for political reasons (Blume, 1971: 35; O'Brien, 1984: 122). Agribusiness capital has also perceived that plantations have become risky in the context of possible nationalisation and land shortage. Commercial strategies are thus increasingly defined in terms of leaving land ownership and production in the hands of the direct producers and exercising control through contracts, managing state settlement schemes or monopsonistic purchasing arrangements (Buch-Hansen and Marcussen, 1982: 16; George, 1976: 70).

Conventional wisdom holds that stability thrives 'on a large participating middle class acting as a buffer between the rich and poor' (Harrison, 1981: 389). This is echoed by American political scientists who lament the absence of a middle class in underdeveloped societies (Kitching, 1972: 334, footnote 15; Markovitz, 1976: 185). The middle peasantry is often lauded as the rural form of a middle class that is conducive to political stability. For example, the World Bank favours the creation of a stable and conservative class of small producers in the Third World (see Hayter, 1981; Williams, 1981a: 37–8). Certainly the middle peasantry does lie between rich and poor peasants, and it is not wholly caught up in exploitative relations between the two. The middle peasantry is also structurally placed to act as a buffer in that it shares simultaneously some of the interests of these two class relations that traverse it. On the other hand, because rich and poor peasant interrelate independently of the middle peasantry, this buffer role is not as great as it might initially appear. Another point to note is that the pressures on the middle peasantry to disintegrate give it an unstable class character. In the light of this, the reason for any politically stabilising role may well lie more in the inability of the class to represent itself (see above), rather than in any inherent stable character.

In the politics of development planning, there is little distinction made between the middle peasantry and simple commodity producers. Both are lumped together as a 'rural middle class' – and kulaks sometimes are assumed to be part of this as well. While all may have the potential to play certain political roles, a focus on the political roles without the economic not only increases the risk of developing unpredictable political monsters: it also has no necessary connection to the development of productive capacity. These problems have not, however, deterred development strategists in Africa from anticipating strong political returns from the planned development of a stable rural middle class. The creation of a rural 'middle class' of 'sturdy yeoman farmers' was 'a vision particularly beloved of various colonial administrations' (Kitching, 1972: 343). In pre-independence Kenya,

the colonial administration saw in land consolidation a means of rewarding those Africans who had supported the Government in putting down Mau-Mau, and of encouraging the growth of a productive rural middle class which would be immune to the cries of militant nationalists and perhaps challenge their leadership in the rural areas after Mau-Mau. (Harbeson, 1971: 236; see also Heyer, 1981: 101)

The 1950s colonial Swynnerton Plan strategy in Kenya was intended to

develop an economic base to sustain the political purpose of rural stabil-
isation. It aimed to promote small farms through individual registration
of tenure and consolidation and enclosure of land (Heyer, 1981: 101).
Swynnerton also advocated a change of emphasis in African farming from
subsistence to cash crops. The provision of extension, inputs, credit and
processing and marketing facilities was another part of the strategy. This
was all to be concentrated on the development of an elite of 'progressive
farmers' as a solid conservative bulwark against Mau-Mau (Heyer, 1981:
101–2; Ruthenberg, 1966: 9–10).[19] The colonial government believed
that a political solution to Mau-Mau would depend on a major change in
the three-tier class structure of big farmer, small peasant and landless
poor peasant (Cliffe, 1977: 198). Some administrators urged an English
two-tier class structure through some kind of enclosure act, in order to
create a class of yeomen farmers 'too busy on their land to worry about
political agitators' (Sorrenson, 1963; 1967). The final solution was a
modified three-tier structure where small middle peasants retained their
land, rather than being dispossessed by a totally free market in land
(Cliffe, 1977: 208–9). The consequence was that many of the landed
peasants came to support the status quo – leaving the land-hungry poor
peasants isolated. In an attempt to pacify the latter and pre-empt uncontrolled seizures of land, the government launched a mass resettlement
programme from 1962–6 in the former white highlands. Indeed, an
accelerated programme (the million acre scheme) did ease the thrust of
rural insurgency (Wilkinson, 1979: 71–2; Kitching, 1980: 326; Ruthenberg, 1966: 64).[20] Similar moves towards trying to create a rural class
interested in maintaining stability and property rights followed political
stirrings in colonial Tanzania and Uganda (Mamdani, 1977: 189, 192–5;
Raikes, 1978: 295, 296; Bryceson, 1980: 306). A 1953–4 commission
advocated an increase in individual land tenure and encouragement of
the 'progressive farmer' aimed at stimulating a political and economic
sense of responsibility. In pre-independence Zambia, the colonial
government set up a scheme modelled on 'the sturdy British yeoman, a
type to be created in Central Africa to give political stability to that
country' (Foster, 1969: 10; see also Muntemba, 1978: 61).[21] Establishing
such political goals is, however, one thing – the question of their being
reached is another.

Politics and rural development

Many of the grandiose political intentions behind rural development are
not necessarily realised. Instead, they come up against both the failure of
the economic base to sustain the political project and resistance by the

people affected. Even where development strategies achieve some economic and political goals, they generate new political conflicts and contradictions. Thus, one of the political aims of rural development planning in post-colonial Africa is the attempt to resolve the food crisis.[22] In the face of the power and political importance of urban constituencies, African governments have implemented policies aimed at keeping food prices down at the expense of local producers. Strategies are adopted to fix food prices and to outlaw marketing outside of state boards (Bates, 1981: 40). But while such policies may be politically expedient, they have not in the longer term been able to resolve the food crisis. Consequently, governments faced with the political need to achieve results have also turned towards a different emphasis – namely large-scale, highly capitalised and mechanised schemes (Dinham and Hines, 1983: 143). While these initiatives have also generally failed to resolve the crisis, they enable governments to claim that they are doing their best. In this regard, there are significant propaganda gains to be made from development. Agricultural schemes serve as a 'visible symbol' of a government's desire to develop the country – as a 'monument to modernity' (Hill, 1977: 28). According to a South African development consultant:

an innovative rural success can have social, political and economic impact out of all proportion to the size of the area or the number of people involved. This impact is upon the local economy, upon traditional attitudes to agriculture, on the standing of the leaders, developers and backers, on the attitudes of the have nots to the developmental efforts of the haves, and last but not least, on the image of South Africa internationally ... What South Africa so desperately needs, what black leaders need, is a number of dramatic success stories in rural development which will stand out as shining examples of how the land can provide acceptable incomes; ... that will be the pride of the sponsors, and of the homeland cabinets.[23] (Venn, 1979: 7)

The political uses of development affect the types of programme that get adopted. Governments could raise prices to encourage producers to expand output but, in addition to being politically costly in urban constituencies, the political benefits of winning broad rural support are often low relative to what can be achieved with a handful of prestige projects. Governments may thus prefer project-based policies to price-based policies even though the latter often yield better economic results (Bates, 1981: 5, 114). Development projects also offer more scope than pricing policies for extending patronage, authority and control by governments over rural people (Heyer et al., 1980: 14; Williams, 1986a: 4; Bates, 1981: 109, 115). Projects are also sometimes seen as an answer to urban unemployment as in western Nigeria where the ruling elite saw unemployed school-leavers as a political threat. A similar situation occurred in Nkrumah's Ghana, demonstrating – as Hill puts it – that a 'public sector peasantry' has political appeal to regimes of varying persuasions (Hill, 1977: 27, 31–4).

If rural development projects do not usually benefit the mass of rural producers, they still do benefit some groups. Bates (1981: 121; 1983: 133) has identified a 'development coalition' of urban owners and workers, political elites, top bureaucrats, large farmers and tenants – all of whom reap the benefits of development choices. Williams (1986a: 6) excludes the urban workers from these beneficiaries, but the point still stands that there are strong vested interests in rural development, often irrespective of economic success or failure. Thus, settlement schemes may end up subsidising the tenants on them while unsuccessful progressive farmer policies still give advantages to groups of kulaks and capitalist farmers (see below). In addition to such beneficiaries, there are also the fertiliser firms, construction companies, bureaucrats, international experts and academics – all of whom are provided with markets, management contracts, jobs and consultancies by rural development (Heyer et al., 1980: 14) Outgrower strategies which involve capital in upstream activities especially benefit international firms who can reap rewards of agricultural production without having to invest in it or take on the political and commercial risks involved.[24] Rural development programmes may in fact function to transfer surplus to entirely non-agricultural activities. Thus, 'in the cases of irrigation projects and support for capitalist farming in northern Ghana and northern Nigeria, subsidies have simply drained money into the hands of contractors, military officers, politicians, civil servants and businessmen' (Williams, 1986a: 3). The costs of rural development do not fall on its beneficiaries. World Bank loans, for example, are not repaid from net returns on projects, but from government revenues and more borrowing (Williams, 1981a: 41). In other cases, aid agencies effectively guarantee payments and therefore eliminate the financial risks to agribusiness (Dinham and Hines, 1983: 144).

The political success or failure of rural class creation can be analysed in terms of its record in defusing conflict and ensuring stability. Land reform, once implemented, can be successful in raising a few peasants above the many, and in co-opting the most militant leaders into the middle classes (Kay, 1981: 501; Harrison, 1981: 123). Progressive farmer strategies may also yield political rewards. In Kenya, according to Currie and Ray :1987: 93–4), the 12 per cent of smallholders farming cash crops are a politically loyal middle peasantry, and the possibility of mass land ownership gives legitimacy to the post-colonial state. In addition, the growth of smallholder production has reduced landlessness and urban drift, thereby diminishing the political threat of both. Settlement schemes may also be politically successful. Despite ongoing unrest in response to the loan-repayment issue in Kenya, political stability was not threatened because, no matter how great their distress, settlers did not want to risk losing their plots (Leys, 1977b: 355; Harbeson, 1971: 249). The community in Tyefu, in South Africa's Ciskei bantustan, was 'notoriously recalcitrant and opposed to authority', but its attitude reportedly changed dramatically as a result of an irrigation settlement scheme (see Proctor-Sims, 1978: 58). The high cost of the project was deemed acceptable because, as one of the consultants involved observed, the scheme's 'most important benefit has been the "winning over" of the local community who are now collaborating with the authorities' (1978: 141).

Aside from these examples, however, there is often a contradiction between the politics and economics of development. In Kenya's Special Rural Development Programme (SRDP), political pressures meant that the SRDP was planned in a hurry, without involving the people to be affected – hence it was not only manipulative but also misinformed (Oyugi, 1981: 133). Short-term political objectives frequently override long-term development goals and as a result the political usefulness of development in the long run tends to be less than it appears to be initially (Dinham and Hines, 1983: 161). Economic failure catches up with, and undermines, political success. Kenya's government reaped short-term political gains by settling large numbers of landless people on high-density schemes. But because loan repayments by the settlers remained outstanding, the scheme *de facto* absorbed such heavy subsidies that the prospects for further political successes were limited by the longer-term economic problems of the strategy (Ruthenberg, 1966: 132, 149). Another instance of the contradiction between the politics and economics of development is the food crisis. African governments often resort to a policy which entails, alongside rural development efforts, importing food in order to avoid political problems. But because the imports keep prices down, rural producers lack an incentive to step up their own production. Many governments also now face the difficulty of costs of food imports rising at the same time as prices are declining for their countries' exports (Dinham and Hines, 1983: 141).

The political uses of rural development also run up against limits by producer resistance to the imposed strategies. In Kenya there are conflict-ridden relations between peasants and capital (both state and private) over the conditions of labour and the distribution and realisation of the value of the product (Bernstein, 1979a: 432). Producers resist by rejecting or sabotaging new production practices, and by refusing to grow or cut back on specific crops. They attempt to withdraw from commercial relations and find alternative income sources (as with coffee growers in

Kenya), as well as evade crop-grading regulations and monopolistic terms of trade (Bernstein, 1979a: 433; Bates, 1981: 82). They also use the labour market to defend themselves rather than produce crops with poor returns, while bribery and corruption are used to counter the effect of pricing and marketing policies (Bates, 1981: 43, 84). Rural producers also resist through political organisation. In Kenya, a policy to control the numbers of coffee trees was delayed because it would have provoked political conflict (Lamb, 1974: 94–111). When it eventually began to take effect, growers mobilised through the co-operatives and political parties to urge that white estates should make the cut-backs. The successful implementation of development strategies may also generate new resistance by the beneficiaries unhappy with the terms of their involvement. The special circumstances of subordination to institutional and agro-industrial capital give rise to settler tenant and outgrower struggles around issues like tenure, control of the immediate labour process, the scope for alternative production, input costs and monopsonistic marketing institutions (Goodman et al., 1984: 205; Williams, 1984: 18).

Development strategies involving land reform especially evoke resistance and conflict – including beatings, evictions, burnings of houses and crops, and even murders (Herring, 1981: 142; Buckley, 1981: 55; Brietzke, 1976: 656). Less violent opposition to land reform was mounted in Kenya by the National Farmers Union, through which capitalist farmers lobbied to ensure that their land was left intact (Bates, 1981: 94). Resistance to land reform comes not only from large landowners but from others who are dispossessed. Nigerian government schemes gave officials and businessmen access to irrigated land, but evoked opposition and even sabotage from the farmers expelled to make way for them (Williams, 1984: 44; Wallace, 1980: 65). Even where land reform does not radically threaten social structure, it may well evoke antagonism. Smallholders have often violently resisted compulsory land rehabilitation and consolidation. In Malawi, the colonial government tried to enforce soil conservation, provoking political unrest which became the rural base of the nationalist movement. Even after independence, riots broke out in response to enforced quotas for tobacco production (Thomas, 1975: 36–8).

Governments' responses typically involve coercion as well as a mixture of additional 'development'. In Kenya, the Institute for Development Studies (IDS) recommended that district level officers be allowed flexibility to deal with 'ethnic, political agitation which tends to become a serious bottleneck' and to 'create a visible success' (IDS, 1972: B–2). The IDS added that 'given the political sensitivity of land holding, adjudication work needs positive political inputs from the M.P.s, D.C., P.C. and District Councillors', and expressed the hope that 'with closer administration these programs will be explained to [*sic*] their perspective' (1972: B–5).

Williams argues that conflict in peasant communities does not rise from internal differentiation so much as from the contradiction between peasants and state (1985: 173). Although this may often be so, development policies also often lead to inequalities that generate increased conflict *within* rural communities. The political success of development strategies needs to be evaluated in terms of the impact within rural communities as a whole. In this regard, development strategies often ultimately have similar results in excluding certain classes or groups from policy largesse. Thus, in Malawi, the colonial government resettled 40,000 people on unused estate land in a bid to deflate unrest in 1946 and 1953 by landless peasants and tenants of estates (Thomas, 1975: 43). But similar unrest erupted at independence from people left out of the plan. Further land was bought and distributed, although this provided two-acre-size holdings that were only enough for subsistence. Pressure to break up the estates has continued, as has rural instability. While land reform can win support where it ends landlord power, in Iran, popular hopes that all would get land were not met and landless discontent constituted another centre of unrest (Halliday, 1979: 136; Greussing and Kippenburg, 1975–6: 126). It is hardly surprising that land reform strategies generate new conflicts between beneficiaries and non-beneficiaries when they deliberately exclude large numbers of people by encouraging a 'rich farming class' at the expense of other classes (Halliday, 1979: 135). The resulting visible inequalities may well generate class tensions. For example, in the Ciskei bantustan, it has been observed that 'to juxtapose the settlers and the people with no land rights . . . could build up problems for the future. The widening of the gap between rich and poor, even at the rural level, makes a conflict situation possible' (McI. Daniel, 1980: 14). In a confidential memorandum, one official noted: 'Is it that in Ciskei we are too obsessed with spectacular capital intensive projects to bother about the masses? Will the day not dawn when the voters of Ciskei will rebel and say "What is there for us in agricultural development?"' (Anonymous, 1979: 4). In Mozambique, competition and even violent conflict between co-operative members and outsiders have erupted over land (Harris, 1980: 345, 349). In Malawi the Salimi lakeshore development project benefits 750 people with incomes seven times higher than the 20,000 poor in the area, giving rise to 'envy and violence, results strikingly similar to those experienced during the "master farmer" schemes in the colonial days' (Thomas, 1975: 38). Where scheme participants hire outside labour, this may be an added source of conflict. At Mumias, workers hired by the company to service outgrower plots have sabotaged harvests on occasion (Mulaa, 1981: 98).

In the light of all this, it is evident that political successes in rural development are by no means unqualified and the economic ramifications may well generate additional political problems. The relationships between rural development and political stability is therefore ridden with contradictions. On the one hand, there is a recognition that political stability requires at least some pay-off for all classes but, on the other hand, the short-term political uses of development policy, plus an inegalitarian development policy, often lead to conflict in the longer term. This contradiction reflects – in an exaggerated form – the distinction between economic and extra-economic definitions of development as discussed in chapter one. It is by identifying 'development' as an economic issue, that one can then show how it is both distinct and inseparable from politics.

Conclusion

This monograph began with an argument for a 'pragmatic' methodological position, on the basis of which my definition of development and my economic concepts were theorised. These were then used to analyse capitalist development, the international capitalist system and the factors underpinning underdevelopment at the periphery. Within this framework, the focus turned to agriculture's role in development, the character of rural social structure and the economics and politics of planned rural development. The arguments are thus cumulative, with each consecutive part depending on those preceding it, but all are intended to contribute in their own right towards understanding the relationship between social structure and development

My basic assumption throughout has been that social structure, as a variable alongside environmental and other factors, is central to development. My aim has been to demonstrate this as a very broad proposition, as well as elaborating upon its significance at levels of abstraction ranging from modes of production in general, through the CMP and the international economy, to the agrarian social structure. This objective required extensive discussion of the concepts of social structure and development. 'Social structure' was analysed in terms of its various economic structures (relations of production, dependence–extroversion, etc.), political structures (the state) and social classes. 'Development' was discussed in terms of its economic significance concerning productive capacity, departments of production and the Agrarian Question. In investigating how these two major issues relate to each other, I have worked with a crucial distinction between the course of a social structure on one hand, and the course of productive capacity on the other. This distinction is sorely lacking in much of the literature, which generally assumes there to be some identity between capitalism and development (be this identity positive or negative in character). The corresponding investigations have tended to confuse the two issues, frequently merging the one into the other and then losing sight of it as a distinct object of analysis. Thus, the *development of capitalism* and *capitalist development* have been taken as meaning one and the same thing. Seldom is it explicitly or clearly recognised that the phrase 'development of *capitalism*', considered rigorously, reflects a vantage point concentrating on the course of a *social structure*, while 'capitalist *development*' emphasises the issue of *productive capacity*. My concern has been to investigate the relationship between social structure and productive capacity, and especially how the former affects the latter. This has necessitated disentangling and separating the two issues precisely in order to discover the terms of their interrelation. For this reason, my approach has generally been to treat social structure separately from development before going on to look at the relation between them. This pattern is evident throughout the structure of the work, as shown by the table below:

Social structure	Development
Moments of production, relations and forces etc.	Productive capacity
Class structure, reproduction, mode of production, articulation	Economic surplus
Capitalist mode of production	Mixed effects on productive capacity
Genesis and expansion of CMP, transformation, conservation-dissolution, new production relations, extroversion, etc.	Dependent growth, growth without development, surplus transfer
Class structure	Use of surplus
Agrarian social structure: capitalist, kulak and simple commodity-producer classes	Rural development, agricultural productivity, Agrarian Question
State	Planned development
Class structures of planned development, politics	Limits and failure of rural development

Central to my analysis of the relation between social structure and development have been what are probably the most original concepts in this monograph, namely the three *Moments of production* (Moment A referring to relations of possession/separation from the means of production, Moment B to relations within the labour process, and Moment C to relations of distribution and utilisation). By distinguishing each Moment, and by emphasising the need to consider all three Moments, I was able to cut through many debates around social structure and development. Thus, to review the key arguments in this work, social relations of production were analysed in terms of the characteristics at Moments A, B and C, in contrast to those writers who refer to only one or two Moments. By reference to this whole, I was able to distinguish between *homogeneous relations* (where there is a class congruency between the three Moments), and *heterogeneous relations* (involving disparate relations at each Moment). These concepts provided the basis for theorising a mode of production and the articulation of its internal and external relations. In addition, by considering how the three Moments of a mode are linked together through *reproduction* of the whole, and through the *system dynamics* deriving from the structure, I was in a position to provide a clear identification of social structure and its significance for productive capacity.

This is important because not only has much analysis confused the issue of social structure with the issue of development as described above; it has also been unclear in its identification of the social structure. This is especially the case concerning capitalist social structure where there has been confusion about the identification of capitalist relations as such. Arguments have flown thick and fast about whether capitalism generates development or underdevelopment in the Third World – but without adequate attention to what is meant by capitalism. There has been a simplistic attempt to label production relations as capitalist due to characteristics such as production for exchange (Frank and the dependency school) or the existence of wage-labour (Laclau). Alternatively, and equally problematically, the appellation has been based on characteristics such as reproduction within a capitalist context (some writers within the articulation approach), or commercialisation of the whole process (Banaji). These analyses concentrate respectively on Moment C, Moment B, reproduction and the system dynamic of the relations of production – and assume that one aspect suffices to describe (and even determine) the whole. Clearly, it is impossible to agree on the relationship between capitalism and development when different things are meant by capitalism. Indeed, much of the debate says more about the different writers' conceptions of capitalism than about development.

My schema gets past many of these problems with its comprehensive concept of mode of production and the articulation of the capitalist mode with non-capitalist structures at all Moments of production (and in terms of reproduction within capitalist relations of distribution and the system dynamics of competition, commercialisation and capital accumulation). Marx's concept of differing subsumption under capitalism (as revised within my framework) offers a way to analyse articulation within the capitalist relations of the CMP which varies according to the character of the forces of production especially at Moment B. Applying these concepts and insights to the international economy, my argument has distinguished between the CMP at the centre and the CMP at the periphery, on the basis of how the two contexts differ in both internal and external CMP relations (at all three Moments). This approach is superior both to articulation theory, which tends to ignore the internal CMP articulation, and to dependency theory, which fails to recognise the external. The different effects of articulation at the centre and periphery, I have argued, go hand in hand with class differences in each situation, and both underpin the differences between central and peripheral states and economic systems.

This framework allows for an analysis of the phenomena of monopoly competition, extroversion–dependence and disarticulation–unevenness at the periphery, and for isolating their particular different contributions to development and underdevelopment. Similarly, the three-tier economic structure characteristic of the periphery is also a facet of this analysis. Conceived in these terms, it provides insight into formal/informal sector model. Relating all this to productive capacity, I have identified and distinguished between dependent growth and growth without development. This involved investigating how the structure of the periphery relates to class structures and practices, and how classes also directly affect development and underdevelopment.

Analysing the role of agriculture in development is also illuminated by the perspective of the three Moments of production and the concepts built upon them. Thus, I argued that factors affecting agricultural productivity (land-size, labour-input and means of production) cannot be understood at the level of labour process alone (Moment B), but are part of a wider context of relations at Moments A and C. Agrarian social structure and its many classes can be characterised and distinguished in a comprehensive manner in terms of the three Moments, reproduction and system dynamics. Analysing the Agrarian Question in these terms means locating it in the articulation between capitalist relations in agriculture and industry, and between both of these sets of relations and the diverse non-capitalist classes in agriculture (middle peasants, kulaks and simple commodity production). On this basis, assumptions that agrarian capitalism is needed to resolve the Agrarian Question are shown to be flawed.

Considering the social structural implications of rural development policies in terms of their impact on the diverse Moments of production gives insight into the distinctions between progressive farmer, marketing board, contract farming and settler-tenant strategies. While writers have been quick to label rural producers as proletarians, peasants, etc., my approach has been to analyse the features at each Moment of production, and in terms of reproduction and system dynamics. This facilitates an assessment of the extent to which the total relations of production involved are capitalist or not, and here my earlier theorisation of the CMP and subsumption is useful. It shows that – despite sharing some characteristics with capitalist classes – progressive farmers, outgrowers and settler tenants also exhibit several heterogeneous non-capitalist relations. Their differing articulation to the dominant CMP is crucial to understanding their dynamics and limitations regarding development. My conclusion to this debate is that much rural social structure at the periphery evidences multi-class characteristics rather than a primary relation of production. The recognition of this complexity is an advance on simplistic labelling and hasty conclusions about the significance of capitalist class relations for development. A more complex set of relations implies a more complex relation to development. This relation needs to be firmly located in the broader context of Moments A, B and C at the levels of the peripheral economy and the international economy as a whole and, furthermore, in a political context. The particular rural class structures in tropical Africa, in conjunction with broader economic and political relations do not, it appears, bode well for productive capacity there.

One aim of this monograph has been to meet certain challenges facing students of development – specifically rural development – which are outlined in the Introduction. While all of these challenges are interrelated, it is now also possible to point to certain arguments I have used which are of relevance to particular challenges. Thus, in response to the first challenge concerning the use of clear philosophical principles, the first part of this monograph is devoted precisely to their role in the production of knowledge and the use of Marxist methodology. It will be evident throughout the work that concepts such as quantity–quality distinctions, interconnections, social process, history and contradiction have informed the arguments. It has especially been a guiding principle throughout that my theorisation deals in abstractions, and while these may help explain reality, by their nature they cannot approximate its particularity, historicity and multi-causal complexity. In this regard, however, it should be recognised that in its emphasis on social *structure*, my argument does not preclude any role for ideology and conscious human volition *vis-à-vis* development. In general, I would hope that my interpretation, development and application of Marxism to economic development demonstrates some of the wider potential of this approach.

In response to the second challenge outlined in the Introduction – i.e. developing comprehensive units of analysis to deal with the relationship between the parts and the whole, the structure of this work with its different levels of abstraction and generality is relevant. All its parts have their place in the overall framework of studying development in the most general terms through to its character in the international capitalist system and, ultimately, to the specific cases of individual rural development strategies. Central to the enterprise of generating comprehensive units of analysis have been the concepts of three Moments of production, reproduction of the whole and system dynamics. These enable one to distinguish between elements or features of capitalism and the capitalist mode as such (and therefore their respective implications for development), while they also help to avoid the pitfalls of concepts of international modes of production and unique modes in each social formation. In addition, they are useful in analysing how articulation can lead to one unit internalising an external relationship within it or being reproduced through articulation to another unit (and what all this means for development). There are also the specific concepts of economic system and modes (and homogeneous/heterogeneous relations) of production which encompass the totality, its parts and the relation between them.

Concerning the third challenge of maintaining an approach where 'development' remains firmly at the centre of the project, I have continuously tried to relate social structure back to the issue of productive capacity. At the same time, my argument clearly shows that the study of development cannot be limited to the discourse of pure economics, and that development is integrally bound up with issues of social relations, social control and politics. However, 'development' in this monograph has been considered as an economic phenomenon in order for it to be related to political factors. This is evident in my discussion of the base-superstructure model, the issue of surplus, the capitalist state, articulation, planned rural development and the failure of development strategies. It will not escape the reader's attention that there is an ironical twist in my conclusion that development *in practice* comes to have a meaning that is anything but purely economic. Yet, it is only by keeping one's eyes on development as an economic category that it is possible to see how and why 'planned development' diverges from the analytical definition and may become, in effect, its opposite.

The fourth challenge outlined in the Introduction concerned synthesising insights from various other studies, and this has been an important part of the entire work. Various debates have been tackled in the course of my argument, whether they be around the base–superstructure model, defining what is internal to a mode of production, or the significance of dependence *vis-à-vis* other factors of underdevelopment. In all of these, I have argued for or incorporated positions based on the theoretical points developed in this monograph. In this way, I have criticised as well as drawn from elements of modernisation theory, Baran's concept of surplus and the theories of the informal sector and the Agrarian Question, integrating them within my overall framework. I have also combined contributions from three different approaches: dependency theory, articulation of modes of production and class struggle emphases. Dependency theory is shown to work with, *inter alia*, inadequate units of analysis and concepts of capitalism; articulation theory is shown to miss the underdeveloped aspects of social structure like dependency and the three-tier structure of the economy. While the class struggle approach is shown, *inter alia*, to underpin many of the various dependence and articulation factors, these are not automatically given by classes, and neither can they be directly reduced to classes. I have therefore tried to show how these different approaches draw attention to different phenomena and, at the same time, how they complement and enrich each other by accounting for some of the blindspots in each other's approach. The conflicting dimensions of these different approaches have not been glossed over. For example, the problem of the relative weight of each of the approaches is discussed in the light of the fact that supporters of each have claimed primacy of account for the particular factors they stress. I argue for the primacy, but not exclusivity, of class structure.

The attempted synthesis of theoretical insights has been complemented by drawing empirical data from a variety of sources and contexts. Both operations have been performed on the basis of my framework in terms of which source material has been evaluated, accepted or rejected. The aim has been an integrated, coherent and consistent whole.

To the extent that I have successfully met all these challenges, this monograph constitutes a wide-ranging theory of the complexities of social structure and development. But, despite the length of the work it is, in a sense, not long enough. Its lack of a discussion of non-capitalist development may perhaps have resulted in a one-sidedness, and even some misconceptions, about the relationship between capitalism and development. A comparative study using the same framework may have avoided some of these problems. At the same time, the three Moments schema may be of value in researching social relations for concerns other than development and rural development. It could perhaps be fruitfully applied to studies concerned with, for example, questions of patriarchy and domestic labour. The monograph also lacks an analysis of development and specifically rural development in social formations that are more difficult to locate in terms of a centre and periphery model – for example, New Zealand, the Scandinavian countries and south-east Asia. How their economic systems developed and provided answers to the Agrarian Question raises important issues for the study of Third World development. Any prognosis for the latter has to take these experiences into account. Further research is needed here.

Furthermore, in order to be fully developed, the arguments in this monograph need to be tested in a detailed empirical research exercise – at macro- and micro-levels. As it stands, the work is limited to being an elaborated prolegomenon to the study of development (specifically, rural development). Subjecting it to extensive empirical research would provide insights into the value of the entire framework, including even my definition of development and social structure (and my use of Marxism).

As a final observation, it can be noted that rural development continues despite its poor record in achieving both its economic and political objectives. This is not only because it is now conventional wisdom that the state should intervene in this way, nor is it only due to the interests it serves. It continues also because there are not the political or social forces with the strength and vision – and, dare I say it, the theoretical apparatus – to come up with an alternative. Although this monograph concentrates on the problems of 'what is', I would hope that it might also be of value in theorising such alternatives.

Notes

1 DEVELOPMENT: DEFINING THE TERRAIN

1 For Kuhn, the 'paradigm', and for Althusser, the 'problematic', refers to the basic assumptions of a particular world view which determine what problems will be selected, and what, conversely, will thereby be excluded (see Althusser, 1971: 113; Popper, 1972; Kuhn, 1962; Carr, 1974: 11; Moore, 1969: 521; Hobsbawm, 1972: 265–6).

2 Weber correctly cautioned against being scientifically content with conventional self-evidentness of very widely accepted value-judgements (Weber, 1948: 77–8; see also Popper, 1973: 213, 222–3). However, it is also true that we cannot wholly escape such judgements.

3 In terms of semiology, an empirical fact can be analysed as a sign which in turn comprises a conceptual signified meaning and a material signifier (such as a symbol, sound and other physical objects with communicative significance). Together, these two dimensions provide knowledge about an aspect of a referent material reality. Between the sign as a whole and the referent reality, there is a dynamic relationship, in terms of which the signifier and/or signified dimensions of the sign may be modified to represent more accurately the reality (see Sebeok, 1975; Fiske, 1979; Coward and Ellis, 1977). As an example of this, for a racist, the generally sorry state of rural development in Africa lies in the nature of the 'black man'. Looking at African farmers, a racist registers skin-colour as a socially relevant signifier and goes on to link it with a specific signified meaning (e.g. low intelligence). In the course of experience and education, it may become necessary for this racist to be more accurate in understanding reality, and therefore to come up with a different signified meaning (e.g. non-biological characteristics – culture, colonial heritage, etc.). And in certain contexts (such as contact with successful black farmers), where in reality skin-colour has no social relevance whatsoever, this signifier may be discarded altogether. Using theory involves applying a set of signs of relatively fixed and inter-connected general meanings to a different and more specific array of signifiers and signs.

4 As Marx noted, the same economic basis can show 'infinite variations and gradations in its appearance even though its principle conditions are everywhere the same' (1974, vol. III, quoted by Baran, 1962: 44).

5 It may be added that the totality should be recognised as differentiated, complex, internally articulated and uneven (Althusser, 1976: 177, 183; Lukacs, 1971: 12).

6 'The properties of things change with changing relations: what is true of a thing in one relationship is not true in another, what is true in one set of circumstances is not true in another' (Cornforth, 1968: 106). This applies to the concepts of various modes of production which cannot be defined as 'combinatories' (Althusser and Balibar, 1970: 7) of a set of ahistorical factors (see chapter two). It also defines my approach to concrete development schemes and rural class relations which rejects analysing them in isolation of their economic (and political) context (see chapter five).

7 This particular way of distinguishing economic growth from 'development' has wide currency in the 'humanist' development literature. For Seers (1979), economic growth refers to per capita incomes and GNP, while development refers, *inter alia*, to the elimination of absolute poverty, reduction of high unemployment, and narrowing of huge social inequalities (cited by Mouzelis, 1979a: 353). Clearly, on these definitions, there can be economic growth without development. There is no inherent reason why development in this sense should automatically follow in a 'trickle-down' sense from economic growth. The latter is a necessary means to socio-economic ends, but it is not adequate by itself. In this view, 'growth' and 'development' are quite distinct (see also Markovitz, 1976: 183).

8 It should be noted that the literature often uses words such as 'undeveloped', 'underdeveloped', and 'developing' interchangeably and without much regard for semantic distinction or consistency. This section attempts to separate out the different meanings involved. Specific references will not be given when the usages discussed are commonplace, but see, *inter alia*, Myint (1971; 1967), Myrdal (1957), Hagen (1962) and Gerschenkron (1965).

9 Although X is already 'developed' in relation to Y, it may also be seen as 'undeveloped', etc. *vis-à-vis* a condition X+. Similarly, Y may be called 'developed' in relation to a pre-Y state. The 'mutuality' of meaning still remains.

10 There is a kind of teleological perspective here: regions, social formations, etc., are categorised and judged as 'undeveloped' etc., in terms of a standpoint which assumes unit X to embody the desirable attributes of the 'developed' ideal (Taylor, 1979). The appellations 'backward' and 'advanced' illustrate this clearly. Even the terms 'undeveloped' and 'underdeveloped' often imply a very particular potential: i.e. defined in terms of the attributes of a 'developed' economic unit.

11 This problem also exists where 'development' is used to designate not merely attributes but also a process. Here development is defined solely in terms of X's history – underdevelopment being *all* other processes.

12 Mouzelis (1979a: 354) tries to get round Eurocentrism by defining development in relation to the conditions of underdevelopment (poverty, etc.). But in doing so, his approach tends to lump together all countries which have better living conditions than the worst ones.

13 Quality, as Afanasyev (1980: 96–7) points out, concerns the attributes that make an object what it is – thereby distinguishing it from other objects. Quantity concerns the intensity, size or value of these attributes. Quantity and quality are a unity representing two sides of the same object and *both* characteristics need to be taken into account.

14 To move away from the artificiality of X and Y being static conditions, they should be seen as *part* of a process (i.e. as not simply entering or ending one). This would be represented as ---X--->, and <---Y---.

15 It is in the analysis of this question – i.e. where development and underdevelopment are directly interrelated phenomena – that further qualitative distinctions can be made (see especially chapter three).

16 See, for example, Harrison, 1981: 419; Suret-Canale, 1977: 134; Berger, 1976: 24; Baran and Hobsbawm, 1961: 275; Kahn, 1978: 133; Hindess and Hirst, 1975: *passim*; Standing, 1981: 186; Friedmann, 1979: 176; Weeks, 1975: 25; Genovese, 1971; Amin, 1974: 8–9; 1977: 157; Baran, 1962: 242.

17 The distinction between 'relations' and 'relationships' comes from Williams (1976a: 257).

18 The Althusserian use of structure has been particularly criticised for presenting a rigid and mechanical Marxist view (Geras, 1972; Miliband, 1972). Indeed, both Althusser (1976) and Poulantzas (1973) make a sharp distinction between structures and what they call their 'social effects' – these latter being individuals or classes who are the supports or agents ('träger') of the structures. Structures are not seen to exist in and through humans, but *vice versa* (Williams, 1976a: 257). The dialectic between structure and practice is lost, and missing entirely is the concept of contradiction.

19 I owe this distinction between relations *of* production and relations *in* production to Nichols (1981. 115) (who uses it to make a different point). In this monograph, relations in both the relations of production *and* the forces of production structures are present in the 'relations in production' (Moment B of production).

20 Within each labour process, these technical social relations exist as an internal division of labour – for example, as a horizontal occupational work specialisation. They may also involve a separation of the functions of organising production from direct productive activity itself, i.e. a vertical division of labour (Galeski, 1972: 40).

21 These sectors in the forces of production should not be confused with the so-called sectors defined by 'mode of production' (e.g. 'capitalist sector') or by 'relations of production' (e.g. 'co-operative sector'; 'public/private sector'; 'subsistence sector'). Such 'sectors' are not part of the structure of *forces* of production.

22 See Marx (1972: 178). However, Marx also often used the term 'productive' in the context of capitalist production where it refers to labour that generates profits, as distinct from labour which consumes revenue. This distinction is independent of the material character of the labour concerned (see Marx, 1976a: 644; 1976b: 1038–41; 1973: 305). This sense is clearly narrower than the general one I am working with.

23 This is especially clear in Banaji's argument (1976a: 315) that the purpose of production (e.g. consumption by a feudal lord, rather than capital accumulation) defines the 'relation of production'. He holds that this is the case *even* if the labour process and immediate relations of exploitation (e.g. wage-labour) usually correspond to a different 'relation of production' (i.e. correspond to a different purpose of production – such as capital accumulation associated with

wage-labour) (see also Banaji, 1980: 516). He quotes the *Grundrisse* (Marx, 1973: 469) for support:

> if a nobleman brings a free worker together with his serfs, even if he resells a part of the whole product, and the free worker thus creates value for him, then this exchange takes place . . . for the sake of superfluity, for luxury consumption.

24 It is evident therefore that classes in the Marxist view only exist in terms of their social relationships with each other (Wright, 1980: 178). In each structure of a set of relations of production, the classes complement and presuppose each other (Godelier, 1972: 335). As Byres (1981: 406) puts it, they cannot be understood without each other. 'They are constituent and mutually determining parts of a whole process. To isolate them from each other is an act of distortion . . .' There is therefore no such thing as a single class (Mamdani, 1977: 8). In other words, class is a relational property of a group of people *vis-à-vis* another group.

25 It is possible that the exploiting class of Moments A and B may also control the means of distribution in C and thereby doubly exploit the producers. Where it does happen, as in the case of certain rural development strategies (see chapter five), the two forms of exploitation still remain conceptually distinct. The 'second round' exploitation is a zero-sum equation of fixed proportions determined by the previous Moments.

26 There are different opinions about the extent to which financial capital can enter into exploitation at Moment B even if, unlike productive capital, it does not bring the labour process fully under its sway. According to Bradby (1975: 146), Rey (1973) holds that finance capital can control social reproduction without getting involved in the immediate process of production. For Roseberry (1978: 23), unlike merchant capital, which by definition is confined to relations of distribution, 'interest-bearing capital' can enter into direct relations with direct producers (see also Howard, 1980: 73). Clearly, it can also enter into direct relations with direct exploiters. However, even though it is in these ways able to dictate certain of the conditions of production (witness the International Monetary Fund), and therefore appears close to exploitation in Moment B, it is still conceptually distinct from class exploitation based on direct immediate possession of the means of production. Joffe (1980: 23) follows Roseberry (1978) in arguing that 'usury capital' can enter into relations with direct producers and become the primary mechanism of exploitation. Hence, she says, it must be considered as a production relation. A more precise conceptualisation, however, would be to see this as a 'heterogeneous' relation of production (see chapter two) in as much as it does not have an integral link with any particular relations (and classes) at Moments A and B.

27 The effect of ideology and consciousness on class practices has also been cogently discussed by Alavi, 1973: 23; Hobsbawm, 1973: 7–8; Byres, 1981: 407; Femia, 1975: *passim*; Awiti, 1973: 231; Hindess and Hirst, 1975: 64; Cabral, 1969: 51.

2 MODE OF PRODUCTION, SURPLUS AND CAPITALIST DEVELOPMENT

1 A mode of production is not a structuralist 'combinatory' of variables – the formal play of which would allow for the deduction or prediction of different modes of production (Althusser, 1976: 130).

2 In referring to certain Third World units of production, Kay (1975: 102) writes:

> It would be wrong not to recognise these undertakings as capitalist, for they possess all its formal qualities. On the other hand they have certain features which suggest that it would not be completely correct to treat them in this way.

After mentioning the features of migrant labour and low capitalisation, he continues, 'of course it may be claimed that neither of these features change the fundamental character of these enterprises as capitalist, but merely define them as a particular type of capitalist enterprise. Whatever one decides . . .' and he goes on to a different point. But in order to explain the specificity of these undertakings, their character and their likely development, it is surely necessary to try to characterise them as accurately as possible.

3 This problem is evidenced by Hindess and Hirst in their view (1975: 82) that the 'ancient' mode of production is based on, *inter alia*, slave production, tax farming, independent peasants and artisans.

4 Friedmann takes an even stricter view than Hindess and Hirst. For her (1979: 160):

> markets in products, labour power, credit and means of production must encompass all units with wage relations in order for the reproduction of each unit to be fully capitalist in form. From this perspective, latifundia employing landless labour in a context of labour immobility are not fully capitalist.

5 That the issue is ridden with problems is evident in the claim by Hindess and Hirst (1975: 21) that variants can correspond to different mechanisms of exploitation – i.e. to diverse sets of relations in production. This clearly runs counter to the schema developed above about the internal elements of a mode of production, as well as to Hindess and Hirst's own stress on integration of Moments A and B.

6 In some respects this discussion below overlaps with the earlier analysis about what makes a labour process internal to a mode *per se*, although it deals with the distinct issue of variations *within internal* labour processes.

7 For Marx, both formal and real subsumptions are variants of a *fully* capitalist labour process, i.e. both subsumptions are fully integrated into capitalist relations of possession/separation, distribution and utilisation, capitalist reproduction and capitalist system processes. Formal subsumption of labour to capital may exist outside of the CMP, but it also may be a stage in the CMP and a foundation for real subsumption (Marx, 1976b: 1034; 1972: 478). As such, formal subsumption in the latter case is not simply wage-labour and commodity production at Moment B, but this in articulation with a capitalist mode as a whole.

8 Wolpe's response to the issue has been to label the dependent 'mode' a 'restricted mode of production' (1980a: 34–8). This he counterposes to an

'extended mode of production' which has its own 'laws of motion' and mechanisms of reproduction. While Wolpe is on the right track in his distinctions, it seems confusing to call both situations modes of production, albeit 'restricted' or 'extended'. In my terminology, Wolpe's 'restricted mode of production' is a heterogeneous relation of production (subordinately articulated to a mode for its reproduction and system processes), and the 'extended mode' is simply a 'mode of production'.

9 It is important to state this because the articulation approach has been criticised for being economistic and ignoring the political level of articulation (see Mouzelis, 1980: 368–9; Foster-Carter, 1978: 243).

10 Poulantzas (1978: 27) also argues that political and ideological relations are present in the constitution of a mode of production and do not only, or functionalistically, enter the picture at the level of reproduction. For him, it is because they are present in this first place, that they play an essential role in reproduction. However, like Muratorio, he confuses the level of the social formation with that of the mode of production.

11 Hindess and Hirst are not entirely consistent on this issue. They sometimes imply that these conditions are part of the mode, as in their analysis of ideological and political relations *vis-à-vis* primitive communism and the ancient mode of production (Asad and Wolpe, 1976: 489, 492).

12 Rey (1973) has been accused of creating a macro-framework of articulation which ignores the distinction which I theorise here as that between internal and external articulation (see Foster-Carter, 1978: 218). In fact, however, Rey does note the difference between the articulation of fully fledged modes of production (with one being introduced from the outside) and when the articulation arises endogamously (see quotation from Rey in Foster-Carter, 1978: 230).

13 For Hilton (1973: 208), even though European capitalism was and is riddled with feudal relics, capitalism and feudalism are distinct social formations because they are based on different modes of production, legitimised by different ideological systems and dominated by struggles between social classes distinctive of each.

14 This perspective enables us to understand how, as Asad and Wolpe (1976: 505) argue, the conditions of existence of one mode in part can be conditions of existence for the elements of another mode – as in the way that the feudal mode provided a market for emerging bourgeoisie of the capitalist mode (Hindess and Hirst, 1975: 296–7; see also Rey, 1973).

15 Hindess and Hirst (1975: 74) reject the concept of surplus because of the lack of any absolute standard for evaluating what is surplus and what is necessary to a society. Taylor (1981: 383) criticises the concept as making it difficult to differentiate between economic systems. Both these criticisms have some validity and are symptomatic of the over-generality of the concept. Nevertheless, the concept is still very useful at an abstract level for designating important overall issues in economic development. (It may be noted that the products of *surplus labour* are not identical to *surplus* in Baran's sense described above. *Surplus labour* in my definition is labour that is surplus only to the immediate reproduction of the producers involved in performing it. It does not necessarily produce surplus products for investment in *growth*.)

16 The discussion about productive labour has another complication added to it with the concept of relative surplus value. Here, what becomes important is labour that produces those specific means of production which in turn reduce the labour-time necessary for the social reproduction of the producers (see next section). Again, however, the key issue is whether this contributes to developing Department I – the production of means of production.

17 At the level of capitalist social formations, there are significant differences in the extent to which various spheres of social life are integrated into the commodity exchange circuit (Poulantzas, 1978: 27). Housework and child-rearing activity straddle the margins of commodity circulation (unlike transport, furniture and even food production, which are far more integrated into the circuit). These diverse relations can profitably be analysed in terms of their articulation to the CMP.

18 Private property in the means of production is an invariant condition of the CMP (Cliffe, 1977: 205). However, it is not necessary that these be privately owned by the capitalists themselves; enough if they can be privately hired. Thus, state- or communally-owned land can be compatible with the CMP (Hindess and Hirst, 1975: 294). This is an important point in evaluating the class character of rural development schemes set up on state or community land and managed by a capitalist company (see chapter five).

19 Of course, in the historical development of capitalism, the capitalist has often had to take part in the labour process (Sohn-Rethal, 1979). However, this labour input may be viewed analytically as the capitalist selling labour-power to him/herself. Clearly, this is a contradictory condition and it is similar to that of kulaks discussed in the next chapter.

20 The piece-work payment system makes no difference to the essentially capitalistic nature of the wage (see Marx, 1976a: 517). It should not be confused with independent simple commodity producers selling to a merchant capitalist. In this latter instance, the capitalist does not possess all the means of production, and to the extent that there is exploitation, it is in Moment C rather than (as in the CMP) in Moment B.

21 This exploitation is distinct from expenditure on labour-power that does not generate any profit but merely transfers income, i.e. labour-power that represents an increase in consumption without any surplus-value exploitation (Amin, 1974: 196). (This shows that not all wage-labour is capitalist: a distinction must be made between revenue (spending profits) and capital (making them).) It is also distinct from that profit-making capital which derives its profits not from wage-labour exploitation, but from surplus transfer within Moment C of production (this latter is – as has been argued – a heterogeneous relation of production).

22 This is not always recognised as relative surplus value in Marxist literature, even although clearly identified by Marx as such (1976a: 530–4).

23 For example, capitalist service, circulation or entertainment enterprises produce profits through absolutely exploiting wage-labour, but only where these activities cheapen the costs of reproducing wage-labour do they contribute to relative surplus value. Luxury and armament production also do not affect the costs of wage-goods and therefore expanded capacity in these sectors cannot directly help reduce the socially necessary labour-time for reproducing

labour-power (see Bullock, 1974: 9). They may develop productive capacity in a different way, i.e. indirectly, where their profits or technology find their way into Department I (the production of means of production) (Amin, 1974: 185), but this is quite distinct.

24 For example, motivations like greed are not natural, but historical products of definite social development (Marx, 1973: 222). See Brenner (1977) for a devastating criticism of *homo economicus* assumptions.

25 It is partly because Chilean market farmers only increased their production in this way that Kay (1981: 489–90) argues (incorrectly in my view) that they were not capitalists even though they employed and exploited wage-labour.

26 Turnover time affecting the rate of profit includes not only production time but also circulation time. Marx cites improved communications (based on new material means of communication) as the chief means of reducing circulation time (1974: 71). There are complex debates about whether advanced means of production do not, paradoxically, also reduce the rate of profit – i.e. Marx's theory of the 'falling rate of profit' (Marx, 1974: part III). Suffice it here to say that Marx believed that as capitalist mechanisation increased, there was a relative decrease in the proportion of new value created in relation to total capital outlay, and the rate of profit would fall in consequence. Among what Marx saw as several countervailing tendencies to this 'falling rate of profit', he noted that mechanisation itself can indirectly increase the rate of surplus-value exploitation through contributing to relative surplus value. However, it may be argued that far from being a mere countertendency, this phenomenon in fact renders problematic the notion of a falling rate of profit *per se*. While the debate is important, it has little direct bearing on my theorisation of capitalist development.

27 The status of the discussion that follows is theoretically informed general-isation from concrete social formations rather than a general theory about the role of the state in capitalist society (see Jessop, 1982: 211).

28 Monetarism and cutbacks in the state's expenditure on welfare are not so much an absence of state involvement in the economy as a specific form of involvement that undermines or resists working-class gains. State involve-ment in monopoly capitalism does not negate competition nor the funda-mental 'anarchy' of capitalist production (Holloway and Picciotto, 1977: 96).

29 This is not to imply that the state has privileged knowledge of the general interest of capital (see Jessop, 1982: 98). It is only when the range of specific interests are articulated and aggregated that the state can serve capital as a whole.

3   CAPITALISM AND UNDERDEVELOPMENT

1 The pitfalls of this approach can clearly be seen with regard to the Frankian argument that the southern United States were capitalist because they were integrated into the world market and produced for profit (see Banaji, 1980: 516). The problem is that if the southern states are called capitalist, it is difficult to explain why their social relations impeded the development of capitalist features across all the Moments of production and inhibited the use

of new means of production (Hindess and Hirst, 1975: 150–2). The situation is better explained as the southern states having a slave mode of production subordinately articulated to the CMP through the international division of labour and world market (1975: 161).

2 Indeed, why stop at each type of social formation having its own mode of production – why not each local or regional economy within a given social formation? This kind of approach makes the same error as the dependency approach (i.e. confusing modes of production with economic systems) – but at a smaller unit of analysis.

3 Related to this, the way that dependency theory conceptualises exploitation and surplus is so general as to obliterate differences within the economic relations of a structure of underdevelopment (Taylor, 1979, cited by Mouzelis, 1980: 382–3; Foster-Carter, 1978: 211; Booth, 1975: 79; Leys, 1977a). Thus, amongst the theory's blindspots, is the mix of economic relations within international (and national) capitalist economic systems. The dependency concepts of centre-periphery and metropole-satellite are also used to refer both to classes and systems (e.g. urban centres) – and this collapsing of spatial and social relations under the same concepts points to a lack of concreteness (Mouzelis, 1979b: 43; Barnett, 1977: 23). The concrete differences between CMP relations and non-CMP relations, and their articulation at various Moments of production are lost sight of. The conflation of class and spatial relations further detracts from the specific role of classes and the state in determining differences between national capitalisms. The important distinction between exploitation in Moment B and Moment C is ignored by Frank (1969a; 1969b).

4 Following Marx (1972, chapter twenty-five), this is sometimes referred to as the *real* process of primitive accumulation (Duggett, 1975: 167; Bryceson, 1980: 280; Brenner, 1977: 66–7).

5 Under colonial articulation, the prior modes of production did not disappear entirely: the CMP was not therefore built on the ruins of the old modes of production, but inserted into their remains with the consequence of preserving some of their effects (Szentes, 1971: 9). In fact, in Uganda, the partial dissolution of the feudal mode of production was followed by an actual decline in capitalist units of production as petty commodity production rapidly gained ground (Mamdani, 1977: 141).

6 This discussion shows the value of integrating the *dependency* theory and *articulation of modes* framework. According to Foster-Carter (1978: 230), it is the contribution of dependency theory to have shown that the progeny of the peripheral articulation is deformed. Foster-Carter seems to advocate merging the 'articulation' framework with dependency theory, and, as shown above, this does add clarity to the analysis, and it allows for specifying types of dependency (Mouzelis, 1979b: 45).

7 In Mamdani's study of Uganda, for example, feudal forms of exploitation remained at Moment B, but the serfs became tenants producing in a heterogeneous relation of production for a merchant class involved in export activity (a restructuring of Moment C). Although the process of production was the same physically (hoe cultivation) and socially (the family unit of production with possession of the means of production – except land), the purpose was no

longer for use, but for trade (a change in the system dynamic) (1977: 138–9, 143; see also Amin, 1974: 360).

8 On the one hand, a merchant class affects production by giving it more and more the character of production for exchange. Through this, the effects of competition are brought to bear on production – enforcing a socially average labour-time for the production of the various commodities (Kay, 1975: 94; Bryceson, 1980: 285). On the other hand, however, merchant capital also has a conservative effect because it depends on the existing class structures for the execution of production (Marx, 1973: 586–7, quoted in Banaji, 1976a: 301; Kay, 1975: 95).

9 One feature of this difference is that while European medieval feudalism was reciprocal and had customary limits to exploitation, in Latin America it was a one-sided relation: the peasant had duties, and the lord had the rights (Harrison, 1981: 105).

10 For example, Mamdani (1977: 5) sees the relation between productive economic units and backward/stagnating ones as one of exploitation whereby the impoverishment of the latter is the condition of the enrichment of the former. Frank (1969b) similarly sees development and underdevelopment as being linked through a process involving a structural transfer of surplus. Development is thus at the expense of underdevelopment: they are different outcomes of an identical process (see also Booth, 1975: 70; Kay, 1975: 96; Arrighi, 1971: 1–2; Bundy, 1972: 388; Legassick, 1976: 436). I will argue later that although this perspective has useful insights, it is not the full story of either development or underdevelopment, and that a *complex of historical processes* is involved – not simply a single zero-sum exploitative one, and that theory needs to reflect *all* of these.

11 It should be noted that the absence of effective competition is in part a result not only of monopoly, but also of the existence of non-capitalist structures that are not integrated into commodity exchange and therefore not dependent on the market to the extent that competitive pressure significantly affects them (see Dobb, 1962: 26; Szentes, 1971: 20–30).

12 Warren (1973:4, footnote 1) provocatively asks if the United States is not highly dependent on Saudi Arabian oil. One could also ask about Japan and her export markets. It can also be noted that despite the subordinate dependence of Canada on the United States, and Australia on Britain, these former colonies did develop their national productive capacity (Barratt-Brown, 1976: 259; Kay, 1975: 104).

13 Amongst many others, Arrighi and Saul (1973: 293) and Girvan and Jefferson (1968: 342) speak in this sense of 'growth without development' – a sense distinct from the moral one described in chapter one.

14 It is useful to examine how the distinctions drawn so far are highlighted by reference to Marxist philosophical principles. Marxism holds that change and movement can be distinguished according to whether it continues within the terms of its structural contradictions; or whether it changes the contradiction itself (Cornforth, 1968: 107). In this light, 'underdevelopment' can be said to undergo quantitative movement insofar as it occurs within the terms of its substructures. It becomes 'development' when it *qualitatively* changes these terms. It may be noted that a qualitative change is, sometimes, the cumulative

effect of a myriad of quantitative changes, although a change in quantity – within certain limits – does not necessarily transform quality (Cornforth, 1968: 107; Afanasyev, 1980: 97).

15 Amin (1974: 606) notes that Latin American analysts tend to stress dependency rather than disarticulation as the main feature of the structure of underdevelopment in their region. According to him, Latin American countries tend to have disarticulation at a national level between industry and agriculture – rather than throughout the economy, and dependency is primarily on imports such as technology.

16 The marginal level is not simply the outcome of articulation between the CMP and the *pre*-capitalist structures. In addition, it comprises groups who are actually *excluded* – i.e. marginalised – from the peripheral CMP itself. Marginal structures are therefore partly created by the *internal* action and character of the peripheral CMP, as well as by its conservation-dissolution relationship with antecedent relations.

17 Productivity and expansion in the monopoly level tend to be predicated on advanced means of production rather than on low wages. This involves not only relatively few labourers, but also a particular quality of labour. Obregon (1974) argues that the skill level required excludes much of the relative surplus population from fulfilling either of the 'growth' functions of a reserve army. However, Arrighi (1977: 172) and Braverman (1974) argue that capital-intensive technology does involve semi-skilled labour (although see Elger, 1979, for a critique of Braverman). These arguments tend to weaken Obregon's point about skill levels but, even so, his model still has general validity – at the very least with regard to the low labour requirements of capital-intensive technology. The marginal level is thus unlikely to aid growth at the monopoly level.

18 It is in this light that one can understand Marx's remark that 'the *so-called* primitive accumulation of capital therefore is nothing else than the historical process of divorcing the producer from the means of production' (Marx, 1972: 668).

19 As discussed in chapter two, the limits on absolute surplus-value exploitation also include the mobility of labour and capital's own need to reproduce its labour force. Neither of these limits would seem to have much weight at the periphery (see Emmanuel, 1972a; Harrison, 1981: *passim*; Elkan, 1978: 137; Szentes, 1973: 192).

4 RURAL DEVELOPMENT

1 Productive capacity in agriculture may be raised through both land and labour productivity, singly or jointly. Prior to the Green revolution, it was argued that raising agricultural productivity referred not so much to raising output per acre, as to reducing the cost of production through labour-saving techniques (Galeski, 1972: 26; Kay, 1975: 495; Byres, 1981: 409; Baran, 1962: xxxii). Clearly, through mechanising production, labour productivity can be increased – even if this does not necessarily raise yields per hectare. Since the Green revolution, not to mention the more recent development of genetic engineering and hormone development, it is clear that land productivity can

also be raised, to some extent independently of labour, through technical advances such as high-yield-variety crops. These advances allow for an increase in the number of crops grown each year – which is equivalent to an extensive expansion of land and labour output (Harrison, 1981: 97).

2 Claims lauding the economic performance of small-size family-run farms often ignore the way that these farms are integrated into a scale unit much wider than their land-size in which relatively few of the functions of production at A, B and C are actually performed by them (Galeski, 1972: 160–1; Vogoler, 1981).

3 This point also applies to the stratification of the peasantry according to income. The danger of the terms 'rich', 'middle' and 'poor' peasants is that they can be interpreted as distinctions based only (or primarily) in Moment C, and only one dimension of this Moment at that.

4 'Peasants' have rights and obligations in a wider economic system which includes 'non-peasants'. In rural Iran, for example, such 'non-peasants' include usurers, pedlars, artisans, teachers, mullahs, absentee landlords, rentiers, village officials and lessors of means of production (Keddie, 1968: 156–7).

5 This narrowness aside, a different problem that this focus involves is that of identifying wage-labour empirically when payment is obscured. Exchange of labour-power can be concealed by non-money wage payments and traditional forms of co-operation and reciprocity (see Spiegel, 1979). Attention to other Moments of production is needed to identify disguised wage-labour.

6 On this basis, Friedmann distinguishes four categories of 'peasant' production (1979: 176): i. household production; ii. sharecropping and related rents; iii. poor, middle and rich peasantry; iv. hacienda. What is common to all these is the possession of land and absence of a labour market.

7 Brass (1980: 451, footnote 15) found in Peru that all producers hired labour at certain junctures. For this reason, he decided to use different criteria for distinguishing class differentiation, namely the fertility of land-holdings and the ownership of means of production.

8 Entrepreneurship similarly does not mean that the producer involved is a capitalist (Howard, 1980: 75–6). For example, a poor peasant remains a poor peasant even when in cash-crop production, and exhibiting an 'entrepreneurial dynamic', if – *inter alia* – the objective is only to meet family needs (Charlesworth, 1980: 262).

9 There are demograp.ic and technological exceptions to this. Friedmann calculates the labour-time necessary at a particular historical juncture for cultivating an acre of wheat in the United States, and concludes that a single household could not supply this labour at a particular historical period (1978: 76). However, with increasing mechanisation, the requisite labour-time dropped, and a single household with a man and one son could operate an expanded unit of production (1978: 78).

10 Mouzelis (1975–6: 489) disputes this, arguing that the experience of the Iberian Peninsula shows that industrial capital can prosper with or without the existence of big agricultural landed property. He further argues that as agriculture becomes an increasingly subordinate part of the economy, it makes little difference for the overall development of the CMP whether landed property persists or is destroyed (1975–6: 488). Mouzelis may be correct in all

this, but in the absence of a detailed analysis of the specifics of the Iberian case (including a critical look at the claim that industrial capital has prospered there), it is difficult to evaluate these points. It may be that a far-sighted landed class has embarked on a 'Junker' route enabling both agrarian development and a transfer of surplus to industry in a manner not unlike Japan's experience (see Geertz, 1963: 47–8; Baran, 1962: 289; Moore, 1969: 246, 251). More likely, however, the situation may be externally induced and result in dependent industrialisation with no relation to the local Agrarian Question (see Poulantzas, 1976b). While more research is clearly needed, it can be stated that while landed property does not preclude *either* scenario developing prosperous capitalist industry, it appears more likely to obstruct rather than facilitate this. This is different to cases where the contradiction between Agrarian Transition and a landed class has been bypassed. Thus, in Chile the national industrial bourgeoisie and the landlords reached a compromise whereby not agriculture but copper mining would subsidise industrial development (Kay, 1981: 493). In other countries there have been similar compromises involving oil or gold (Hiro, 1978: 289; Halliday, 1979: 129).

11 Super-profit based on absolute rent exists irrespective of the productivity of the land – and in this regard is distinct from super-profit based on another type of rent which is found *only* in agriculture and which is discussed below (see Hindess and Hirst, 1975: 186).

12 In industry, super-profits may be made by capitalists who use exceptional machinery and can produce below the normal costs of production. On this basis, they can sell at the going price and, through the relative increase in the surplus value they realise (see chapter two), achieve a super-profit. But capital mobility means that this super-profit is usually transitory (Kautsky, 1976: 16–17). Through competition, such industrial super-profits are constantly erased as more capitalists catch up and the super-rate becomes the new average (Tribe, 1977: 78).

13 Rey similarly holds that transformation of agriculture into capitalist relations has only really been completed in the United States (Bradby, 1975: 144). But even these claims overestimate the extent of CMP relations in American agriculture. In 1900, nearly 80 per cent of American agricultural producers were self-employed and used unpaid family labour, and this had declined only to 67 per cent in 1960 (Friedmann, 1978: 93). In the economy as a whole, this status was 51 per cent in 1900 and it had dropped to 17 per cent by 1960.

14 The rich peasant and simple commodity producer models are both directly relevant to tropical Africa where historically the absence of a large landed class has precluded a 'Junker' type of transformation (Amin, 1974: 364; Byres, 1977, cited by Kay, 1981: 486). In view of this, I therefore leave aside other Third World experiences, including the 'strategic' path as in Taiwan and South Korea (Harrison, 1981: 103; Hamilton, 1983: *passim*; Hiro, 1978: 289); the Latin American experience (Kay, 1981: 487; Amin, 1974: 362; Harrison, 1981: 112–13); the Middle East and Gulf region (Keddie, 1968: 152; Halliday, 1979: 117–19; Greussing and Kippenburg, 1975–6: 126; Amin, 1974: 168); and south-east Asia (Harrison, 1981: 79–80).

15 There are sometimes countertendencies to this polarisation – such as impoverishment caused by the sub-division of rich peasant farms among family

members. Likewise with certain systems of land tenure, inheritance laws, land shortages, marketing restrictions and legislation.

16 Demographic variables are not an alternative to class factors as underlying causes of social differentiation; family structure and size still clearly play a role in determining inequalities among middle peasants. However, it would be wrong to follow Chayanov in seeing family size as the major factor or as a biologically autonomous one. Patnaik (1979: 381) points out that Chayanov's correlations of demography and wealth are, in fact, consistent with the Marxist proposition that economic variations in land-size and scale of production cause variations in family size, rather than *vice versa* (see also Hunt, 1979: 277, 280). Richer peasants can support a larger family and, in Africa and the Middle East, also acquire more wives (see Galeski, 1972: 63; Raikes, 1978: 291).

17 Kautsky (1976: 14) argues that such a subsidy is not surplus value. He argues that there can be no surplus value when the labour that generates the surplus product is not commoditised and does not itself possess a value. To the extent that one is considering the labour of the simple commodity producer himself, this much can probably be granted. As against an ahistorical 'labour theory of value', I would argue that it is only meaningful to speak of labour-time creating value where this is evident in exchange-value. In other words, only where there is commodity exchange can one talk of value, and only where labour-power is a commodity, of surplus value (see also Williams, 1981a: 32). However, I leave aside a detailed discussion of these issues, as they are not fundamental to my argument.

18 Friedmann (1979: 169, 172) disputes any subsidising role by simple commodity production. She argues that a capitalist and a simple commodity producer exist in the same price market in their relations to merchant capital, finance capital and land-owners – because of the mobility of factors of production, and because of competition, in a capitalist economic system. Like capitalists, simple commodity producers only pay capitalist rates of interest, rent and merchant costs. Friedmann acknowledges, however, that simple commodity producers may experience unequal exchange, and that an indirect subsidy to the CMP can be transferred in this way. This is especially possible at the periphery where there is not a universal price market because of the lower capital mobility and because of the presence of non-capitalist relations as well. Further, at the periphery, the strength of finance, merchant and landlord capitals in relation to simple commodity producers is greater than that in relation to capitalists, and monopoly-based exploitation is hence more likely for the simple commodity producers.

19 For example, rural development for the World Bank, while not conceived in terms of the Agrarian Question, is seen explicitly as a *strategy* aimed at people in rural areas (World Bank, 1975: 3) (my emphasis).

20 As Datoo and Gray (1979: 258–61) describe the differences, *additive planning* is an incrementalism within a given structural context and does not in itself ensure sectoral integration; *growth-centre* strategy derives from diffusionist theory and sees development as spreading from selected growth poles. In contrast to this approach, *structural transformation* implies a holistic approach

that encompasses qualitative change in relations as well as forces of production.

21 The depth and strength of this assumption is evident in Sano's review (1982) of a book by Heyer et al. (1981a). Sano fails to see the significance of the book's critique of such a view. Acknowledging the problems of much development policy, he writes that '[t]o set rural development in motion might in every case be to set a process of contradictions in motion, to which there can be no perfect solutions, but only relatively "good" policies, i.e. policies that to the greatest extent possible seek to compensate for the fact that they are initiated by agencies based outside the rural areas' (1982: 115). One could point out in response to this, that it is not possible to 'compensate' for a view which implies that no rural development takes place until it 'is set in motion' and indeed that contradictions wait upon such input to be activated.

22 Taking all these factors into account helps to explain why Africa stands out as a prime case of the failure of peripheral capitalist development. In Latin America, classes have been strong enough to constitute authentic ruling (as opposed to merely governing) classes. In these cases, the character of the state has been given more by the influence of the dominant class(es), than by the class composition of members of its apparatuses, and the autonomy of the bureaucracy is far more limited. In Peru, for example, contrary to some interpretations that the military government was creating – against the interests of the 'dominant' landed and mercantile classes – an industrial bourgeoisie *ex nihilo*, this government actually represented the interests of an already existing and powerful industrial bourgeoisie (Ferner, 1979: 272–3).

23 In the literature, the debate over the Kenyan state concerns largely the question of *industrial* capitalist development, unlike the focus here and in the next part of this monograph which is on rural development. However, the same arguments about the distinctions between class character, class relations, the state and development apply equally to agriculture.

24 For example, one company engaged in direct contract farming in Kenya is BAT (Kenya) Developments Ltd which since 1976 has a strictly controlled contract chicken-growers scheme. Twenty contract farmers take 10,000 chicks a week, rear them and return them to BAT(K) for slaughtering, processing, packaging and marketing (Dinham and Hines, 1983: 109). BAT(K) also contracts small producers to grow tobacco at a set quality using company loans and technical inputs – and is the sole buyer of leaf tobacco in Kenya (Buch-Hansen and Marcussen, 1982: 94).

5 SOCIAL STRUCTURE AND FAILED DEVELOPMENT

1 This trend may explain the decline of the wage-labour sector in agriculture by 1.7 per cent annually between 1972–80 at the same time as output rose at 3 per cent annually over the same period (Currie and Ray, 1987: 94).

2 On the Ugandan group farms, farmers became indebted through the use of government credit, marketing, tractors and mortgages (Seidman, 1978: 164). In Mozambique's Eduardo Mondlane co-operative, the same thing happened through renting various means of production from the state (Harris, 1980:

342). At Mumias in Kenya, services were given on credit to outgrowers by the company on credit, and charged at 8 per cent interest (Mulaa, 1981: 91).

3 It appears that the only difference between outgrowers and proletarians which Currie and Ray (1987: 95) are prepared to concede is an ideological one: for them, 'whereas the wage relation conceals the expropriation of surplus value, the producer price is a different ideological relation. It conceals the farmer's subsumption to transnational capital, and the fact that ownership of productive property has become more formal than real.'

4 In post-1973 Chile, middle peasants became contracted to agro-export industries, having little control over their farms as a result. Despite still having formal ownership of the land, they were, according to Kay (1981: 510), ultimately indirect wage-labourers for capital. Williams says that the dependence of outgrowers on capitalist owners of means of production is close to that of the proletariat (1981a: 34–5).

5 One pointer to capitalist features is evident in the attitude of workers hired by the company to service outgrowers' plots. At Mumias, they expect outgrowers to reproduce them while on the job (Mulaa, 1981: 98).

6 Not all settlement schemes involve control of land. In the case of Nigeria's Kano River irrigation project, political and economic considerations ruled out removing producers' title to the land. Control shifted from the issues of access to other vital means of production – water, seeds, fertilisers, tractors and knowledge. (When these failed in the case of the Bakalori irrigation scheme, it involved the violent use of means of coercion (Wallace, 1980: 63–5).) Such controls are similar to those exercised over outgrowers, and the analysis in the previous section applies here.

7 This often needs to be seen in the context of widespread separation from means of production in the rest of the social formation. In these conditions (i.e. CMP relations at Moment A):

the general peasant population can then be relegated to the political-economic position of an 'agrarian reserve army' useful for maintaining discipline among and control over those who participate in the government agricultural scheme. (Hill, 1977: 27)

8 The IDS reports describe how the Mbere cotton blocks project was implemented (1972: 26–7):

1 Cotton blocks started in the absence of information on environmental suitability for cotton, and in face of expert advice against the project.
2 Target acreage reduced from 500 acres to 280 acres due to unwillingness of the clans to lease land for the project.
3 178 acres cleared, 169 ploughed, and only about 48 acres planted. Despite lateness of the rains the 'optimal' planting date was rigidly applied so (a) what was planted failed to germinate, and (b) clearing and ploughing stopped before it was really necessary.
4 The project was declared a failure, and the land was left unused.

The 'Special 4K' project at Tetu aimed to attract youths to farming and increase output through the demonstration effect on parents and neighbours, using hybrid maize. An earlier survey of the region, had it been consulted, would have shown that 60 per cent of 4K members' families already grew hybrid maize (1972: 29–30). In another case, at Vihiga, the absence of integrated planning meant that:

... pigs were fed maize which was needed to feed the local population. Coordinated planning would have indicated that a livestock project dependent on the generation of local crop surpluses was premature. In Mbere, hybrid maize and cotton production were introduced before adequate experimentation had been carried out on a spectrum of crops appropriate for dry areas, and the results were not successful.' (IDS, 1975: 20–9; see also Harrison, 1981: 339; Amin, 1974: 289; Heyer et al., 1980: 12; Williams, 1986a: 7; 1986b: 19).

9 For example, in 1957, smallholders produced only 9 per cent of marketed coffee. By the late 1960s, they were growing over 50 per cent, and their numbers also rose from 3,000 to 133,000 in central province over this period (Kitching, 1980: 317–18; Blume, 1971: 83; Carlsen, 1980: 11, 38; Ruthenberg, 1966: 12).

10 This articulation contributed to the failure of a state credit policy aimed at smallholders. The households preferred the available option of remittances to the debt associated with the state scheme (Heyer, 1981: 113–14).

11 This restricted peripheral simple commodity production has also been different from the new centres in Canada and Australia. The latter were dominated by simple commodity production and therefore had the capacity to evolve independently into a fully developed CMP (Amin, 1974: 393; see also Barratt-Brown, 1976: 259).

12 In pre-independence Sri Lanka, some of the wealthy peasants became petty rentiers through subletting rather than turning to productive capitalism (Herring, 1981: 169, footnote 56). In Iran, middle peasants did not pass through the rich-peasant stage of continuing to take part in the labour process at the same time as hiring labour: instead, they ceased work entirely because of the cultural value of non-labour, and also because of social pressures to provide employment. The overall effect was to reduce their incomes and therefore their potential to expand production (Keddie, 1968: 160–1). A further reason why they ceased working was because of the lack of alternative investment opportunities in the face of monopoly competition. This has also been the situation in Ismani, Tanzania (Feldman, 1975: 165).

13 According to Stavenhagen (1964: 92), attempts by the most diverse governments at different periods in the underdeveloped areas have failed to generate a workable system of medium-sized family farms supplying the internal market. Malawi's experience of 'progressive farmer' policies is interesting in this regard. Promoting this strategy in 1969, the Malawian government gave a select group of farmers the bulk of extension, credit and subsidies. But only 260 'progressive farmers' – not the 3,000 targeted – actually emerged. Evidently, the particular mixture of social and technical reform in the context of Malawi's underdevelopment and articulation to the CMP was not suitable. Consequently, by 1972, the state itself was forced to intervene directly with a different development strategy, and large state farmers began to be developed instead (Thomas, 1975: 38). Similarly in Iran, land was distributed to richer peasants, and there was also the creation of moishavs and co-operatives (Halliday, 1979: 113). Yet none of this was economically successful: the richer

peasants' incomes rose – but these were used for consumption rather than reinvestment (1979: 129). Thus, the state had to intervene at the point of production by becoming directly involved in co-operatives, farm corporations, and joint ventures with 'agribusiness' (1979: 113). Evaluating such state strategy in the form of settlement and outgrower schemes is the subject matter of the next section.

14 In comparison, outgrower and contract farmer schemes absorb fewer inputs. In the case of Kenyan coffee, small producers are only half as productive as estates, but they also have far fewer expensive inputs (Dinham and Hines, 1983: 54). Likewise with outgrower tea farmers who plant about two-thirds of the total tea area, although they produce only a third of the total output (tea plantations growing most of the remainder) (Buch-Hansen and Marcussen, 1982: 22–3, 26).

15 On the Keiskammahoek irrigation scheme, it is held to be 'conceivable that one day the management staff will work not for the Department of Agriculture and Forestry, but for a Keiskamma Farmers Cooperative' (Proctor-Simms, 1978: 138). For this reason, 'it is intended that settlers be involved in decision making from the beginning and that increasing responsibility for the project affairs be delegated ...' (1978: 138). However, as the scheme's management admits, there is no formal training to this end, and weekly meetings between management and settlers concern only immediate production issues (1978: 93). As one commentary notes: 'decision-making is largely based with managers at central unit ... [the settlers'] "wage" is dependent upon their co-operation with the central unit [management] in producing as they are told to do' (PADRI, 1979: 12).

16 As Barnett (1977: 175) notes about the Gezira scheme:

The tenant has to operate in terms of the superior rationality of the total system. The organisation, based on the elaborate irrigation scheme, is elaborately interdependent and ponderously 'other' than the tenant. It is as independent of him as is the factory for a motor car assembler.

17 Even in the United States, it is noteworthy that the Tennessee Valley Authority 'was created in April 1933, at the crest of the wave of Roosevelt's New Deal – the nearest the USA has ever been to a social revolution' (Sohn-Rethal, 1979: 187).

18 More recently, the United States has promoted land reform in Thailand as a counter to insurgency (*Time*, 1981: 27). 'Aggressive rural-development programs are being launched. To win peasants to its side, Bangkok provided new varieties of rice, and imported silkworms ...' (1981: 27). The United States has been pressurising El Salvador's landowner government to institute land reform as a means of reducing peasant support for the Left (Buckley, 1981: 43) – with successful results according to the government (1981: 50). The CIA has promoted land reform in the Philippines (Krinks, 1983: 108–9).

19 From 1952–65, Kenya's entire rural development practice (i.e. including extension, settlement, etc.) was strongly motivated by political considerations. 'A prosperous middle class society of farmers, firmly established on the land, was expected to exercise a stabilising influence on politics in Kenya' (Ruthenberg, 1966: 14).

20 Interestingly, large-scale irrigated farming was initiated in Kenya to resettle political detainees (Williams, 1986a: 13).

21 Other examples where political motives have played a part in formulating rural development plans have been colonial Mozambique (Harris, 1980: 344) and Senegal (Kom, 1977: 161).

22 'No government can ignore the social and political disruption caused by food production failures on this scale. Virtually all African governments have intervened in the production and the marketing of food in order to improve availability and to control prices' (Dinham and Hines, 1983: 137).

23 The Ciskei's Keiskammahoek irrigation project has been visited by diplomatic personnel from at least fifteen countries, and has featured prominently in South African government propaganda media (author's fieldwork observation, May 1979).

24 For example, in Kenya, BAT(K) contracts small producers to grow tobacco on terms that include conditions on quality and inputs (Currie and Ray, 1987: 94). The farmers carry the losses when bad weather or market conditions yield adverse returns on production. As sole purchaser of leaf tobacco, BAT(K) has major bargaining power over the price it pays producers. In addition, BAT(K) is protected against labour disputes or sabotage, though it still exercises managerial control through an extension scheme. And since it does not own land, it is less threatened by nationalisation (1987: 94).

References

Adelman, I., and Taft-Morris, C. 1967. *Society, Politics and Economic Development. A Quantitative Approach*. Baltimore, Johns Hopkins.

Adler, T. (ed.) 1977. *Perspectives on South Africa – a collection of working papers*. Johannesburg, African Studies Institute, University of the Witwatersrand.

Afanasyev, V. G. 1980. *Marxist Philosophy, A Popular Outline*. Moscow, Progress Publishers.

Alavi, H. 1972. The state in post-colonial societies. Pakistan and Bangladesh. *New Left Review*, no. 74.

1973. Peasant classes and primordial loyalties. *Journal of Peasant Studies*, 1, no. 1.

1975. India and the colonial mode of production. *Socialist Register*. London, Merlin Press.

Allan, W. 1949. Studies of African land usage in Northern Rhodesia. *Rhodes-Livingstone Institute Papers*, No. 14.

Almond, G., and Coleman, J. (eds.) 1966. *The Politics of the Developing Areas*. Princeton, Princeton University Press.

Althusser, L. 1969a. *For Marx* (trans. Ben Brewster). London, Allen Lane, Penguin.

1969b. Contradiction and overdetermination. In Althusser, 1969a.

1971. *Politics and History*. London, New Left Books.

1976. *Essays in Self-Criticism*. London, New Left Books.

Althusser, L., and Balibar, E. 1970. *Reading Capital*. London, New Left Books.

Amin, S. 1974. *Accumulation on a World Scale. A Critique of the Theory of Underdevelopment*. Vols. I and II combined. New York, Monthly Review Press.

1977. The dynamic and limitations of agrarian capitalism in Black Africa. In Gutkind and Waterman, 1977.

Amin, S., and Vergopoulos, K. 1974. *La Question paysanne et le capitalisme*. Paris, Anthropos.

Anonymous, 1979. Untitled memorandum criticising Ciskei agricultural policy (probably written by a Ciskei politician).

Anyang'Nyong'o, P. 1981. Middle peasantry in Nyanza. *Review of African Political Economy*, no. 20, Jan.–Apr., 17–26.

Apter, D. E. 1965. *The Politics of Modernization*. Chicago, Chicago University Press.

Arrighi, G. 1971. The relationship between the colonial and the class structures: a critique of A. G. Frank's theory of the development of underdevelopment. Mimeograph.

1977. Foreign investment patterns. In Gutkind and Waterman, 1977.

Arrighi, G., and Saul, J. 1968. Class formation and economic development in tropical Africa. In Bernstein, 1978.

1970. International corporations, labour aristocracies and economic development in tropical Africa. In Rhodes, 1970.

1973. *The Political Economy of Africa*. New York, Monthly Review Press.

Asad, T., and Wolpe, H. 1976. Concepts of modes of production. *Economy and Society*, 5, no. 4.

Awiti, A. 1973. Economic differentiation in Ismani, Iringa region. *African Review*, 3, no. 2.

Balibar, E. 1970. The basic concepts of historical materialism. In Althusser and Balibar, 1970.

Banaji, J. 1972. For a theory of colonial modes of production. *Economic and Political Weekly*, 7, no. 52.

1976a. The peasantry in the feudal mode of production: towards an economic model. *Journal of Peasant Studies*, 3, no. 3.

1976b. Summary of selected parts of Kautsky's *The Agrarian Question. Economy and Society*, 5, no. 1.

1980. Gundar Frank in retreat? *Journal of Peasant Studies*, 7, no. 4.

Baran, P. 1952. National economic planning. In O'Neill, 1969.

1962. *The Political Economy of Growth*. New York, Monthly Review Press.

Baran, P., and Hobsbawm, E. J. 1961. A non-communist manifesto. In O'Neill, 1969. (Also in *Kyklos*, 14, no. 2.)

Barnett, T. 1975. The Gezira scheme: production of cotton and the reproduction of underdevelopment. In Oxaal et al., 1975.

1977. *The Gezira Scheme. An Illusion of Development*. London, Frank Cass.

1981. Evaluating the Gezira scheme. Black box or Pandora's box? In Heyer et al., 1981a.

Barratt-Brown, M. 1976. *The Economics of Imperialism*. Harmondsworth, Penguin.

Bates, R. H. 1981. *Markets and States in Tropical Africa: Political Basis of Agricultural Policies*. Los Angeles, University of California Press.

Bates R. H. 1983. *Essays on the Political Economy of Rural Africa*. Cambridge, Cambridge University Press.

Beckford, G. L. 1969. The economics of agricultural resource use and development in plantation economies. In Bernstein, 1978.

Beckman, B. 1980. Imperialism and capitalist transformation: critique of a Kenyan debate. *Review of African Political Economy*, no. 19, Sept.–Dec., 48–62.

Berg, E. 1964. Socialism and economic development in tropical Africa. *Quarterly Journal of Economics*, 67, no. 4.

Berger, J., and Mohr, J. 1975. *The Seventh Man*. Harmondsworth, Penguin.

Berger, P. L. 1976. *Pyramids of Sacrifice. Political Ethics and Social Change*. London, Allen Lane.

Berle, A. A., and Means, G. C. 1932. *Modern Corporation and Private Property*. London, Macmillan.

Bernstein, H. 1971. Modernization theory and the sociological study of development. *Journal of Development Studies*, 7, no. 2.

1977. Notes on capital and peasantry. *Review of African Political Economy*, no. 10, Sept.–Dec., 60–73.

(ed.) 1978. *Underdevelopment and Development. The Third World Today*. Harmondsworth, Penguin.

1979a. African peasantries: a theoretical framework. *Journal of Peasant Studies*, 6, no. 4.

1979b. Sociology of underdevelopment vs. sociology of development? In Lehmann, 1979.

Bernstein, H., and Campbell, B. K. (eds.) 1985. *Contradictions of Accumulation in Africa*. Sage series on African Modernization and Development, x. London, Sage.

Bettelheim, C. 1972. Theoretical comments. In Emmanuel, 1972a.

Bienefeld M., and Godfrey M. (eds.) 1982. *The Struggle for Development: National Strategies in an International Context*. London, John Wiley and Sons.

Biermann, W., and Kössler, R. 1980. The settler mode of production: the Rhodesian case. *Review of African Political Economy*, no. 18.

Birnberg, J. B., and Resnick, S. R. 1975. *Colonial Development: an Economic Study*. New Haven, Yale University Press.

Black, P. A. 1977. Economic development for the Ciskei. Paper presented to workshop on the Ciskei. Institute for Social and Economic Research. Grahamstown. Rhodes University.

Blackburn, R. (ed) 1972. *Ideology in Social Science: Readings in Critical Social Theory*. London, Fontana/Collins.

Blume, H. 1971. *Organisational Aspects of Agro-industrial Development Agencies*. Munich, Weltforum Verlag.

Booth, D. 1975. André Gundar Frank: an introduction and appreciation. In Oxaal et al., 1975.

Bottomore, T., Harris, L., Kiernan, V. G., and Miliband, R. (eds.) 1985. *A Dictionary of Marxist Thought*. Oxford, Basil Blackwell.

Bradby, B. 1975. The destruction of natural economy. *Economy and Society*, 4, no. 2.

Brandt, H. et al. 1973. Report on development possibilities of Gwembe South Region, Zambia. Berlin, German Development Institute.

Brass, T. 1980. Class formation and class struggle in La Convencion, Peru. *Journal of Peasant Studies*, 7, no 4, 427–58.

Braverman, H. 1974. *Labor and Monopoly Capital. The Degradation of Work in the Twentieth Century*. New York, Monthly Review Press.

Brenner, R. 1977. The origins of capitalist development: a critique of neo-Smithian marxism. *New Left Review*, no. 104.

Brett, E. A. 1973. *Colonialism and Underdevelopment in East Africa*. London, Heinemann Educational.

Brietzke, P. 1976. Land reform in revolutionary Ethiopia. *Journal of Modern African Studies*, 14, no. 4.

Bryceson, D. F. 1980. Changes in peasant food production and food supply in relation to the historical development of commodity production in pre-colonial and colonial Tanganyika. *Journal of Peasant Studies*, 7, no. 3.

Buch-Hansen, M., and Marcussen, H. S. 1982. Contract farming and the peasantry: cases from western Kenya. *Review of African Political Economy*, no. 23, Jan.–Apr., 9–36.

Buckley, T. 1981. Letter from El Salvador. *The New Yorker*, 22 June 1981.

Bullock, P. 1974. Defining productive labour for capital. *Bulletin of the Conference of Socialist Economists*, no. 9.

Bundy, C. 1972. The emergence and decline of a South African peasantry. *African Affairs*, 71, no. 285.

Burton, F., and Carlen, P. 1979. *Official Discourse*. London, Routledge and Kegan Paul.

Byres, T. J. 1977. Agrarian transition and the agrarian question. *Journal of Peasant Studies*, 4, no. 3.

    1981. The new technology, class formation and class action in the Indian countryside. *Journal of Peasant Studies*, 8, no. 4.

Cabral, A. 1969. *Revolution in Guinea*. London, Stage 1.

Carchedi, G. 1975. On the economic identification of the new middle class. *Economy and Society*, 4, no. 1.

Cardoso, C. 1976. The colonial mode of production. *Critique of Anthropology*, nos. 4 and 5.

Cardoso, F. H. 1967. The industrial elite in Latin America. In Bernstein, 1978.

    1972. Dependency and development in Latin America. *New Left Review*, no. 74.

Carlsen, J. 1980. *Economic and Social Transformation in Rural Kenya*. Uppsala, Scandinavian Institute of African Studies.

Carr, E. H. 1974. *What is History?* Harmondsworth, Penguin.

Caute, D. 1975. *Fanon*. London, Collins.

Charlesworth, N. 1980. The 'middle peasant thesis' and the roots of rural agitation in India, 1914–1947. *Journal of Peasant Studies*, 7, no. 3.

Chayanov, A. V. 1966 (1925). *On the Theory of Peasant Economy* (D. Thorner et al., eds.). Homewood, American Economic Association.

Clammer, J. (ed.) 1978a. *The New Economic Anthropology*. London, Macmillan.

Clammer, J. 1978b. Concepts and objects in economic anthropology. In Clammer, 1978a.

Clegg, I. 1977. Workers' control: the Algerian experience. In Gutkind and Waterman, 1977.

Cliffe, L. 1977. Rural class formation in East Africa. *Journal of Peasant Studies*, 4, no. 2.

    1978. Labour migration and peasant differentiation: Zambian experiences. *Journal of Peasant Studies*, 5, no. 3.

Cliffe, L., and Cunningham, G. 1972. Ideology, organisation and the settlement experience in Tanzania. In Cliffe and Saul, 1977.

Cliffe, L., and Saul, J. (eds.) 1977. *Government and Rural Development in East Africa*. The Hague, Institute of Social Studies.

Club of Rome, 1974. *The Limits to Growth*. London, Pan.

Cohen, D. L. 1981. Class and the analysis of African politics: problems and prospects. In Cohen and Daniel, 1981.

Cohen, D. L., and Daniel, J. (eds.) 1981. *The Political Economy of Africa: Selected Readings*. London, Longman.

Cohen, G. A. 1978. *Karl Marx's Theory of History; A Defence*. Oxford, Clarendon.

Colletti, L. 1975. Marxism and the dialectic. *New Left Review*, no. 93.

Cooper, R. G. 1978. Dynamic tension: symbiosis and contradiction in Hmong social relations. In Clammer, 1978a.

Cornforth, M. 1968. *The Open Philosophy and the Open Society*. London, Lawrence and Wishart.

Coulson, A. 1981. Agricultural policies in mainland Tanzania 1946–76. In Heyer et al., 1981a.

Coward, R., and Ellis, J. 1977. *Language and Materialism*. London, Routledge and Kegan Paul.

Cowen, M. 1976. Capital, class and peasant households, Nairobi. Mimeograph.
    1981a. The agrarian problem: notes of the Nairobi discussion. *Review of African Political Economy*, no. 20, Jan.–Apr., 57–73.
    1981b. Commodity production in Kenya's central province. In Heyer et al., 1981a.

Cox, T. M. 1979. *Rural Sociology in the Soviet Union*. London, C. Hurst and Company.

Crouch, C. 1977. *Class Conflict and the Industrial Relations Crisis*. London, Heinemann.

Currie, K., and Ray, L. 1987. The Kenya state, agribusiness and the peasantry. *Review of African Political Economy*, no. 38, Apr.

Cutler, A., Hindess, B., Hirst, P., and Hussain, A. 1977. *Marx's "Capital" and Capitalism Today*. London, Routledge and Kegan Paul.

Datoo, B. A., and Gray, J. A. 1979. Underdevelopment and regional planning in the Third World: a critical overview. *Canadian Journal of African Studies*, 13, nos. 1 and 2.

Davies, R. J. 1977. Notes on the theory of the informal sector with reference to Zimbabwe. *South African Labour Bulletin*, 3, no. 6.

de Oliveira, F. 1972. A economia Brasileira: crítica a razão dualista. *Estudos Cebrap*, no. 2.

de Villiers, A. 1977. A new approach to the planning and development of smallholder irrigation schemes in Southern Africa. *South African Journal of African Affairs*, no. 2.

Dias, G. M. 1978. New patterns of domination in rural Brazil: a case study of agriculture in the Brazilian north-east. *Economic Development and Cultural Change*, 27, no. 1.

Dinham, B., and Hines, C. 1983. *Agribusiness in Africa*. London, Earth Resources Unit.

Dobb, M. 1951. Some aspects of economic development. In Dobb, 1968.
    1962. Some problems in the history of capitalism. In Dobb, 1968.
    1968. *Papers on Capitalism, Development and Planning*. London, Routledge and Kegan Paul.

Dos Santos, T. 1969. The crisis of development theory and the problem of dependence in Latin America. In Bernstein, 1978.

1970. The structure of dependence. *American Economic Review*, 60, no. 2.

Duggett, M. 1975. Marx on peasants. *Journal of Peasant Studies*, 2, no. 2.

Dupré, G., and Rey, P. P. 1973. Reflections on the pertinence of a theory to the history of exchange. *Economy and Society*, 2, no. 2.

Dutkiewicz, P., and Williams, G. 1987. 'All the king's horses and all the king's men couldn't put Humpty-Dumpty together again'. *IDS Bulletin*, 18, no. 3. Sussex, Institute of Development Studies.

Ehrensaft, P. 1971. Semi-industrial capitalism in the Third World. *Africa Today*, 18, no. 3.

Eisenstadt, S. N. (ed.) 1968. *The Protestant Ethic and Modernization*. New York, Basic Books.

Elger, T. 1979. Valuation and deskilling: a critique of Braverman. *Capital and Class*, no. 7.

Elkan, W. 1978. *An Introduction to Development Economics*. Harmondsworth, Penguin.

Emmanuel, A. 1972a. *Unequal Exchange: A Study of the Imperialism of Trade*. London, New Left Books.

1972b. White settler colonialism and the myth of investment imperialism. *New Left Review*, no. 73.

Ennew, J., Hirst, P., and Tribe, K. 1977. 'Peasantry' as an economic category. *Journal of Peasant Studies*, 4, no. 4.

Evans, P. 1977. Multinationals, state-owned corporations and the transformation of imperialism: a Brazilian case study. *Economic Development and Cultural Change*, 26, no. 1.

Feldman, R. 1975. Rural social differentiation and political goals in Tanzania. In Oxaal et al., 1975.

Femia, J. 1975. Hegemony and consciousness in the thought of Antonio Gramsci. *Political Studies*, 23, no. 1.

Ferner, A. 1979. The dominant class and industrial development in Peru. *Journal of Development Studies*, 15, no. 4.

Fieldhouse, D. K. 1967. *Theory of Capitalist Imperialism*. London, Longman.

Fine, B. 1978. On the origins of capitalist development. *New Left Review*, no. 109.

Fiske, J. 1979. *Introduction to Communication Studies*. London, Methuen.

Fitzgerald, F. T. 1983. Sociologies of development. In Limqueco and McFarlane, 1983.

Forrest, T. 1981. Agricultural policies in Nigeria 1900–78. In Heyer et al., 1981a.

Foster, G. M. 1969. *Applied Anthropology*. Boston, Little, Brown and Company.

Foster-Carter, A. 1978. Can we articulate 'articulation'? In Clammer, 1978a.

Frank, A. G. 1969a. *Latin America: Underdevelopment or Revolution*. New York, Monthly Review Press.

1969b. The sociology of underdevelopment and the underdevelopment of sociology. In Frank, 1969a.

1969c. *Capitalism and Underdevelopment in Latin America*. New York, Monthly Review Press.

Fransman, M., and Davies, R. 1977. The South African social formation in the early capitalist period circa 1870–1939. Some views on the question of hegemony. In Adler, 1977.

Friedmann, H. 1978. Simple commodity production and wage labour in the American Plains. *Journal of Peasant Studies*, 6, no. 1.

1979. Household production and the national economy: concepts for the analysis of agrarian formations. *Journal of Peasant Studies*, 7, no. 2.

Fröbel, F., Heinrichs, J., and Kreye, O. 1980. New international division of labour. *South African Laour Bulletin*, 5, no. 8.

Furtado, C. 1964. Elements of a theory of underdevelopment – the under-developed structures. In Bernstein, 1978.

Galeski, B. 1972. *Basic Concepts of Rural Sociology*, Manchester, Manchester University Press.

Gallagher, J., and Robinson, R. E. 1953. *Africa and the Victorians*. London, Macmillan.

Gallisot, R. 1975. Precolonial Algeria. *Economy and Society*, 4, no. 4.

Geertz, C. 1963. Java and Japan compared. In Bernstein, 1978.

Genovese, E. 1971. *The World the Slaveholders Made*. New York, Vintage.

George, S. 1976. *How the Other Half Dies*. Harmondsworth, Penguin.

Geras, N. 1972. Althusser: an account and assessment. *New Left Review*, no. 71.

Gerschenkron, A. 1965. *Economic Backwardness in Historical Perspective*. New York, Praeger.

Giglioli, E. G. 1965. Staff organisation and tenant discipline on an irrigated land settlement. *East African Agricultural and Forestry Journal*, 30, no. 3.

Girvan, N., and Jefferson, O. 1968. Corporate v. Caribbean integration. In Bernstein, 1978.

Godelier, M. 1969. *Sur le mode de production asiatique*. Paris, Editions Sociales, Centre d'Études in Recherches Marxistes.

1972. Structure and contradiction in *Capital*. In Blackburn, 1972.

Godfrey, M. 1982. Kenya: African capitalism or simple dependency. In Bienefeld and Godfrey, 1982.

Goncharov, L. V. 1977. On the drain of capital from African countries. In Gutkind and Waterman, 1977.

Goodman, D., Sorj. B., and Wilkinson, J. 1984. Agro-industry, state policy and rural social structures: recent analyses of proletarianisation in Brazilian agriculture. In Munslow and Finch, 1984.

Greussing, K., and Kippenburg, H. G. 1975–6. Response to *The German Peasant War of 1525, Journal of Peasant Studies*, 3, no. 1.

Grove, A. T. 1979. *Africa*. Oxford, Oxford University Press.

Gutkind, P., and Wallerstein, I. (eds.) 1976. *The Political Economy of Contemporary Africa*. Beverly Hills, Sage.

Gutkind, P., and Waterman, P. (eds.) 1977. *African Social Studies*. London, Heinemann Educational.

Gutto, S. B. O. 1981. Law, rangelands, the peasantry and social classes in Kenya. *Review of African Political Economy*, no. 20, Jan.–Apr.

Habakkuk, H. J. 1967. *American and British Technology in the Nineteenth Century*. Cambridge, Cambridge University Press.

Hagen, E. E. 1962. *On the Theory of Social Change*. Homewood, Dorsey Press.

Halliday, F. 1979. *Iran. Dictatorship and Development.* Harmondsworth, Penguin.

Hamilton, C. 1983. Capitalist industrialization in the four little tigers of East Asia. In Limqueco and McFarlane, 1983.

Harbeson, J. W. 1971. Land reforms and politics in Kenya, 1954–70. *Journal of Modern African Studies*, 9, no. 2.

Harris, L. 1980. Agricultural co-operatives and development policy in Mozambique. *Journal of Peasant Studies*, 7, no. 3.

Harris, R. (ed.) 1975a. *The Political Economy of Africa*, Cambridge, Mass., Schenkman.

Harris, R. 1975b. Underdevelopment or revolution? In Harris, 1975a.

Harrison, P. 1981. *Inside the Third World.* Harmondsworth, Penguin.

Hayter, T. 1981. *The Creation of World Poverty.* London, Pluto in association with Third World First.

Heilbroner, R. L. 1981. The demand for the supply side. *New York Review of Books*, 28, no. 10.

Hellman, G. 1979. Historical materialism. In Mepham and Ruben, 1979.

Herring, R. J. 1981. Embedded production relations and rationality of tenant quiescence in tenure reform. *Journal of Peasant Studies*, 8, no. 2.

Heyer, J., Roberts, P., and Williams, G. 1980. Rural development. Photocopied essay. Circulated at Rhodes University, Grahamstown in the Political Studies department.

(eds.) 1981a. *Rural development in Tropical Africa.* London, Macmillan.

1981b. Rural development. In Heyer et al., 1981a.

Heyer, J. 1981. Agricultural development policy in Kenya from the colonial period to 1975. In Heyer et al., 1981a

Hill, F. 1977. Experimenting with a public sector peasantry: agricultural schemes and class formation in Africa. *The African Studies Review*, 20, no. 3.

Hill, P. 1963. Cocoa-farming and the migratory process in Ghana, 1894–1930. In Bernstein, 1978.

1970. *Studies in Rural Capitalism.* Cambridge, Cambridge University Press.

Hilton, R. 1973. Medieval peasants: any lessons? *Journal of Peasant Studies*, 1, no. 2.

Hindess, B., and Hirst, P. Q. 1975. *Pre-capitalist Modes of Production.* London, Routledge and Kegan Paul.

Hiro, D. 1978. *Inside India Today.* London, Routledge and Kegan Paul.

Hobsbawm, E. J. 1972. Karl Marx's contribution to historiography. In Blackburn, 1972.

1973. Peasants and politics. *Journal of Peasant Studies*, 8, no. 1.

Holloway, J., and Picciotto, SD. 1977. Capital, crisis and the state. *Capital and Class*, no. 2.

Hoselitz, B. F. 1964. Social stratification and economic development. *International Social Science Journal*, 16, no. 2.

Howard, R. 1980. Formation and stratification of the peasantry in colonial Ghana. *Journal of Peasant Studies*, 8, no. 1.

Hughes, G. 1977. Preconditions of socialist development in Africa. In Gutkind and Waterman, 1977.

Hunt, D. 1979. Chayanov's model of peasant household resource allocation. *Journal of Peasant Studies*, 6, no. 3.

Hymer, S. 1972. The multinational corporation and the law of uneven development. In Radice, 1975.

IDS (Institute for Development Studies), 1972. *An Overall Evaluation of the Special Rural Development Programme.* Occasional paper no. 8. University of Nairobi, Institute for Development Studies.

    1975. *Second Overall Evaluation of the Special Rural Development Programme.* Occasional paper no. 12. University of Nairobi, Institute for Development Studies.

International Labour Organisation, 1972. Employment, incomes and equity: a strategy for increasing productive employment in Kenya. Geneva, ILO.

Jessop, B. 1982. *The Capitalist State. Marxist Theories and Methods.* Oxford, Martin Robinson.

Joffe, A. L. 1980. Towards a more thorough understanding of underdeveloped social formations. Industrial sociology honours essay, unpublished. Johannesburg, University of the Witwatersrand.

Joshi, P. C. 1981. Fieldwork experience relived and reconsidered. The agrarian society of Uttar Pradesh. *Journal of Peasant Studies*, 8, no. 4.

Kahn, J. S. 1978. Marxist anthropology and peasant economics: a study of the social structures of underdevelopment. In Clammer, 1978a.

Kahn, J. S., and Llobera, J. R. 1980. French Marxist anthropology: twenty years after. (Review article) *Journal of Peasant Studies*, 8, no. 1.

Kaplan, D. 1977. Capitalist development in South Africa, class conflict and the state. In Adler, 1977.

Kaplinsky, R. 1980. Capitalist accumulation in the periphery – the Kenyan case re-examined. *Review of African Political Economy*, no. 17, Jan.–Apr., 83–105.

Kautsky, K. 1976. The Agrarian Question. In Banaji, 1976b.

Kay, C. 1981. Political economy, class alliances and agrarian change in Chile. *Journal of Peasant Studies*, 8, no. 4.

Kay, G. 1975. *Development and Underdevelopment.* London, Macmillan.

Keddie, N. R. 1968. The Iranian village before and after land reform. In Bernstein, 1978.

Kitching, G. 1972. The concept of class and the study of Africa. *The African Review*, 2, no. 3.

    1980. *Class and Economic Change in Kenya: the Making of an African Petty Bourgeoisie, 1905–1970.* New Haven, Yale University Press.

    1982. *Development and Underdevelopment in Historical Perspective: Populism, Nationalism and Industrialization.* London, Methuen.

    1985. Politics, method, and evidence in the 'Kenya Debate'. In Bernstein and Campbell, 1985.

Kollontai, V. 1970. Planning problems in the 'Third World'. *Problems of Economics*, 13, no. 1.

Kom, D. 1977. The co-operative movement in the Cameroons. In Gutkind and Waterman, 1977.

Krinks, P. 1983. Rectifying inequality or favouring the few? Image and reality in Philippine development. In Lea and Chaudri, 1983a.

Kuhn, T. 1962. *The Structure of Scientific Revolutions*. Chicago, Chicago University Press.

Laclau, E. 1971. Feudalism and capitalism in Latin America. *New Left Review*, no. 67.

1979. The specificity of the political. The Poulantzas–Miliband debate. *Economy and Society*, 4, no. 1.

Lall, S. 1975. Is 'dependence' a useful concept in analysing underdevelopment? *World Development*, 3, nos. 11 and 12.

Lamb, G. 1974. *Peasant Politics. Conflict and Development in Muranga*. Lewes, Julian Friedman.

Larrain, J. 1979, *The Concept of Ideology*. London, Hutchinson.

Lea, D. A. M., and Chaudri, D. P. 1983a. *Rural Development and the State*. London, Methuen.

1983b. The nature, problems and approaches to rural development. In Lea and Chaudri, 1983a.

Le Brun, O. 1973. Fundamental aspects of underdevelopment and aims of development. *Universities' Quarterly*, 27, no. 3.

Lecourt, D. 1977. *Proletarian Science? The Case of Lysenko*. London, New Left Books.

Leech, G. N. 1974. *Semantics*. Harmondsworth, Penguin.

Legassick, M. 1976. Perspectives on African underdevelopment. (Review article) *Journal of African History*, 17, no. 3.

Legassick, M., and Wolpe, H. 1976. The bantustans and capital accumulation in South Africa. *Review of African Political Economy*, no. 7.

Lehmann, D. (ed.) 1979. *Development Theory. Four Critical Studies*. London, Frank Cass.

Lenin, V. I. 1960a. *Collected Works*, vol. III. Moscow, Foreign Languages Publishing House.

1960b (1899). The development of capitalism in Russia: the process of the formation of a home market for larger-scale industry. In Lenin, 1960a.

1964a. *Collected Works*, vol. XXII. Moscow, Progress Publishers.

1964b Imperialism: the highest stage of capitalism. In Lenin, 1964a.

Leo, C. 1979. The failure of the 'progressive farmer' in Kenya's million-acre settlement scheme. *Journal of Modern African Studies*, 16, no. 4.

Leys, C. 1973. Interpreting African unemployment. Reflections on the ILO report on employment, incomes and equality in Kenya. *African Affairs*, 72, no. 289.

1975. *Underdevelopment in Kenya*. London, Heinemann.

1976. The 'overdeveloped' post-colonial state: a re-evaluation. *Review of African Political Economy*, no. 5.

1977a. Underdevelopment and dependency: critical notes. *Journal of Contemporary Asia*, 7, no. 1.

1977b. Political implications of the development of peasant society in Kenya. In Gutkind and Waterman, 1977.

1978. Capital accumulation, class formation and dependency: the significance of the Kenyan case. *Socialist Register*, 1978.

1980. Kenya: what does dependency explain? *Review of African Political Economy*, 17, Jan.–Apr.

Leys, C. 1983. Underdevelopment and dependency: critical notes. In Limqueco and McFarlane, 1983.

Lieberson, J. 1981. The silent majority. *The New York Review of Books*, 17, no. 16.

Limqueco, P., and McFarlane, B. 1983. *Neo-Marxist Theories of Development*. London, Macmillan.

Locke, G. 1976. Introduction. In Althusser, 1976.

Long, N., and Richardson, P. 1978. Informal sector, petty commodity production, and the social relations of the small-scale enterprise. In Clammer, 1978a.

Lukacs, G. 1971. *History and Class Consciousness. Studies in Marxist Dialectics*. London, Merlin Press.

Luton, H. 1976. The satellite/metropolis model. A critique. *Theory and Society*, 3, no. 4.

Luxemburg, R. 1951. *The Accumulation of Capital*. London, Routledge and Kegan Paul.

Mafeje, A. 1977. Neo-colonialism, state capitalism. In Gutkind and Waterman, 1977.

Magubane, B. 1971. A critical look at the indices used in the study of change in colonial Africa. *Current Anthropology*, 12, nos. 4 and 5.

Mamdani, M. 1977. *Politics and Class Formation in Uganda*. London, Heinemann.

Mandel, E. 1968. *Marxist Economic Theory*. 2 vols. London, Merlin Press.
    1975. *Late Capitalism*. London, New Left Books.

Mann, S. A., and Dickinson, J. M. 1978. Obstacles to the development of a capitalist agriculture. *Journal of Peasant Studies*, 5, no. 4.

Mao Tsetung, 1977. *Five Essays on Philosophy*. Peking, Foreign Languages Press.

Maré, P. G. 1977. An exploration of marginalisation theory in relation to the contemporary South African social formation. Bachelor of Arts honours dissertation, Johannesburg, University of the Witwatersrand.

Markovitz, I. L. 1976. Bureaucratic development and economic growth. *Journal of Modern African Studies*, 14, no. 2.

Mars, T., and White, G. (eds.) 1986. *Developmental States and African Agriculture. IDS Bulletin*, 17, no. 1.

Marx, K. 1965. *The German Ideology*. London, Lawrence and Wishart.
    1969. *Theories of Surplus Value*. London, Lawrence and Wishart.
    1971. *Capital*, vol. II. London, Lawrence and Wishart.
    1972. *Capital*, vol. I. London, Lawrence and Wishart.
    1973. *Grundrisse*. Harmondsworth, Penguin/New Left Review.
    1974. *Capital*, vol. III. London, Lawrence and Wishart.
    1976a. *Capital*, vol. I. Harmondsworth, Penguin/New Left Review.
    1976b. Results of the immediate process of production. Appendix to Marx, 1976a.
    1977a. *A Contribution to the Critique of Political Economy*. Moscow, Progress Publishers.
    1977b. The eighteenth brumaire. In Marx and Engels, 1977.

Marx, K., and Engels, F. 1977. *Selected Works in One Volume*. London, Lawrence and Wishart.

1986 (1848). *The Communist Manifesto*. Moscow, Progress Publishers.

McI. Daniel, J. B. 1980. Agricultural development in the Ciskei: review and assessment. Presidential address to South African Geographical Society, 25 July 1980.

Meillassoux, C. 1960. Essai d'interprétation des phénomènes économiques dans les sociétés traditionelles d'autosubsistence. *Cahiers d'études africaines*, no. 4.

1970. A class analysis of the bureaucratic process in Mali. *Journal of Development Studies*, 6, no. 2..

1972. From reproduction to production. A Marxist approach to economic anthropology. *Economy and Society*, 1.

Mepham, J., and Ruben, D-H. (eds.) 1979. *Issues in Marxist Philosophy*, vol. II, *Materialism*. Brighton, The Harvester Press.

Miliband, R. 1972. The capitalist state. In Blackburn, 1972.

Moore, B. Jr. 1969. *Social Origins of Dictatorship and Democracy,. Lord and Peasant in the Making of the Modern World*. Harmondsworth, Peregrine.

Morris, M. L. 1976. The development of capitalism in South African agriculture: class struggle in the countryside. *Economy and Society*, 5, no. 3.

Mouzelis, N. 1975–6. Capitalism and the development of agriculture. (Review article) *Journal of Peasant Studies*, 3, no. 4.

1979a. Peasant agriculture, productivity and the laws of capitalist development: a reply to Vergopoulos. *Journal of Peasant Studies*, 6, no. 3.

1979b. *Modern Greece. Facets of Underdevelopment*. London, Macmillan.

1980. Modernization, underdevelopment, uneven development: prospects for a theory of Third World formations. (Review article) *Journal of Peasant Studies*, 7, no. 3.

Mulaa, J. 1981. The politics of a changing society: Mumias. *Review of African Political Economy*, no. 20, Jan.–Apr., 89–107.

Munslow, B., and Finch, H. 1984. *Proletarianisation in the Third World*. London, Croom Helm.

Muntemba, M. S. 1978. Expectations unfulfilled: the underdevelopment of peasant agriculture in Zambia, the case of Kabwe Rural District, 1964–1970. *Journal of Southern African Studies*, 5, no. 1.

Muratorio, B. 1980. Protestantism and capitalism re-visited. The rural highlands of Ecuador. *Journal of Peasant Studies*, 8, no. 1.

Murray, R. 1971. The internationalization of capital and the nation state. In Radice, 1975.

Myint, H. 1967 *The Economics of Developing Countries*. London, Hutchinson.

1971. *Economic Theory and the Underdeveloped Countries*. Oxford, Oxford University Press.

Myrdal, G. 1957. *Economic Theory and the Underdeveloped Regions*. London, Duckworth.

1968. The 'soft-state' in underdeveloped countries. *UCLA Law Review*, 15.

Nafziger, E. W. 1979. A critique of development economics in the U.S. In Lehmann, 1979.

Njonjo, A. L. 1981. The Kenya peasantry: A re-assessment. *Review of African Political Economy*, no. 20, Jan.–Apr., 27–40.

Nichols, T. 1981. A little marxism. *New Society*, October 15.

Nolan, P. 1976. Collectivization in China: some comparisons with the USSR. *Journal of Peasant Studies*, 3, no. 2.

Nolan, P., and White, G. 1979. Socialist development and rural inequality: the Chinese countryside in the 1970s. *Journal of Peasant Studies*, 7, no. 1.

Obregon, A. Q. 1974. The marginal pole of the economy and the marginalised labour force. *Economy and Society*, 3, no. 4.

O'Brien, P. J. 1975. A critique of Latin American theories of dependency. In Oxaal et al., 1975.

1984. The political economy of semi-proletarian isolation under colonialism: Sudan 1925–50. In Munslow and Finch, 1984.

O'Dowd, M. 1977. The stages of economic growth and the future of South Africa. In Schlemmer and Webster, 1977.

O'Keefe, P. 1984. Poverty, proletarianisation and the production of uneven development: a Kenyan village. In Munslow and Finch, 1984.

O'Neill, J. (ed.) 1969. *The Longer View. Essays towards a Critique of Political Economy, Paul A. Baran*. New York, Monthly Review Press.

Owen, R., and Sutcliffe, B. (eds.) 1972. *Studies in the Theory of Imperialism*. London, Longman.

Oxaal, I., Barnett, T., and Booth, D. (eds.) 1975. *Beyond the Sociology of Development. Economy and Society in Latin America and Africa*. London, Routledge and Kegan Paul.

Oyugi, W. O. 1981. *Rural Development Administration. A Kenyan Experience*. New Delhi, Vikas.

PADRI (Pietermaritzburg Agricultural Development Research Institute), 1979. Does mechanization = development? The Ciskei experience. *Nux*, Pietermaritzburg, University of Natal.

Palloix, C. 1973. The internationalization of capital and the circuit of social capital. In Radice, 1975.

Parsons, T. 1966. *Societies: Evolutionary and Comparative Perspectives*. Englewood Cliffs, Prentice Hall.

Patnaik, U. 1979. Neo-populism and Marxism. The Chayanovian view of the Agrarian Question and its fundamental fallacy. *Journal of Peasant Studies*, 6, no. 4.

Peel, Q. 1982. Aid medicine upsets. *The Star*, 31 August 1982.

Perelman, M. 1979. Obstacles to the development of a capitalist agriculture. A comment on Mann and Dickinson. *Journal of Peasant Studies*, 7, no. 1.

Petras, J., and La Porte, R. Jr, 1970. Two approaches to agrarian reform in Latin America – re-distribution v. incremental change. In Bernstein, 1978.

Phillips, A. 1977. The concept of 'development'. *Review of African Political Economy*, no. 8.

Popper, K. R. 1972. *Objective Knowledge. An Evolutionary Approach*. Oxford, Oxford University Press.

1973. *The Open Society and its Enemies*. Vol. II. The high tide of prophecy: Hegel, Marx, and the aftermath. Revised and enlarged edition. London, Routledge and Kegan Paul.

Post, K. 1977. Peasantization in West Africa. In Gutkind and Waterman, 1977.

Poulantzas, N. 1973. On social classes. *New Left Review*, March–Apr.

1976a. The capitalist state. A reply to Miliband and Laclau. *New Left Review*, March–Apr.

1976b. *The Crisis of the Dictatorships*. London, New Left Books.

1978. *State, Power, Socialism*. London, New Left Books.

Proctor-Simms, J. (ed.) 1978. *Ciskei Development Conference*. Pretoria, Conference Associates.

Radice, H. 1975. *International Firms and Modern Imperialism*. Harmondsworth, Penguin.

Raikes, P. 1978. Rural differentiation and class formation in Tanzania. *Journal of Peasant Studies*, 5, no. 3.

Ranger, T. 1968. Connections between primary resistance and modern mass nationalism. *Journal of African History*, 9, no. 3.

Rey, P. P. 1973. *Les Alliances des classes*. Paris, Maspero.

Rhodes, R. I. (ed.) 1970. *Imperialism and Underdevelopment: A Reader*. New York, Monthly Review Press.

Richards, P. 1979. A green revolution in Africa? *African Affairs*, 78.

Roberts, P. 1981. 'Rural development' and the rural economy in Niger, 1900–75. In Heyer et al., 1981a.

Rodney, W. 1972. *How Europe Underdeveloped Africa*. Dar es Salaam, Bogle l'Ouverture.

1977. Technological stagnation and economic distortion in pre-colonial times. In Gutkind and Waterman, 1977.

Roseberry, W. 1978. Peasants as proletarians. *Critique of Anthropology*, 3, no. 11.

Rostow, W. W. 1965. *The Stages of Economic Growth*. Cambridge, Cambridge University Press.

Roxborough, I. 1976. Dependency theory in the sociology of development. Some theoretical problems. *West African Journal of Sociology and Political Science*, 1, no. 2.

Rudebeck, L. 1979. Development and class struggle in Guinea–Bissau. *Monthly Review Press*, January.

Ruthenberg, H. 1966. *African Agricultural Production Development Policy in Kenya 1952–1965*. Berlin–Heidelberg–New York. Springer–Verlag.

Sahlins, M. 1974. *Stone Age Economics*. Chicago, Aldine.

Sano, H. O. 1982. Review of Heyer et al. (1981a). *Review of African Political Economy*, 23, 112–15.

Saul, J. S. 1974. The state in post-colonial societies: Tanzania. *Socialist Register*. London, Merlin Press.

Schlemmer, L., and Webster, E. (eds.) 1977. *Change, Reform and Economic Growth*. Johannesburg, Ravan Press.

Sebeok, T. A. (ed.) 1975. *The Tell-Tale Sign. A Survey of Semiotics*. Lisse, Peter de Ridder Press.

Seers, D. 1979. The meaning of development. In Lehmann, 1979.

Seidman, A. 1977. Agricultural stagnation in Uganda. In Gutkind and Waterman, 1977.

Seidman, R. B. 1978. *The State, Law and Development*. London, Croom Helm.

Shanin, T. (ed.) 1971. *Peasants and Peasant Societies*. Harmondsworth, Penguin.

Shaw, W. H. 1978. *Marx's Theory of History*. London, Hutchinson.

Shivji, I. G. 1977. The mixed sector and imperialist control in Tanzania. In Gutkind and Waterman, 1977.

Sklair, L. 1979. Relations of production, productive forces, and the mass line in the formation of the Rural People's Communes in China. *Journal of Peasant Studies*, 6, no. 3.

Smith, A. 1937. *An Inquiry into the Nature and Causes of the Wealth of Nations*. New York, The Modern Library.

Sohn-Rethal, A. 1979. *Intellectual and Manual Labour. A Critique of Epistemology*. London, Macmillan.

Sole, K. 1977. Footnote on Hofmeyer. *Work in Progress*, no. 2.

1978. Analogy and aberration. *Work in Progress*, no. 4.

Sorrenson, M. P. K. 1963. Counter-revolution in Mau-Mau: land consolidation in Kikuyuland 1952–60. East African Institute of Social Research conference.

1967. *Land Reform in the Kikuyu Country*. Oxford, Oxford University Press.

Spiegel, A. C. 1979. Rural differentiation in Lesotho. *Work in Progress*, no. 8.

Stalin, J. V. 1940a. *Leninism*. London, Lawrence and Wishart.

1940b. Dialectical and historical materialism. In 1940a.

Standing, G. 1981. Migration and modes of exploitation: social origins of immobility and mobility. *Journal of Peasant Studies*, 8, no. 2.

Stavenhagen, R. 1964. Changing functions of the community in underdeveloped countries. In Bernstein, 1978.

Steeves, J. S. 1978. Class analysis and rural Africa: the Kenya Tea Development Authority. *Journal of Modern African Studies*, 16, no. 1.

Suret-Canale, J. 1977. The economic balance sheet of French colonialism in West Africa. In Gutkind and Waterman, 1977.

Sutcliffe, B. 1972. Imperialism and the industrialization of the Third World. In Owen and Sutcliffe, 1972.

Sweezy, P. 1976. *The Transition from Feudalism to Capitalism*. London, New Left Books.

Szentes, T. 1971. Tropical Africa. In Wyilas, 1978.

1973. *The Political Economy of Underdevelopment*. Budapest, Akademiai Kiado.

Tanzania, 1971. The TANU Guidelines (Mwongozo wa TANU). Dar es Salaam. *The Nationalist*, February.

Taylor, E. 1984. Peasants or proletarians? The transformation of agrarian production relations in Egypt. In Munslow and Finch, 1984.

Taylor, J. 1979. *From Modernization to Modes of Production: A Critique of the Sociologies of Development and Underdevelopment*. London, Macmillan.

1981. Underdevelopment and modes of production: a reply to Nicos Mouzelis. *Journal of Peasant Studies*, 8, no. 3.

Terray, E. 1974. Long-distance exchange and the formation of the state: the case of the Abron Kingdom of Gyaman. *Economy and Society*, 3, no. 3.

Thomas, S. 1975. Economic developments in Malawi since independence. *Journal of Southern African Studies*, 2, no. 1.

Time, 1981. Thailand. Peace festival. Success against an insurgency. No. 36, September.

Tipps, D. C. (n.d.) Modernization theory and the comparative study of societies. Roneo copy issued by Political Studies Department, Rhodes University, Grahamstown. Source unknown.

Todaro. M. R. 1983 (2nd ed.) *Economic Development in the Third World.* Harlow, Longman.

Tribe, K. 1977. Economic property and the theorisation of ground rent. *Economy and Society*, 6, no. 1.

Tsoucalas, C. 1979. Review of *Modern Greece. Facets of Underdevelopment* by Nicos P. Mouzelis. *Journal of Peasant Studies*, 7, no. 1.

Van Zwanenberg, R. 1974. The development of peasant commodity production in Kenya, 1920–40. *Economic History Review*, 27, ser. 11.

Venn, A. C. 1979. A prescription for private participation in successful rural development. Paper presented at The Urban Foundation (Natal Region) workshop: The urbanisation process in Natal and Kwazulu and the need for a total development strategy, Royal Hotel, Durban, 10 August 1979.

Vogoler, I. 1981. *Myth of the Family Farm: Agribusiness and Dominance of US Agriculture*. Westview Press.

Wallace, T. 1980. Agricultural projects and land in northern Nigeria. *Review of African Political Economy*, no. 17, Jan.–Apr., 59–70.

1981. The Kano River project, Nigeria. The impact of an irrigation scheme on productivity and welfare. In Heyer et al., 1981a.

Wallerstein, I. 1971. The state and social transformation: will and possibility. In Bernstein, 1978.

1974. The rise and future demise of the world capitalist system: concepts for comparative analysis. *Comparative Studies in Society and History*, no. 16.

1977. Civilization and modes of production: conflicts and convergences. Mimeograph.

Wallman, S. 1976. The modernization of dependence: a further note on Lesotho. *Journal of Southern African Studies*, 3, no. 1.

Warren, B. 1973. Imperialism and capitalist industrialization. *New Left Review*, no. 81.

Weber, M. 1948. *The Methodology of the Social Sciences*. (Trans. and edited by E. A. Shils and H. A. Finch.) New York, Free Press.

Webster, D. 1978. Migrant labour, social formations and the proletarianization of the Chopi of southern Mozambique. *Africa Perspective*, no. 1.

Weeks, J. 1975. Fundamental economic concepts and their application. In Clammer, 1978a.

Wilkinson, A. R. 1979. The land issue and Kenyan independence. *Africa Today*, 26, no. 3.

Williams, G. 1976. Taking the part of peasants: rural development in Nigeria and Tanzania. In Gutkind and Wallerstein, 1976.

1977. Class relations in a neo-colony: the case of Nigeria. In Gutkind and Waterman, 1977.

1981a. The World Bank and the peasant problem. In Heyer et al., 1981a.

1981b. Nigeria: the neo-colonial political economy. In Cohen and Daniel, 1981.

1982. Equity, growth and the state. (Review article) *Africa*, 53, no. 3.

Williams, G. 1984. Why is there no agrarian capitalism in Nigeria? Draft of article written for *Journal of Historical Sociology*.

  1985. Marketing boards in Nigeria. *Review of African Political Economy*, no. 34, Dec.

  1986a. Introduction: farmers, herders, and the state. *Rural Africana*, Spring–Fall.

  1986b. Rural development: partners and adversaries. *Rural Africana*, Spring–Fall.

  1987. Primitive accumulation: the way to progress? *Development and Change*, 18.

Williams, R. 1976a. *Keywords. A Vocabulary of Culture and Society*. London, Fontana/Croom Helm.

Woddis, J. 1977. Is there an African national bourgeoisie? In Gutkind and Waterman, 1977.

Wolfe, A. 1974. New directions in the marxist theory of politics. *Politics and Society*, 4, no. 2.

Wolpe, H. 1972. Capitalism and cheap labour-power. From segregation to apartheid. *Economy and Society*, 1, no. 4.

  1975. The theory of internal colonialism. In Oxaal et al., 1975.

  1980a. *The Articulation of Modes of Production*. London, Routledge and Kegan Paul.

  1980b. Towards an analysis of the South African state. *International Journal of the Sociology of Law*, no. 8.

World Bank, 1975. *Rural Development: Sector Policy Paper*. World Bank, Washington D.C.

Wright, E. O. 1980. Class and occupation. *Theory and Society*, 9, no. 1.

Wyilas, J. (ed.) 1978. *Tropical Africa: The Changing Face of the Third World*. Leyden, Sijtholt.

Zeitlin, I. M. 1968. (2nd ed.) *Ideology and the Development of Social Theory*. Englewood Cliffs, Prentice Hall.

Ziemann, W., and Lanzensdörfer, M. 1977. The state in peripheral societies. *Socialist Register*. London, Merlin Press.

Index

Printed in the United Kingdom
by Lightning Source UK Ltd.
130857UK00001B/153/P